DIVERSITY

Diversity: A Key Idea for Business and Society introduces an idea that proliferates business and society, having been incorporated into mainstream theory and practice. Beyond this multidisciplinary setting, how diversity is defined, framed, managed and regulated is also exposed to considerable social, economic, political and ideological interpretation and manipulation. This volume explores definitions of diversity, its various manifestations and interdisciplinary influences that shape how diversity is researched. The text turns to workforce diversity as a particular case of diversity and explores antecedents, correlates and consequences of workforce diversity.

The author considers power, inequality and intersectionality to illuminate the subject from the key manifestations, including class, gender, ethnicity, sexuality and disability. With insights from an array of fields from economics, through management to biology, the author also highlights the various cases against diversity alongside analysis of how to navigate the diversity jungle in practice.

This concise, authoritative book will be essential reading for students, researchers and reflective practitioners interested in workforce diversity as well as unique supplementary reading across the social sciences.

Mustafa F. Özbilgin is Professor of Organisational Behaviour at Brunel University London, UK; Co-Chair of Management and Diversity at the University of Paris Dauphine, France; and Visiting Professor of Management at Koç University, Istanbul, Turkey.

KEY IDEAS IN BUSINESS AND MANAGEMENT
Edited by Stewart Clegg

Understanding how business affects and is affected by the wider world is a challenge made more difficult by the disaggregation between various disciplines, from operations research to corporate governance. This series features concise books that break out from disciplinary silos to facilitate understanding by analysing key ideas that shape and influence business, organizations and management.

Each book focuses on a key idea, locating it in relation to other fields, facilitating deeper understanding of its applications and meanings, and providing critical discussion of the contribution of relevant authors and thinkers. The books provide students and scholars with thought-provoking insights that aid the study and research of business and management.

For more information about this series, please visit: www.routledge.com/Key-Ideas-in-Business-and-Management/book-series/KEYBUS

DIVERSITY

A KEY IDEA FOR BUSINESS AND SOCIETY

Mustafa F. Özbilgin

Routledge
Taylor & Francis Group

LONDON AND NEW YORK

Designed cover image: filo

First published 2024
by Routledge
4 Park Square, Milton Park, Abingdon, Oxon OX14 4RN

and by Routledge
605 Third Avenue, New York, NY 10158

Routledge is an imprint of the Taylor & Francis Group, an informa business

British Library Cataloguing-in-Publication Data
A catalogue record for this book is available from the British Library

ISBN: 978-0-367-42426-8 (hbk)
ISBN: 978-0-367-42360-5 (pbk)
ISBN: 978-0-367-82404-4 (ebk)

DOI: 10.4324/9780367824044

Typeset in Baskerville
by Apex CoVantage, LLC

Access the Support Material: www.routledge.com/9780367423605

I would like to dedicate this book to my late father, Nihat Özbilgin, for his love and unwavering support.

CONTENTS

FOREWORDS

I feel privileged to have two of my academic muses, whose values, engagement and humanity inspire me to write forewords that lend energy, reflection and appeal to this book. Without further a word, I will let the forewords motivate you to read on.

FOREWORD BY PROFESSOR TRISH GREENHALGH

I Googled diversity – and wished I hadn't. Diversity, I learnt, is synonymous with 'variety'. If diversity boxes are ticked, this 'empowers' people. Diversity, in an acronym sandwich between equality and inclusion (EDI), is 'a business opportunity' that will make your company and its products and services more attractive and profitable. Diversity can – according to Google – be measured unproblematically by counting the numbers of people with different ethnic backgrounds, sexual orientations, [dis]abilities and genders at different levels of a hierarchical organisation. Lack of diversity can be fixed by setting targets to balance these numbers. Diversity can be 'activated' by celebrating people's differences. And so on.

Enter the critical social sciences. If the word diversity is to mean anything beyond the populist slogans in which it is so ubiquitously found these days, it must be deconstructed, de-reified, stripped of its neoliberal connotations and analysed in all its various contexts of use (including its overuse, misuse and abuse). The academic study of diversity must go beyond traditional categories and become – among other things – post-binary, post-feminist, post-colonialist and even posthuman. That is the ambitious task that Professor Özbilgin has taken on.

He begins in Chapter 1 by highlighting the fundamentally relational nature of diversity. I am a cis woman. The injustices that angered my late-1970s university feminist group emerged and gained purchase in a particular cultural and historical context. We – unconsciously perhaps – defined our identities in relation to just two groups: other cis women ('sisters', who could be 'gay' or 'straight') and cis men (some 'chauvinist pigs', some 'allies'). Looking back, what we then defined as diversity now appears naive, privileged, self-absorbed and dualistic, as I contemplate the multiplicity of new kinds of relations that have emerged in recent decades between different genders, each with their unique personal and collective histories.

In our 1977 consciousness-raising group, we believed that the fight in which we were engaged (against men and against patriarchy) was fought for all women and for all time. A decade later, Kimberlé Crenshaw (1989) demonstrated the flaws of what she called the 'single axis' approach to researching diversity in which someone was considered underprivileged or oppressed by virtue of either their race or their gender but not both. Others have written on how the feminism of young, able-bodied, educated white women was self-serving, excluding as it did the experiences of those whose lives were shaped not only by gender but also by race, ethnicity, material poverty, disability and other constraints on opportunity (Hennessy and Ingraham, 1997). To properly study diversity and its links to systems of power and privilege, we need to unpack the 'crosscutting and mutually reinforcing systems of domination and suppression' (Anthias, 2005) which play out in complex ways for different individuals and in different historical and geographical contexts.

All these and more themes are rigorously explored by Professor Özbilgin in this timely book. In Chapter 2, he describes the complex and intersecting ways in which diversity is manifest (including but not limited to the categories imposed upon it by academics and wider society).

Chapter 3 considers how different academic disciplines from biology to business studies have conceptualised diversity. The next two chapters take 'the workforce' (and 'the workplace') as a case study to examine how diversity has been theorised and empirically studied from a critical social science perspective. On the one hand, we need to acknowledge and measure diversity in order to become conscious of it and attempt to mitigate the disadvantages associated with it (Chapter 4). On the other hand, making diversity visible may have unintended negative consequences, especially for the most vulnerable (Chapter 5). Chapter 6 considers the different ways in which diversity might be managed, including a salutary subsection (6.8) on illustrative failures. Chapter 7 asks whether diversity should be regulated and if so, to what extent. Özbilgin cites the unashamedly neoliberal self-help book *Lean In* by Sheryl Sandberg (Chief Operating Officer of Facebook), which argues forcefully against the need for any form of regulation apart from the self-regulation of a woman who has a firm grip on herself, her ducks in order and her various networks in place. He then offers a withering critique of the discourse of 'responsibilisation' on which such arguments are based.

I have a memory of marching beside my feminist sisters in 1977 with our heads high, our voices raised and our whole adult lives ahead of us, demanding that all Cambridge colleges admit women on equal grounds to men. Thus, we framed diversity when I was 18. We didn't think about whether we would ever grow old, ever be poor, ever develop work- or life-limiting illness, ever live in a place where girls who demand education get shot in the head, ever be invited by people of colour, trans people, non-binary people or people who lack full citizenship status to check our privilege or ever contemplate that one group's gain might be another group's – or the planet's – loss. To immerse in these and other complex themes, read on.

Trish Greenhalgh is Professor of Primary Care Health Sciences at the University of Oxford. She is dual qualified in medicine and social sciences and leads a research unit in interdisciplinary research in healthcare. Her wide research interests include the health needs and illness narratives of minority and disadvantaged groups.

FOREWORD BY PROFESSOR KURT APRIL

The book is impressive because it progresses our understanding of equality, diversity and inclusion away from narrow thinking and workshop/training suggestions by drawing on core/established and the latest, non-siloed interdisciplinary perspectives and interpretations. It is a real contribution to the social sciences, law, environmental, engineering, computer sciences and business and management. In particular, Prof Özbilgin (an established scholar and engaged practitioner with a respected global reputation in his fields of expertise) has provided a unique approach to expanding our lenses into 'diversity' – the constructive but also the destructive ways in which diversity is regulated and used. He successfully moves our thinking from the espoused to a reimagined, enacted understanding of how diversity ought to, and will be, managed (and how it should be regulated). The ideas and experiences shared by the author speak directly to the troubling, embedded and reproduced individual, group, organisational and systemic prejudices and inequities that persist in our world. The author rightly calls into question people's values and the values of organisations, communities and nation-states. He discusses the rise of individualism to enact a transformation in the quest for fair/kind spaces since the neoliberal project globally has seen the decrease and weakening of group and union bargaining power (in favour of labour market dynamics). This rise has led to a new understanding and framing of diversity, namely, through an individual lens (libertarian orientation) – but which ultimately rendered and stalled the shift from inequities and injustices for the masses and specific groups. The author insists on a shift in the responsibility for change from individuals, especially those from atypical socio-demographic backgrounds who are often not central and do not have the power to bring about real change to that of organisations. In addition, Özbilgin rightfully cautions against the financialisation of equality, diversity and inclusion efforts. Because conversations and workplace foci have shifted from moral, common good, human rights and legal perspectives to one that centres on the bottom-line, productivity and competitive logic. This shift has not just been between organisations but also between individual employees, colleagues and groups, thereby forever soiling their interrelationships and teamwork.

As a result, Özbilgin explores the topic of diversity through various important lenses: political, social, economic and technological and also encourages the use of collectives and social movements to forward transformation toward more equitable states. He does caution us about the inevitable pushbacks and setbacks and reminds the reader that it is parring for the course when change and transformation are involved. People, especially those with social, economic and positional power, fight back (in simple, overt ways but also more subtle and covert ways) when they feel like they are going to 'lose something' and would prefer the status quo, untroubled positionality, their cherished privileges to remain untouched and continue living and working in their comfort zones. Often, their thinking is based on Calvinistic heuristics and rules – thinking and reasoning that highlights either-or and absolutes: us versus them, my belief system versus yours, in-group versus out-group, heterosexual versus others, white versus others, cis-gender versus others, able-bodied versus those who are not, you are with us or against us – whereas, the author encourages us to delve into the messiness and ambiguous nature of diversity and to resist simplification of today's complex relationships and power constructions. The author refreshingly calls for intersectional solidarity between human diversity, biodiversity and techno diversity in order to innovatively address our most pressing problems, with a radical proposal to recognise natural environments and algorithmic systems as legal entities to challenge the enduring power structures and its concomitant economic-ownership structures in order to further conjoining agendas. Özbilgin, committed to establishing greater levels of justice, fairness, kindness and inclusion in the world, goes some way in helping us deconstruct, reimagine, reinterpret, reconstruct and reinvent a social and workplace future that we desire for future generations.

Kurt April is Allan Gray Chair, endowed Professor in Leadership, Diversity and Inclusion and Director of the Allan Gray Centre for Values-Based Leadership at the Graduate School of Business, University of Cape Town.

PREFACE

The process of writing this book was nothing but conventional. I was supposed to deliver the book in 2020 when I lost my father and could not attend his funeral in Istanbul due to Covid19 pandemic travel restrictions. I started identifying the book with my father's loss as I worked on it when I received the news. I buried my sorrow in academic work for two years. However, I pushed this book aside and even used other work to procrastinate. At the end of 2022, I decided that I should either complete the book and dedicate it to my father or bow out before the end of the year. One of my friends, Sarah Caton, suggested that maybe the reason I could not complete the book is that I work in isolation on the book, and I should consider getting feedback. I requested feedback from the book series editor and completed the remaining chapters.

This is a long-overdue book, which required reframing my emotions, taking critical advice, reading literature from disparate fields of work and holding many discussions with colleagues and friends on what I should include in the book. The resulting monograph is interdisciplinary but seeks to contribute to how we define and mobilise diversity across disciplines of science, humanities and arts. Although I have almost given up hope on completing the book, I was lucky to have a supportive editorial team and friends, who nudged me to complete it. Once I completed the main body of writing, I invited many of my friends in the field of diversity to comment and suggest their recent work for inclusion to liven up the text. This second phase has brought many critical voices and perspectives, and I was able to revise the book.

What diversity is and how it is defined and treated across science disciplines are the central themes we seek to expand on in this monograph. The expansion we offer to diversity literature emanates from the collapse of the old deal between human diversity, biodiversity and technological diversity. The uneven nature of this tripartite relationship requires us to consider how biodiversity and the rights of the natural environment may not be simply subsumed under the needs of humans and the future of human generations alone. Similarly, disruptive technological innovations now challenge human governance and complicate and distort social, economic and political life, with a deep impact on human diversity. Therefore, in this book, we propose a new deal between humans, the natural environment and technology to reframe the moral and regulatory landscapes of diversity. Focusing on workforce diversity and its management and regulation, we broaden the repertoire of diversity interventions by including new and novel insights from contemporary studies.

There are many alternative texts on diversity. This one takes on a unique approach that adds to the definition, manifestations, management and regulation of diversity. As part of the Key Ideas Series of Routledge, this volume presents a critical approach that introduces, contextualises and develops how diversity is, ought to and will be managed and regulated in the future.

ACKNOWLEDGEMENTS

I am grateful to colleagues and friends Steward Clegg, Cihat Erbil, Mine Karatas Ozkan, Gokce Dervisoglu, Sarah Caton, Refika Bakoglu, Kristleifur Daðason and others who wish to remain anonymous for providing constructive feedback that contributed to the development of this book.

I would like to acknowledge the moral support of my families of choice and lineage, and collegiate support of friends who commented on the text and institutions that invited me to give talks on some of the contents in this book. I have travelled to four continents to discuss aspects of this book. These invitations have helped me find time, inspiration and energy to develop the book.

INTRODUCTION

In its broadest sense, diversity is the availability of differences, variations, separations, disparities and divisions in human populations, among life forms, inanimate objects and technology. In biological sciences, diversity often refers to biodiversity, the availability of different and varied life forms. Social sciences have developed the notion of diversity to explore how biological and social differences are socially and culturally received, treated and (de)valued among human populations. In physical sciences, diversity refers to objects having different physical qualities. The interest in diversity is evident across many scientific disciplines, including biology, chemistry, physics, social sciences, humanities and the arts. Nevertheless, diversity studies in each discipline remained relatively siloed, with very few scholars viewing diversity as a transdisciplinary construct. Following calls for building diversity science that draws on interdisciplinary insights (Plaut, 2010; Roberson, 2013; Chanlat et al., 2013; Bruna and Ducray, 2018), this book broadens the definition of diversity beyond the confines of human diversity in the social sciences and offers new and innovative ways of managing and regulating diversity.

Besides an interdisciplinary approach, diversity management also needs a critical turn which attends to uneven power relations to raise awareness about and end inequality, exploitation, exclusion, discrimination and loss of dignity that individuals and groups face based on their diversity and difference. Calvard (2020) argues that framing diversity along the lines of power relations and politics would enrich diversity studies. However, the expansion of the diversity field over time has brought in less political and uncritical diversity frames, such as cognitive diversity, behavioural diversity and functional diversity (Kirton and Greene, 2021). The framing of diversity without power diverts attention from historical power struggles for equality, inclusion, solidarity and social justice that have given meaning and impetus to critical studies of diversity in the social sciences. In line with the transformative and critical tradition of diversity studies, this book also lends support to the expansion of diversity science and research to support equality and inclusion, viewing diversity not as an isolated end in itself but a path to the transformation of societies and institutions towards equality and inclusion.

Although one would expect a positive slant on diversity in a book on diversity (Ahmed and Swan, 2006), diversity continues to surface as a divisive construct at the heart of most hateful acts, conflicts, disagreements, atrocities and wars among human populations. In line with the Gramscian adage of the pessimism of the intellect and optimism of will (Antonini, 2019), in this book, we explore diversity and its pessimistic manifestations with a strong commitment to social and political change to repair the uneven power relations in diversity. Understanding how diversity and power intersect is essential in revealing how diversity is treated and how diversity could be regulated and governed in more democratic and inclusive ways (Özbilgin, 2019a). In his book *Gulliver's Travels, Jonathan Swift* tells the story of a war between fictional states of Lilliput and Blefuscu. They are two fictional nations with a major dispute and long wars about a major issue of diversity for these two nations, notably, at which end one should break their egg before citizens eat eggs (Jonathan Swift, *Gulliver's Travels*, 1826, p. 49). On this significant diversity concern, wars were waged, and thousands have died to defend their egg-based identity. What Swift presents in *Gulliver's Travels* as the diversity that causes major disputes between two nations is a satire about the long-standing historical disagreements between the French and English and between the Catholic and Protestant churches. This dispute, now long resolved and forgotten among common people in both countries, was based on an impossibly insignificant doctrinal difference, which we find rather futile today. In the same satirical way as described by Swift,

DOI: 10.4324/9780367824044-1

diversity continues to be the source of many conflicts and disputes across social and institutional settings, sometimes due to misunderstandings, ignorance and intolerance of diversity (Taksa and Groutsis, 2010, 2013a, 2013b; Groutsis et al., 2018b; Saba et al., 2021). Yet the will of people and institutions can overcome conflicts based on diversity. This book has a chapter on resistance, backlash and setbacks against diversity. However, we would do a gross injustice to diversity if we were to consider only some of its miserly consequences. Diversity is, at the same time, the reason for much of human achievements and accomplishments. We owe to diversity the diversity of intellectual and moral contributions and the varied richness of the world. There are many positive individual, institutional, social and environmental consequences of diversity if diversity is framed and managed well. In this book, we also attend to the management and regulation of diversity from multiple perspectives.

Diversity often refers to human diversity in traditional social sciences. Diversity studies have the underlying assumption that human diversity is superior to other forms of diversity, such as biodiversity and techno diversity. There is little recognition of how biodiversity and techno diversity contribute to and sustains life on earth in studies of social diversity. The old deal on diversity mainly focuses on a limited number of categories of human diversity based on social differences by gender, ethnicity, sexuality and class, among other emic categories. The fundamental assumption of the old deal is the dominion of human diversity over the natural environment and technology, two significant factors that will radicalise the diversity landscape soon. The old assumption of the dominion of humans and human diversity over the natural environment and technology has failed. For example, the earthquakes that tore apart more than ten cities in southeastern Turkey and northern Syria on February 6, 2023, led to immeasurable damage to all forms of life and collapse of the technological framework. Lax building regulation measures, amnesty for illegal buildings and common bribery led to devastating loss of life (Tol, 2023; Özbilgin et al., 2023c). This case illustrates that the domination of humans over nature and technology when left to operation of market forces alone collapses, and this relationship requires regulation. We explicate how the relationship between human diversity, biodiversity and techno diversity fails on two accounts. First, there is an environmental crisis due to excessive human impact. Climate change, the extinction of some species and environmental destruction of the natural environment induced by human consumption are giving warning signals, such as environmental disasters. Climate migration, water and food shortages and global warming are alarming concerns for social scientists, social movements and policymakers internationally. There is also a divide regarding human impact between the Global North and the Global South. The Global South produces most of what the Global North consumes. As a result of the production-generated impact on the environment, the Global South suffers a worse environmental impact than the Global North, which offshores its environmental impact. The environmental crises put extra pressure on politically, socially and economically disadvantaged groups of human diversity. The superiority of human diversity over biodiversity concerns becomes questionable, as human consumption has an unsustainable, devastating impact on nature and biodiversity, which in turn has an uneven impact on human diversity.

Second, techno diversity, which refers to the full range of disruptive technological innovations, such as artificial intelligence (AI), algorithmic system-led platform and gig economies, undermine and evade human control, regulation and governance. In many sectors of work, such as derivatives work in the financial services sector, artificial intelligence replaces human decision-making. It is impossible for a single individual or team to fully control complex algorithmic systems to ensure algorithmic justice. An increasing number of incidents of algorithmic inequality, injustice and bias are now reported in the media (Gulson et al., 2021). Disruptive technologies that lead to techno diversity rely on historical and old data. In the absence of regulatory measures for fair and equal impact on human diversity, techno diversity internalises, normalises and entrenches the biases inherent in the historical data. Vassilopoulou et al. (2022) explain that there is a governance and regulatory gap that leads to algorithmic biases being overlooked. The relationship between techno diversity and human diversity proves to be a skewed one, where the governance of techno diversity leads to the deterioration of this relationship. Thus, the old deal between human diversity, biodiversity and techno diversity shows signs of strain. We attend to this strain and possible venues for addressing it in later sections of this book.

In this introduction, we explore the crisis of diversity among life forms, human populations and institutional settings further in some detail. The competition for limited resources and untamed human greed and consumption have put biodiversity, human diversity and institutional diversity at risk. Global warming and depletion and contamination of natural sources are forcing species in the biodiversity to compete for limited resources. There are over 8 billion people worldwide (UN, 2022) and more than 9 million types of plants, animals, insects, protists and fungi (Cardinale et al., 2012). One million species face extinction by 2050 and beyond with devastating consequences due to human environmental impact (Tollefson, 2019). Crises of diversity due to human activity manifest as the extinction of species, maltreatment of ecosystems, discrimination and exploitation at work and life and deterioration of some forms of institutions and sectors of work and employment.

Ecological, human and institutional diversity is threatened due to excessive human activity worldwide. The demise of biodiversity is brought to public attention with social movements such as the #extinctionrebellion (Taylor, 2020) and the #fridaysforfuture (Soliev et al., 2021) of climate strikes in September 2019 (Laville and Watts, 2019), Gezi Park Movement in Turkey (Turkmenoglu, 2016), the billion tree afforestation drive in Pakistan (Sabir et al., 2022) and initiatives of the United Nations in recognition of the threat to biodiversity and climate change. Human diversity has always been the focus of historical struggles for power, resources, recognition and legitimacy among different groups. Intersectional solidarity emerges across social movements, which move beyond single-identity categories, such as #blacklivesmatter, #metoo and Pride marches. Furthermore, international declarations, such as the Universal Declaration of Human Rights, and conventions, such as the Convention on Elimination of All Forms of Discrimination Against Women (CEDAW) and the Convention on the Elimination of All Forms of Racial Discrimination (CERD), and part of UN Sustainable Development Goals and other initiatives are gaining intersectional character, embracing multiple agendas for change towards complex forms of diversity beyond human diversity alone.

There are serious threats to ecological and human diversity in the institutional context. The socio-political and economic organisation of societies and institutional arrangements are intricately interlinked with biodiversity and human diversity. Historically, institutional diversity manifested, as diverse institutional arrangements were made available in advanced democratic states to cater for varied social, political and economic needs. For example, public institutions are formed to provide equal and unhindered access to public goods, such as healthcare, education and justice. Welfare systems were originally located within the public sector provision in countries with established democratic regimes. Voluntary sector institutions are formed to provide solutions where the private and public sectors leave a gap in supporting public needs. Since the 1970s, diversity in these institutional arrangements has come under considerable threat with the expansion of the neoliberal system, which brought private sector logic to public and voluntary sector institutions (Özbilgin and Slutskaya, 2017; Kamasak et al., 2023). For example, competition and financialisation, dominant paradigms in the private sector institutions (Palpacuer et al., 2006), are promoted as ideal ways of managing and operating the public sector, non-governmental sector and voluntary sector institutions. Adopting private sector logic brings competition, deregulation, financialisation and individualisation to other sectors. It derails institutional diversity from a wide range of rationales and aims, such as public, charitable, solidaristic and compassionate service (Özbilgin and Slutskaya, 2017). In one of his many controversial statements during the Covid19 pandemic, the British Prime Minister of the time, Boris Johnson (BBC, 2021), boasted that 'capitalism' and 'greed' have helped Britain to buy and administer vaccinations. This tongue-in-cheek statement highlights how neoliberal logic has now become dominant in politics, impacting not only private sector institutions but also public sector decisions, converging the rationale by which public sector, non-governmental sector, charities and voluntary sector organisations run with competitive corporate rationales. The neoliberal turn internationally undermines the traditional diversity of institutions of regulation, commerce, philanthropy, community and worker collectives to the extent that it converts all institutions into private sector institutions (see, for instance, Groutsis et al., 2023).

The corrosive nature of the expansion of capitalist interests (Sennett, 1998), particularly through neoliberal ideology, continues to threaten institutional diversity and undermine solidarity, human rights and human diversity by marketising and commercialising everything in its path (Stiglitz, 2000, 2012, 2016). Anti-capitalist social movements, international debates around controlling the power and greed of global enterprises and voluntary initiatives, such as the Global Compact and the Sustainable Development Goals (SDGs) of the United Nations (UN), which promote sustainable development and accountability for global organisations, present as modest steps towards protecting institutional diversity. What brought this turn has been the unprecedented growth of the private sector's political power that undermined the traditional tripartite deal between workers, employers and the state. Growing recognition of serious threats to institutional diversity at multiple levels has galvanised interest in support of diversity, even if some commentators dismiss this international- and national-level resistance to loss of institutional diversity as feeble and suggest that more needs to be done to avert the crisis.

Technological advances, developments in transportation systems and changes in social mores and human demography, such as ageing populations, have engendered possibilities of diverse encounters among human populations and individuals. However, social diversity is also threatened by wars, famines, epidemics and many other crises and social injustices, which result in uneven distribution of limited resources. The human population has grown from 1 billion in the 1800s to 8 billion in 2021 (UN, 2022), and the human population now presents the single most significant threat to the depletion of natural resources, the destruction of biodiversity and the deterioration of institutions that help support different forms of diversity.

Humans are capable of not only destruction but also much creativity in developing technologies, arts and cultures, systems and institutions that improve their lives beyond measure over time. Most notably, humans created technologies to help them with their needs for security, sustenance and wealth and institutions, such as families and friendships that fulfilled their needs for shelter, nourishment and sociality, and many other institutions that supported their needs for education, healthcare, security, justice and work. Institutions have great diversity in terms of their forms and have significant power and influence in the access and distribution of natural and social resources. How some institutions are structured and legally defined allows them great power over and above other institutions. For example, private sector institutions, such as corporations, were given legal status, responsibilities and power to invest and accumulate wealth, similar to human beings. While some institutions, such as public sector organisations, are built for the protection and effective distribution of the public good, others, such as voluntary sector organisations, were created to provide charitable, philanthropic and voluntary contributions towards some social ends. Institutional diversity is not only necessary for healthy social, economic and political systems, it is also important for ensuring sustainable futures.

The asymmetric nature of power bases of different forms of institutions which were founded to protect different kinds of interests, such as the interests of the public, the environment or private investors, are also threatening the balance of access to resources for biodiversity and human beings. For example, the public sector institutions, such as the welfare state, which are founded to promote the public good, came under considerable attack by economic ideologies which are underpinned by a misguided belief that economic markets and private sector institutions could effectively manage the public good and the common ground by using market models of government, which essentially moulds the public sector into a market enterprise (Box et al., 2001). Economic liberalisation and its concomitant drives to bring competitive logic to public sector work and deregulation and privatisation of state enterprises started with Ronald Reagan in the USA and Margaret Thatcher in the UK and many others in the Global South who subscribed to market liberalisation ideas. The expansion of the neoliberal ideology has hit the public sector hard. Voluntary and social enterprise sectors are invited to fill the void that the deterioration and part-privatisation of social welfare systems have caused, where neoliberal ideology took root (Nicholls and Teasdale, 2017). Beyond the national-level threat to diversity in institutions and sectors of work, the global support afforded to commercial enterprises and corporations has given global corporations unprecedented power, allowing them to grow in economic resources and political power greater than average-sized nation-states and all international institutions, such as the UN and the International Labour Organisation (ILO). Thus, institutional diversity is also under threat at the global institutional level, as there is a limited range of measures to curb the exploitative potential of global corporations. As such, global corporations, such as Amazon, remain grossly unaccountable in terms of their impact across their value chains, causing inequalities and injustice across human populations and institutions with which it interacts (Mergen and Ozbilgin, 2021b). There is little governance of the value chains of global organisations (Gibbon et al., 2008), which have the significant political power to influence national- and international-level regulations today (Groutsis et al., 2015; Özbilgin et al., 2016; Underhill et al., 2016; van den Broek et al., 2016). Brabet and Beierlein (2017) explain that how multinational corporations operate through their value chains remains a problematic black box. The opacity of the value chains of global organisations, particularly with the advance of technology-led global businesses, make it difficult to reveal and question their monopolistic and oligopolistic uneven impact on diverse communities and stakeholders.

In this dystopian context where the old deal of human diversity, biodiversity and techno diversity is failing with the unprecedented decline of institutional diversity, what could be a source of hope? Social movements, which support human diversity, need to recognise the collapse of the old deal to establish a new deal between human diversity, nature and technology. The possibility of such a new deal could strengthen the human diversity perspectives and open possibilities for intersectional solidarity with other social movements (i.e. eco-feminism and techno-feminism) to ultimately recognise nature as a legal entity that can be defended by social movements and the public in legal systems. Furthermore, the problems with effective governance of techno diversity require a closer look at the responsibilisation of technology. Such a responsibilisation could be achieved by transforming ownership structures of technology, attending to technological impacts across the value chain and taxing algorithmic systems for redistribution of wealth across the value chains of technology. These radical ideas are yet to be tested, although there are early signs of progress towards these radical propositions.

Biodiversity, human diversity and institutional diversity are in constant flux and under threat due to unprecedented challenges that increasing human populations and depletion of resources and expansion of the capitalist system through disruptive technological innovations and resultant changes in the climate are posing. In this context, biodiversity and techno diversity emerge as global challenges that need to be addressed in the future. In the first half of this book, we focus on diversity among human populations with specific reference to workforce diversity. Focusing on institutional diversity, we question how institutions could undermine or foster diversity. The latter part of the book focuses on the management and regulation of diversity, highlighting the emergence of the new deal between human diversity, biodiversity and techno diversity, which could potentially allow diversity scholarship to expand beyond human diversity. The new deal refers to possibilities of regulating human diversity, biodiversity and techno diversity. The final chapter proposes radical solutions, such as recognising nature and biodiversity as legal entities and building solidarity between social movements and environmental movements to protect biodiversity and promote human diversity together. In terms of techno diversity and its algorithmic governance with diversity in mind, the chapter proposes not only legal rights for techno diversity but also legal responsibilities as a legal entity to challenge the uneven model ownership in the value chain of techno diversity, which benefits the owners and investors at the expense of all other actors in the technological value chain.

This book has seven chapters which explore diversity from critical and transdisciplinary perspectives. The first chapter defines diversity and identifies its origins, manifestations and frames. The chapter has an illustrative case of the gene delusion. Chapter 2 focuses on generic, (i.e. etic) and locally meaningful (i.e. emic) categories of diversity and how these forms of diversity are examined. The illustrative case explains the migration of diversity constructs and categories over time and across countries. Chapter 3 explains how each discipline of science has contributed to the development of diversity science as a transdisciplinary and multifaceted field of research. The illustrative case in this section explores the significance of interdisciplinarity for science and diversity in particular. Diversity and its consequences are explored in Chapter 4 based on pro-diversity research. The illustrative case attempts to broaden the frame of diversity from human diversity to posthuman diversity. Chapter 5 of this book explores the resistance, backlash and setbacks against diversity across micro, meso and macro levels. The illustrative case focuses on the denial of institutional racism in the UK. Chapter 6 presents approaches and techniques for diversity management. It highlights how diversity management approaches lead to certain choices of techniques to be adopted. The chapter highlights the failure of diversity management interventions with examples of international research. The final chapter of the book is on the regulation of diversity, exploring voluntary, coercive and relational variants of regulation. The chapter delineates the new deal for diversity in light of the collapse of the old deal between humans, the environment and technology. The new deal between human diversity, biodiversity and techno diversity is illustrated in a case study on responsibilisation for posthuman diversity.

CHAPTER 1

DIVERSITY AND ITS ORIGINS

Diversity, which is defined as the availability of difference and variation, is a concept that finds use across all disciplines of science, humanities and the arts. Diversity is an inclusive concept in its essence, based on the assumption of coexistence of differences and variations in social, environmental, symbolic and material worlds. The plurality of its definitions and uses is the main strength and limitation of the concept of diversity. It is possible to adopt a definition of diversity to serve almost any end. For example, diversity could be considered a strength or a weakness, a reason for solidarity or conflict, a source of inspiration or threat. Therefore, it is important to understand the history of diversity, the politics of defining diversity and the emergence of its varied forms. In this chapter, we explore the power and politics of defining diversity. First, we define diversity from multiple frames and multilevel perspectives, focusing on struggles for dominance and power that shape how diversity manifests across time and places. Second, we examine manifestations of diversity in different settings and explore the biological and social construction of diversity through the nature-nurture debate. Third, we explore key categories of biological and social diversity, including gender and sex, ethnicity and race, social and economic class, sexual orientation and gender identity and disability. The chapter ends with an illustrative case of gene delusion.

DEFINING DIVERSITY

Diversity has been framed differently depending on the socio-historical context in which it was used. Diversity is a relational concept like all other social concepts (Kyriakidou and Ozbilgin, 2006; Özbilgin and Vassilopoulou, 2018; Syed and Özbilgin, 2009). As a relational concept, diversity gains new meanings and content depending on the particular time, place, socio-cultural, institutional and symbolic setting and human population in which it is discussed (Tatli et al., 2012; Chanlat et al., 2013). Therefore, for example, the kinds of diversity issues that are considered in Australia would be different to those in China, shaped by their unique historical, regulatory and cultural contexts. Critical diversity studies focus on the unresolved nature of the historical injustice against the indigenous people and the rampant historic anti-immigration politics in Australia. These forms of ethnic inequity are instituted as forms of labour market protection for the white settlers that initially colonised the country. This historical context and current challenges shape how diversity is framed in Australia (Syed and Kramar, 2010; Taksa and Groutsis, 2017). However, in the case of China, critical diversity work would focus on the changing dynamics of China's approach to its extremely diverse ethnic composition, which is made up of 56 ethnic groups (China ABC, 2021), which leads to very different sets of critical considerations. Critical diversity studies in the USA (McDonald, 2010) focus on the uneven power relations rather than instrumental rationales for promoting diversity. Therefore, understanding diversity critically is about understanding the context in which diversity manifests. Özbilgin and Chanlat (2017) illustrate how workforce diversity manifests as a phenomenon which is historically and geographically specific yet dynamically changing based on current socio-demographic and political trends.

Local customs; cultures; religious and belief systems; legal, political and economic conditions; institutional arrangements; and human geography shape how diversity is framed relationally. Similarly, the kinds of diversity issues that are discussed in one particular location change

DOI: 10.4324/9780367824044-2

over time. For example, aspects of human diversity that were covered and protected by laws in the 1970s in the UK were limited to gender, ethnicity and disability. In the 2000s, the categories of diversity that are protected by law have expanded to include sexual orientation, age, marriage and civil partnership, gender reassignment, pregnancy and maternity and religion and belief (EHRC, 2021). The expansion of the categories of diversity, which are protected against discrimination by law, has grown considerably in the last 30 years. We owe these legal developments partly to a general increase in public demands for social justice internationally in a world facing considerable challenges to all forms of diversity and which suffers entrenched forms of inequality and exploitation across many dimensions. The demand for social justice is at an all-time high worldwide, characterised by strong social movements for and backlash against diversity (Özbilgin and Erbil, 2021b). International Labour Organisation (ILO), which was founded to promote equality and fairness in the world of work and labour, explains how social justice is even more urgent a demand today:

> The aspiration for social justice, through which every working man and woman can claim freely and on the basis of equality of opportunity their fair share of the wealth that they have helped to generate, is as great today as it was when the ILO was created in 1919. As the ILO celebrates its 100th anniversary in 2019, the importance of achieving social justice is ever more pressing, with the rise in inequality and exclusion, which is a threat to social cohesion, economic growth and human progress. With climate change, demographic changes, technological development and, more generally, globalization, we are witnessing a world of work that is changing at an unprecedented pace and scale. How can these challenges be addressed to offer possibilities for the achievement of social justice in an ever more complex world of work?
>
> (ILO, 2021, p. 1)

Diversity is a universally recognised but contextually shaped phenomenon. As such, it is formed by the circumstances in which it is located. For example, Tatli et al. (2012) illustrate that when diversity travelled from North America to Britain, France and Germany, it gained unique meanings in each country. Diversity gains new meanings in new locations depending on the priorities, customs and regulatory requirements in that location. Diversity sometimes loses relevance in new contexts because each context has silences, taboos and hegemonic frames. For example, it is difficult to discuss class diversity in the UK, religious diversity in France and ethnic diversity in Germany due to the historical struggles which render these categories of diversity contentious in the mainstream. Diversity also bends and gains new meanings depending on national priorities and frames by which diversity is defined. In the UK, the dominant discourse of multiculturalism has shaped the diversity discourse. The French revolution and its values of equality, universalism and fraternity-based solidarity have shaped how diversity is framed in France (Chanlat, 2017; Bruna et al., 2017). However, Brabet et al. (2019) explain the resilience of racism and the low outcomes that minority ethnic individuals face in the French employment context. Despite divergent paths that the use of terms have taken across national borders, when explored critically, labour market outcomes of disadvantaged groups remain poor. In the German context, diversity is locked into the integration of migrants, which has been its central effort in the post-war era (Vassilopoulou, 2011; Vassilopoulou et al., 2019). While among three countries with relatively strong cultural, political and economic ties as Britain, France and Germany, diversity gains diverse meanings, when diversity travels to other less familiar locations, it gains more surprising meanings and interpretations yet. For example, Küskü et al. (2021) demonstrate that in a country with ceremonial laws on equality, no state support for diversity and general social hostility, diversity is left unattended in discourses and policies in organisations. All these examples highlight the interplay between definitions of diversity and the circumstances of the setting that gives meaning to diversity.

The relationship between humans and their circumstances informs how diversity is defined in agentic and structural terms and from multiple levels. At the macro level, there is global, international- and national-level diversity. The macro-level diversity is sometimes framed as social diversity, shaped by civil liberties, human rights and social movements that demand equality for all. At the macro level also exist decentralised autonomous organisations (DAOs), which bring together individuals towards common yet improbable goals, such as eradicating poverty, building unity in diversity, eliminating inequality or combating global warming. Many social movements today turn into DAOs to effect changes towards shared concerns and to improve their impact with limited resources (Marquez, 2021). Macro-level structures regulate the politics of how diversity is defined formally. The macro-level definitions of diversity help formalise diversity in national and international policy. Drawing on the example of the MeToo movement and the need for the movement to secure intersectional character to retain its transformative power, Ozkazanc-Pan (2019) explains that collective and intersectional agency could provide that impetus to social movements to gain transformative power and intersectional character. Meliou and Mallett (2022) draw upon the intersectional theorising of McCall's (2005) and Archer's (2003) work on human reflexivity to develop the concept of 'intersectional reflexivity'. Intersectional reflexivity reveals a sense of self that emerges where the past meets the present and where social structures collide. Their analysis shows how older women negotiate their concerns in relation to gendered ageing and realise self-employment.

At the meso level, definitions of diversity are at the organisational and institutional levels. Institutional definitions of diversity locate diversity in either individual demography or in structures, systems, processes and routines of organisations. When diversity is defined as relational demography of individuals, it can help organisations shape employee behaviours in inclusive ways (Harrison et al., 1998). When diversity is defined in institutional ways, it can help organisations consider the consequences of their institution making practices on diversity. For example, Acker's (2006) theory of inequality regimes focuses on how relatively innocuous-looking routines, structures and practices in organisations could lead to discriminatory outcomes. Healy et al. (2011) show how inequality regimes manifest in public sector organisations in the UK. Drawing on inequality regimes, the definition of diversity at the meso level would map diversity in practices, systems and structures of institutions. Meso-level definitions of diversity locate responsibility for diversity-related change variably in employees or institutions.

At the micro level, diversity is defined as a set of individual characteristics based on their demographic background, biological and social constitution and their relational difference to the group (Tsui et al., 1992). For example, Linnehan et al. (2006) measure individual attitudes, beliefs and behaviours of diversity. The micro-level definitions of diversity tend to locate responsibility for change on individuals who are different to seek inclusion or the dominant group members to adopt inclusive behaviours. The level at which diversity is defined informs where the responsibility for protecting diversity resides. If diversity is framed as a macro-level concept, it is often regulated through the pressures of social movements, international regulatory interventions and national laws. If diversity is framed as a meso-level concept, the definition straddles individual- to organisational-level responsibility for diversity and inclusion. If diversity is framed as an individual-level construct, it deals with diversity as cognition, affect and behaviours. Syed and Özbilgin (2009) explore the multilevel nature of diversity through a relational framework, where diversity issues at each level of analysis impact other levels through time and place. For example, national- and social-level diversity priorities are transposed into laws and adapted by organisations as diversity interventions experienced by individuals at work. Similarly, the micro-individual beliefs may lead to institutional structures (Ridgeway, 2001) and turn into the organisational design by change agents (Nentwich et al., 2015) and moral entrepreneurs (Greenhalgh, 2019), whose opinions are taken up by general public, critical actors and followers. Therefore, definitions of diversity at different levels are co-constitutive, as each definition influences the definitions of diversity in other levels.

Defining is a political act. Diversity is defined depending on the politics of the context. Each definition has implications for key actors and relations of power, and it sets intentions and motivates stability or change (Özbilgin and Erbil, 2023a, 2023d). Defining diversity as a political act could be a force for progress towards equality, equity, inclusion and social justice, if those definitions capture effective agendas for change, fit for the circumstances. There are fine distinctions, semantic differences and populist divisions in use of these terms. For example, the choice of the terms of equality versus equity is remarkable. While equality and equity have varied definitions and approaches, these terms are sometimes defined in narrow ways to serve populist agendas to undermine the value of either. Cook and Hegtvedt (1983) unpack differences and complementarity between equality and equity, showing that what it means to be equal includes objective equality of having equal amounts, subjective equality, relative equality (i.e. equity), rank order equality and equal opportunity. Failing to see intra-conceptual variations could lead to misinterpretations and misappropriations. Similarly, the terms diversity and inclusion are sometimes presented as polarised terms. However, diversity and inclusion are interdependent concepts, which could be used together rather than in isolation. Diversity without inclusion and inclusion without diversity both sustain uneven power relations and divert from the value of having diversity and inclusion. Diversity and inclusion are interdependent and complementary concepts.

Defining diversity needs to attend to the conceptual universe of diversity and related terms, such as inequality, discrimination, exclusion, bias, equality, equity and inclusion. The choice of any of these terms in referring to diversity highlights the politics of diversity in any setting. Definitions of diversity could include critical, progressive or conservative lenses. Critical approaches to diversity include social justice concerns, such as inequality, exclusion and discrimination that individuals from diverse backgrounds experience. Progressive approaches may focus on the direction of change, such as equality, equity and inclusion. Conservative approaches to diversity may resist progressive diversity and social justice demands. The coexistence of conservative, progressive and critical approaches to defining diversity is why defining diversity is a highly contested and political issue. The terms diversity and inclusion are often used together in social policy. Some scholars make a distinction between diversity and inclusion. For example, a diverse workforce may not be very inclusive (e.g. Kirton and Greene, 2021) nor grant voice and representation (Peterson and Gardner, 2023) and that inclusion has a stronger positive impact on organisational outcomes than diversity alone (Mor Barak et al., 2016; Nishii, 2013; Shore et al., 2011). In the same way, Bourke and Espedido (2019 and 2020) suggest that inclusive interpersonal behaviours and inclusive leadership are good for business. Yet more recent work shows that even inclusive leadership has a curvilinear relationship with organisational performance, for which too little or too much inclusion could result in lower performance outcomes (Ma and Tang, 2022). Exploring diversity with its allied concepts, such as inclusion, expands our understanding of diversity through different lenses.

The politics of defining diversity has some traps. For example, diversity could be defined as a threat or the identity characteristic of an individual. Defining diversity as an individual identity consideration alone may derail possibilities of connecting diversity with common good, solidarity and communities. Similarly, defining diversity as a national or organisational concern may undermine the role of individual actors in promoting equality and inclusion. Defining diversity is a multifarious act, enriched when the definition takes on the board contextual, relational, multilevel and political aspects of diversity. When faced with a definition of diversity, we can ask simple questions, such as what, where, when, how, why, for whom and by whom to flesh out the interests and the relations of power that shape that particular definition. Through such an awareness, we may develop a critical reflexivity that transcends the naive treatment of defining a simple, innocuous and disinterested act. Definitions of diversity can shed light on how diversity is treated and what remains silent and unattended in that definition.

HOW DOES DIVERSITY MANIFEST?

In his theory of emergence, Pepper (1926) explains that there are cumulative, epiphenomenal, alongside predictable and unpredictable ways that any social phenomenon emerges. If we adopt this framework of emergence, workforce diversity may have a cumulative emergence. Cumulative emergence is about the emergence of multiple forms of a phenomenon. For example, diversity manifests along generic diversity categories. Each individual would be located along generic demographic diversity lines based on their gender, ethnicity, age, sexual orientation, disability and class. Therefore, each individual would have a cumulative experience of their demographic diversity categories. In Chapter 2, we explore further the concept of intersectionality that accounts for the cumulative emergence of diversity.

Diversity may manifest in an epiphenomenal way (i.e. unique to its context). There are diversity categories which are unique to certain geographies, such as the caste system in the Indian subcontinent. Deshpande (2015) explains that the caste system is a form of emic diversity which is locally meaningful. Tatli and Özbilgin (2012a) present a framework to investigate emic categories of diversity by tracing how power, privilege and resources are allocated in a given context. Through the identification of historically and locally meaningful processes through which the elites obtain and retain their unearned privileges, emic categories could be named. The authors explain that class presents an emic diversity category in the UK, which affords unearned privileges and penalties to individuals by virtue of their inherited class position. Epiphenomenal manifestations of diversity shed light on local struggles for power and privilege in any context.

Diversity manifests also in predictable ways. Most diversity concerns are historically embedded, and the future patterns are often path dependent. For example, the legacy of slavery and colonialism shapes how ethnic diversity manifests. Colonialism is a relationship of extraction of resources and exploitation of colonised territories and peoples by colonising forces (Georgiadou et al., 2021). Yalkin and Özbilgin (2022) explain that ethnic diversity as experienced in academia requires an understanding of colonial history and its path-dependent influence on modern institutions. The authors show that there are neocolonial knowledge hierarchies between academics from colonised territories and academics from colonising countries. Predictable manifestations of diversity require an appreciation of the history, culture, geography and symbolism that informed the original struggles for power to understand how that form of diversity manifests now.

Diversity may also take unpredictable manifestations. There are path-breaking legitimations of new forms of diversity. For example, neurodiversity, which emerged in the late 1990s as a concept capturing the diversity of cognitive and mental functionalities in the human brain, has been the outcome of path-breaking advancements in neuroscience (Pisano, 2017). In the final chapter of this book, we explain the previously unpredicted emergence of biodiversity and techno diversity as human diversity concerns. Devastation of the natural environment and the challenge of governing disruptive technological innovations, these two manifestations of diversity are now legitimated and considered as part of unpredictable, and yet-to-be-regulated, concerns of human diversity. Although we attended to the historical emergence of diversity, history alone cannot help us understand how we should craft our social and economic lives, shape organisational designs and change systems and structures to make them welcoming of diversity.

Diversity emergence also requires foresight (Tatli and Özbilgin, 2009), future crafting and co-design which constitute the less predictable manifestations of diversity. Newly legitimated forms of diversity bring the new normal (Samdanis and Özbilgin, 2020) to our social and economic lives and significant institutions, such as family, education and employment. Therefore, it is important to theorise afresh to capture the new normal that emerges with diversity.

To understand the manifestation and emergence of workforce diversity, we need to explore these four different routes through which diversity categories could have developed. However, beyond the Popperian emergence of diversity, the nature versus nurture debate is the most classical dichotomous pathway to studying manifestation of diversity (Durham, 1991). The nature argument of the nature-nurture debate takes a biological stance and refers to certain inherited qualities of diversity, such as the colour of skin and some disabilities, to account for manifestation of diversity. The nature argument often refers to biology, ecology, genetic makeup and nature to explain manifestations of human diversity (Blazer and Hernandez, 2006). The nature arguments tend to be essentialist, arguing for the deterministic role of human nature and biological and genetic makeup. The nature argument has been used against demands for equality and inclusion for some groups.

Proponents of the nurture argument suggest that diversity issues emerge from socialisation, schooling and acculturation of individuals from early childhood in families to educational institutions and beyond (Ceci and Williams, 1999). The nurture argument highlights the explanatory role of the environment in shaping the emergence of human diversity. Although genetic inheritance accounts for some of our physical qualities, personality and psychology, research on the role of nature highlights how our circumstances shape our differences and diversity. The nature-nurture debate is often underpinned by biological versus social constructions of how difference codes manifest. One prominent example of the nature-nurture debate is the distinction between sex and gender. Sex is often viewed as a biologically determined category of diversity, manifesting from nature arguments (Hird, 2000). In many countries, sex is based on a binary distinction between women and men (Dea, 2016). However, there are developments in the field of social policy highlighting that such frames of sex are merely social constructions (Dea, 2016). For example, intersex and non-binary individuals, who fall out of this binary conception of sex, are now increasingly recognised in advanced democratic countries (Wilchins et al., 2020). There is now wider recognition of intersex and trans individuals in legal terms in countries such as Germany, which permits a third category or a possibility of changing sex in its national registration, passport and legal system. Monro et al. (2021) outline that there is an interplay between the well-being of intersex individuals and their inclusion as fully recognised social actors and citizens. In contrast to often rigid and binary definitions of sex, gender diversity is defined as a social construction of being women and men in each society. Therefore, gender diversity, as a social construct, would gain new meanings and changes across place and time (Tsouroufli, 2018a; Gezici Yalçın and Tanriverdi, 2018). While sex often refers to nature, gender tends to refer to the nurture aspects of the debate. Similar issues exist between race and ethnicity: while race is often attributed to arbitrary markers, such as colour and bloodline, ethnicity is how such supposed differences among people are socially attributed to different meanings and values. Today, sex and gender, race and ethnicity are often used interchangeably for convenience reasons, and some of the differences that have led to their emergence from the nature-nurture debate have transformed or disappeared in their contemporary use.

There is also a historical dimension to human diversity. Foley and Lahr (2011) explore the emergence of human diversity and identify that human diversity emerged in the last 100,000 years when humans first moved out of Africa and spread around the world. Authors argue that human diversity presents a genetic and cultural paradox. While intragroup genetic diversity is apparently high based on genome studies in human populations, intergroup genetic diversity appears varied. Conversely, intragroup cultural diversity is low among human populations, when intergroup cultural diversity could be high or low. Authors explain that as markers of human cultural diversity, there are slightly less than 7,000 distinct languages and approximately 3,800 distinct cultures that social scientists have identified. Central to the emergence of human diversity is the ability of human beings to shape their environments, capture resources and craft their conditions, norms and ways of life and transfer of such knowledge to new generations.

Since its early beginning, the emergence of diversity is historically embedded, as it gains shape and meaning depending on time and place. Diversity concerns remain idiosyncratically local because of differences that diversity emergence has had across different geographies and over time. The emergence of diversity as a cultural artefact in early times has gained new form with the emergence of diversity as a result of changes in the moral landscape, fostered by social movements, historical turning points and disputes about the distribution of power and resources (Uygur, 2021). For naive commentators, the emergence of diversity may appear infinitely relative due to its complexity, as forms, manifestations and rationales for diversity are highly varied. Implicit to such relativism is a subtle invitation to end commitment to progress towards universal human rights and values of equality and inclusion (Macklin, 1999). However, if we explore diversity through the lens of power relations, we could transcend such relativism that could otherwise disarm emancipation and commitment to universal human rights. This cautionary note about relativism in manifestations of diversity is critically important for engaged scholars who are committed to human rights, equality and inclusion. Relativism is an anti-progressive stance. Not all forms of diversity matter in the same way. Gender, ethnic and sexual orientation diversity emanate from social movements that wish to end inequality. They cannot be treated in the same way as functional diversity in teams, which does not require a commitment to human rights but may serve corporate interests in contribution to the bottom line alone. Therefore, it is important to distinguish between diversity categories that manifested out of the struggles for human rights and those that manifested based on corporate demands for competitiveness, innovation and performance.

CATEGORIES OF DIVERSITY

There are many established and generic categories of human diversity, such as gender, ethnicity, class, sexual orientation, disability, religion and belief, among others. Categories of diversity emanate from different sources. First, some diversity categories, such as gender, ethnicity and sexual orientation, emanate from human rights, civil liberties and social movements, such as the feminist movement, anti-racist movement and the LGBT+ movement (Özbilgin et al., 2017). Second, some categories of diversity originate from organisational demands for high performance, innovation and competition, such as the team- and organisational-level differences, such as functional diversity and diversity based on seniority and education. The former cluster of diversity categories is mainly considered in relation to equality, justice and inclusion concerns at work and in life. The second cluster of diversity categories is often apolitical and considered mainly in response to performative demands in organisations. In this book, our emphasis is on the former categories of diversity that involve a commitment to human rights, civil liberties and justice for all. The uneven relations of power and influence are fundamental to the emergence of social movements that promote diversity, equality and inclusion. Individuals and groups that experience inequalities, discrimination and exclusion have historically demanded inclusion, equality and equity. With such social demands, critical categories of diversity emerged. April et al. (2023) outline how diversity categories relate to experiences of exclusion. Later, with the expansion of the diversity discourses, other less critical and more instrumental categories of diversity, such as job roles, are added to the long lists organisations are using today to monitor and manage diversity.

We can distinguish etic and emic categories of diversity (Tatli and Özbilgin, 2012a; Palalar Alkan et al., 2022). Etic diversity categories are based on generic and established perspectives studied across multiple locations. The two sets of diversity categories outlined earlier are termed etic categories of diversity because they are studied extensively across all countries and regions of the world (Özbilgin and Chanlat, 2017). Etic categories include gender, ethnicity, class, age, sexual orientation, and disability, among others, which are recognised as diversity categories in international agreements across different countries and regions. Emic categories of diversity are idiosyncratic and specific to localities, and they are not generic in nature. Emic categories of diversity emanate from an understanding of local explanations, which are often not meaningful in other locations. Emic categories of diversity cannot easily travel across different local environments. Emic categories of diversity emerge as a local setting is explored in terms of unique ways power and privileges are negotiated between the haves and have-nots. One specific example of the emic diversity category from Turkey would be the concept of *hemseri*, which roughly translates to people born in the same city. *Hemseri* (individuals with the same birthplace) owe each other a moral duty of care above and beyond the duty of care they have for other acquaintances born elsewhere in Turkey. Thus, a *hemseri* would be afforded (by other *hemseris*) better access to social and work networks than a non-*hemseri*. The *hemseri/non-hemseri* category of diversity does not travel outside Turkey, as it would lack explanatory power. Thus, it is considered an emic category of diversity, which operates as a discriminatory system where hemseri networks could determine access to resources and positions of power and privilege (Kamasak et al., 2019). Most diversity research focuses on etic categories of diversity that cuts across different geographies. Emic diversity categories may remain silent, particularly in countries and regions underexplored by diversity scholars. Another example of the emic category of diversity is postcode diversity in France. Postcodes are marked with ethnic and religious differences in France. Therefore, when studying the French context, it is possible to include emic terms, such as postcode diversity and discrimination (Kiwan, 2011), when such a concept would not generate meaningful results in the same way in the UK, where postcodes do not have the same ethnic and religious markers (Tunstall et al., 2014).

Not all diversity categories are similarly treated in research and practice across countries. Gender is the most commonly studied category of diversity internationally. Due to several initiatives, such as the CEDAW (Convention on Elimination of Discrimination Against Women) and the SDGs (Sustainable Development Goals), which focus on and include gender diversity in their content, most countries and organisations have mechanisms that monitor and manage gender diversity. The same international drive only partly applies to ethnic diversity, even though there are international conventions to eliminate racism (Özbilgin, 2019a; D'Almada-Remedios et al., 2021). One reason why ethnic diversity is less emphasised internationally has been the complexity of ethnic counting practices (Karakas and Özbilgin, 2019). Diversity based on disability is one of the less studied subjects internationally due to significant differences in how disability is treated and accommodated as a biological, social, religious, spiritual and cultural phenomenon. Eliminating disability discrimination is a significant concern ratified by most nation-states. Diversity based on sexuality and sexual orientation–based diversity is also complicated by significant variations in the way it is historically treated, socially constructed and locally regulated and sometimes protected or criminalised. There is limited focus on sexual orientation diversity outside the developed and democratic countries. There emerges a pecking order between categories of diversity in terms of the research conducted, social and national legislative support that they receive and the recognition and resources that they are given in organisations. Therefore, focusing on categories of diversity rather than considering diversity as a monolithic body of knowledge may help combat these hierarchies of knowledge and practice among categories of diversity.

DIVERSITY AND ITS MULTIPLE FRAMES

Diversity is a broad concept that means different things to different people. The divergence of frames of diversity is most evident in how diversity is defined and measured. The most dominant frame of diversity is that of numbers and numerical representation. Diversity in numbers relates to the proportionate representation of individuals from disadvantaged backgrounds. Numbers of women in positions of power and authority, representation of minority ethnic groups across different domains of economic and social life and proportions of out lesbian, gay, bisexual and trans (LGBT+) individuals in different sectors and labour markets are examples of how numerical framing of diversity could be used. When diversity is framed in terms of numerical representation, vertical and horizontal segregation could be used. Vertical segregation refers to the proportionate representation of people in positions of power and privilege (Poggio, 2010). Kanter (1977) famously coined the term tokenism to refer to the ceremonial and limited representation of diversity in positions of power and leadership. Horizontal segregation refers to the proportionate representation of people across different categories of work, such as the demographic composition of doctors, nurses, administrators and auxiliary staff, to identify over and underrepresentation of certain demographic groups (Charles, 2003). Numerical framing of diversity with headcounts provides a partial understanding of the value attributed to diversity in different settings. Headcount and numerical framing of diversity tends to omit the complexity of subjective experience of individuals from diverse backgrounds.

Diversity could also be framed as relations of power and used to examine the uneven power relations among different groups of people by the majority and minority dynamics, historical privilege and disadvantages and through social justice lenses (Nkomo et al., 2019; Zanoni, 2011). For example, in the case of South Africa, the struggle for equality and racial emancipation could be studied with the frame of diversity as power relations. In contrast to the usual majority and minority dynamics based on headcounts alone, South Africa is a country where the minority ethnic group (whites) dominated the majority ethnic (black South Africans and other black communities) historically. Workforce and social diversity in South Africa, when studied from numerical and power relations perspectives, provide contrasting insights, as the minority-majority dynamic does not always translate to relations of power (April et al., 2012; Myeza and April, 2021). Thus, there is utility in drawing on more than one frame of diversity to understand a particular human population. Similarly, studies on gender composition and power relations in the boardroom indicate that increased gender representation has not radically shifted the gender order and power relations based on traditional gender hierarchies (Sayce and Özbilgin, 2014; Kakabadse et al., 2015; Georgiadou et al., 2021).

Diversity is also studied as a set of psychological concerns, including affect, cognition and behaviours (Jones et al., 2013). For example, issues such as bias, stereotyping, harassment, bullying and stigma are constructs which frame diversity issues from a psychological perspective. Psychological framing of diversity tends to explore diversity as an individual-level construct that occurs at the point of experience, cognition and behavioural choices (Blaine and Brenchley, 2020). Psychological framing of diversity is the dominant paradigm in studies of equality, diversity and inclusion, and it informs much of the awareness raising, training and education interventions for diversity management in organisations. Although raising awareness is a widely used diversity intervention, it is criticised for its tendency to locate the responsibility for diversity awareness and intervention at the individual level, as it is underpinned by the assumption that changing individual cognitive, affective and behavioural frames would be sufficient to support diversity. Authors such as Dobbin and Kalev (2016, 2018, 2022) and Noon (2018) have been critical of the domination of the psychological frames in the design and delivery of diversity interventions. Authors argue that without institutional- and organisational-level development, individual psychology-level interventions are not adequate measures for managing diversity.

This leads us to the next frame of diversity (i.e. institutional and organisational frames of diversity). For example, Zhang (2020) calls for moving beyond individual and psychological framing of diversity to changing and transforming organisations. Institutional framing of diversity often draws on sociological notions and underlines how organisational development interventions should be considered frames for diversity management. For example, the stepwise model for making progress on diversity by April (2021) or the maturity model of diversity management by Jonsen and Özbilgin (2014) posit that diversity interventions would move from training and education towards deeper level structural and organisational development activities as diversity gains legitimacy, recognition and maturity in an organisation. The framing of diversity as a psychological or an institutional construct leads to a spectrum of choices of actions, placing responsibility on individuals or organisations respectively.

There are process frames of diversity also. In these frames, diversity is explored in terms of its antecedents, correlates and consequences (Nishii et al., 2018). Antecedents of diversity include normative pressures from social movements, organisational leaders and the preparedness of organisational culture and climate for diversity. Process frames of diversity include activities and correlates of diversity, such as training and education, through which diversity competencies are offered; engagement of stakeholders in defining terms and conditions of diversity; and implementation of diversity interventions across the organisation (Bruna, 2016a, 2016b, 2020, 2022; Koall, 2001). The process frames also show how effective diversity management may lead to positive outcomes, such as improved innovative potential, employee engagement and lower levels of turnover intention, among others (Nishii and Özbilgin, 2007). Process frames may focus on individual, team and organisational outcomes of diversity (Roberson et al., 2017a). The curious aspect of the process frames is that the way diversity is regulated across time and place varies extensively. As a result, process frames would hold only when the context could be fixed and when a single diversity context is studied.

Legal, cultural and historical context shapes how diversity is defined and practised in organisations. For example, despite their geographic and democratic proximity, there are marked differences in how diversity is defined, measured and regulated between Britain, France and Germany. Notably, the national history in terms of colonisation, state ideology, economic systems and market ideology shape to a wide extent the way diversity is viewed in these countries (Karatas-Ozkan et al., 2010; Tatli et al., 2012). Syed and Özbilgin (2009) provide a relational framework that locates diversity in its history and multilevel context, including regulatory-, cultural- and market-level dynamics at the macro level; organisational processes and contingencies at the meso level; and individual choices and chances at the micro level. Framing diversity from multiple vantage points locates individual and institutional actors in different fields of social, political and economic relations. It helps us identify the respective levels of responsibility these actors may have in supporting diversity.

ILLUSTRATIVE CASE: THE GENE DELUSION

'For' has become a dangerous word in genetic science (Ball, 2020). Popularised versions of genetic science refer to 'genes for' something, such as 'genes for intelligence, genes for mental illness, genes for cancer', among others. This trend has also been fuelled by under-informed politicians, some of whom claimed that identifying genetic sequences for certain illnesses would lead to personalised remedies. On a more sinister note, the ultra-right wing has usurped the term 'genes for' on two ill-founded accounts: First, to assert biologically deterministic approaches to eugenics (Sear, 2021) to justify sexism, racism, ableism and classism. Second, to highlight genetic differences, rather than discrimination, to account for poor health, lowly educational attainment levels and failure to reach positions of power and status for individuals from atypical backgrounds. Some studies on 'gene for' have gone to the extreme to claim an explanation of the political beliefs of people in terms of right-wing or left-wing political affiliations. Zaraska (2016) reported that genes could explain 40 per cent of our political choices while the environment has 60 per cent explanatory power in predicting political attitudes.

The misappropriation of advances in genetic science in this way is called gene delusion (Ball, 2020). Another aspect of gene delusion occurs in the field of neurodiversity, where biological constructs and explorations are used to account for human behaviour. In the case of neurodiversity, in contrast to biologically deterministic claims, authors such as Kirby and Gibbon (2018) suggest that environmental factors play a significant role in how neurodiversity is experienced. There is a dangerous trend to subvert the message of science also in the nature-nurture debate and the use of this debate for divergent ends to suggest that genetic makeup and human nature account for the deeply entrenched forms of discrimination, such as sexism, racism, classism and sexual orientation and disability discriminations. For example, during the Covid19 pandemic, there were discourses suggesting that some races were genetically more susceptible to infection and death in the UK and the USA. Morgan (2020) explains that it is not genetics but structural and systemic discrimination and disadvantage that account for the adverse impact on black and minority ethnic communities in both countries. Szabados (2019) suggests that the populist war on science subverts science for its own purposes. Oliver (2020) explains that racism, xenophobia and other forms of hate of outgroup members have biological and environmental reasons. In particular, the amygdala region of the human brain controls the fear and hate of the unexpected. The author explains that tribalism, which may emerge as negative biological responses to atypical or uncommon others in society, could be moderated by education on human rights and equality. The nature-nurture debate, although dated now, continues to shape and sometimes warp our understanding of the interplay between innate and earned qualities of human diversity.

The evidence suggests that the social and institutional environment in which individuals live and work accounts for much of the variation. In the case of South Africa, April (2021) explains how genetic reasoning is wrongly used and how that makes race relevant to the context:

> genetics account for less than half a percent of the characteristics associated with 'race', thus no inferences can be made to cultural and behavioural practices. Notwithstanding this assertion, race is a construct which cannot be ignored in the discourse of South African identity formation and processes of socialisation, by virtue of the fact that the Population Registration Act of South Africa during Apartheid was premised on "racist and segregationist assumptions", and prejudice and discrimination are customary and dominant categories of thought in society.
>
> (April, 2021, p. 3)

Based on this brief illustrative case, it is possible to note that the way diversity is defined, framed and considered is vulnerable to struggles for power. Therefore, engaging with diversity science requires a degree of caution, as advances in one aspect of science (i.e. genetics) could be misappropriated for discriminatory ends. Diversity suffers from dichotomous frames which could enhance our understanding if treated as dualities rather than in polarised ways.

CONCLUSION

Understanding diversity is not different from eating a pineapple. How do we eat a pineapple? Of course, we need to dissect it into bite-size chunks. In order to understand diversity, we need to define it, understand its aspects and dimensions. In this chapter, we examined the origins of diversity and examined its varied definitions, categories and frames. The chapter shows the power and poverty of defining and framing diversity in certain ways, accounting for the historical development of the diversity frames. The chapter offers an illustrative case of how the nature-nurture debate in diversity is misappropriated by recent developments in genetic science and why it is important to consider multiple frames of diversity to understand its complex meanings and categories. The next chapter focuses on manifestations of diversity.

CHAPTER 2

MANIFESTATIONS OF DIVERSITY

In this chapter, we examine manifestations of diversity across etic and emic categories and simultaneous manifestations of multiple diversity categories. Etic categories of diversity are the ones which are commonly covered in studies of diversity, such as gender, ethnicity, sexual orientation, class and disability. We focus in this chapter on the manifestation of those etic categories of diversity which are widely recognised and regulated worldwide. The chapter also explores manifestation of emic categories, which are specific to local settings, such as accent diversity, caste- and tribe-based diversity and other categories which are idiosyncratic to specific locations. As diversity manifests not in single category form but in the plural and intersectional ways, the chapter explores the manifestation of multiple categories of diversity.

It is impossible to do justice to all manifestations of diversity across its etic, emic and multiple categories in a short chapter. You could find in other diversity texts longer lists of diversity categories. We explore how a few forms of diversity emerge and how they are treated in practice and theory. The chapter starts with gender diversity, distinguishes between gender and sex and explains how gender diversity manifests and is framed, defined and measured. The second form of diversity that the chapter tackles is ethnic diversity and its manifestations. This section compares ethnicity and race and explains how ethnic diversity is framed, regulated and promoted in different cultural and organisational settings. Sexual orientation, class and disability diversity are also discussed in this chapter. The chapter also considers locally meaningful emic categories of diversity and discusses manifestations of multiple forms of diversity. There is an illustrative case at the end of the chapter on manifesting diversity as a migrating concept.

ETIC CATEGORIES OF DIVERSITY

Some categories of diversity are universally recognised. For example, gender, ethnicity, sexual orientation, class and disability diversity are well-studied internationally, and many of these etic categories of diversity are protected by international conventions and national laws (Syed and Ozbilgin, 2019). In this section, we explore how these generic (i.e. etic) categories of diversity are defined and how they manifest in different settings. One cautionary note about etic forms of diversity is that although each etic category is recognised internationally, their manifestations across locations are highly varied. For example, how gender or ethnic diversity manifests would be different in each location. Therefore, the universal naming of diversity categories as etic categories does not mean that the manifestation of these categories is the same across time, geography and cultural and symbolic contexts.

Gender diversity

Gender is a social construct, which suggests that the meanings and roles attributed to women, men and intersex individuals are dynamically shaped by the social, historical and political context in which they are located (Nanda, 2014; Saglam, 2019). Gender is different to sex, which is a biological construct. Even the notion of sex, which is supposed to be the biologically deterministic and binary account of being women or men traditionally, is subject to much social and legal progress, including the intersex and non-binary categories, which freed

DOI: 10.4324/9780367824044-3

sex from its binary shackles (Rubin et al., 2020). It is only recently that intersex is recognised as a separate category of sex in a limited number of countries (Garland and Travis, 2018). Although both gender and sex are used interchangeably today, they are different constructs. Gender is a geographically and historically shaped social construct, which has universal relevance due to the interconnected nature of women's historical struggles for equality with men. Gender diversity is the range of meanings, representations and social roles given to different genders across time and in different geographies. It is different to sex diversity which is often biologically based and traditionally assigned at birth based on a medical and legal model. Historical and cultural definitions of gender, which come from cis-gender, male-dominated cultures, religiously informed binary norms and functionalist or instrumental ideas of political economy, have not been supportive of the full spectrum of gender diversity and gender equality (Gezici Yalçın and Tanriverdi, 2020). In some cultures, binary conceptions of gender, as limited to women and men, are considered fixed and unchanging. However, in other cultural settings, gender diversity includes trans, non-binary, intersex and other expressions of gender identity (Köllen, 2016). Even though it is predominantly in binary lines, gender equality and gender diversity are advancing internationally, despite the resilience and resistance of traditional gender norms.

Research on gender diversity inherits much of its insights from the gender equality debates and struggles of feminist movements and ideals, which are now consequently enshrined in the Universal Declaration of Human Rights and more recent international agreements, such as the CEDAW (Convention on Elimination of All kind of Discrimination Against Women). Feminist and women's political activism provided foundations for developing gender diversity discourses (Englehart and Miller, 2014). Gender equality is studied across all aspects of life and work regarding feelings, cognitions, behaviours, experiences, opportunities, access, representations, power and resources and outcomes in life and work (Squires, 2007; Meliou and Edwards, 2018). Gender diversity is also studied across similar domains with a focus on issues of material, numerical and symbolic representations of gender diversity in different groups, organisations and across time (Nanda, 2014).

Gender diversity does not manifest in the same way in the Global North and Global South. Even among advanced democracies, gender diversity efforts have taken divergent paths shaped by local histories and social-political demands. For example, today, gender diversity practices in Scandinavian countries are based on issues of representation in positions of power, and the modernisation of parenthood as a shared responsibility, that seeks to transform gender hierarchies at home and work (Ellingsæter and Leira, 2006). Similarly, von Doussa et al. (2020) explore extension of the family concept to trans parenting in the case of Australia. Nevertheless, across other countries of the Global North, the same concerns do not manifest in the same way. For example, in the UK, the dominant paradigm is voluntarism for parenting which places the onus on women for parenting, culturally freeing fathers, organisations and the state of substantive responsibility. As a result, women struggle between motherhood and careers as the state and organisations do not share the responsibility in a substantive way (Kircal Şahin, 2023, 2022; Gash, 2009). Mothering offered as Hobson's choice leads to loss of professional standing and careers for women who stay in the labour market and face career detriments (McIntosh et al., 2012). Women who exit the labour market for child care also suffer economic and social exclusion and career detriments (Kanji and Cahusac, 2015; Cahusac and Kanji, 2014). Due to a lack of policy on social contribution to childcare costs (UK has the second highest costs in the OECD), gendered norms, responsibilities and roles at work and in life, the UK have also remained resistant to change. While in France, similar to Scandinavian countries, pro-natal policies have transformed motherhood into parenthood (Portier-Le Cocq, 2019), easing gendered norms around motherhood.

If we turn our attention to manifestation of gender relations in parenting in the Global South, Carmichael et al. (2022) explain that gendering of the domestic work and ideas about parenting start in early childhood years in the Global South. When we examine the situation in exposure to labour market, Kamasak and Palalar Alkan (2023) demonstrate how female academics struggle to execute their jobs and parenthood responsibilities due to their gendered roles in Turkey. Özbilgin et al. (2022a) explain the lack of legal supports for gender diversity in terms of recognition of trans, intersex and non-binary identities and rights in Turkey. However, it is interesting that in some emerging democracies, women's representation in senior posts is higher than in countries in the Global North (Healy et al., 2005). One particular issue in the Global South has been the subdued and subjugated nature of feminist movements. Although women achieve equality with a long struggle also in the Global South, often, these achievements are attributed to reforming men, who at the time were in positions of power in most countries. For example, Begum Rakoya in Pakistan (Roy and Hossain, 2015) and Nezihe Muhittin in Turkey (Özsoy et al., 2022; Cin, 2017) pushed for and organised women for gender equality. Subsequently, their demands and achievements for gender equality were usurped and attributed to modernising male leaders in their countries. Such usurpation is not unique to the Global South alone. While the broad-based feminist movement (i.e. MeToo), which was started by a black woman, has galvanised more support for white middle-class women (Leung and Williams, 2019) and failed to combat inequalities experienced by migrant, refugee, working-class, lesbian and trans women. When examining gender diversity, it is very important to take an inclusive view, as the earlier examples show. To understand how gender diversity manifests is to acknowledge its multiple frames. Intersectionality complicates such analyses of gender diversity.

Gender diversity is the most widely studied construct among all categories of diversity internationally. Most diversity management efforts focus on gender diversity and show less emphasis on other categories, even in most inclusive organisations (OECD, 2021). The reason for this has been the strength of the feminist movement, which pushed for the representation of women at work and in life across positions of hierarchy. Of the studies that explore gender diversity, most common are the ones that focus on numerical representation based on headcounts of women and men. Several approaches have been developed to explore gender diversity. First, to capture and account for the low representation of women in positions of power, concepts such as the glass ceiling (Powell, 1999), glass cliff (Ryan et al., 2016) and sticky floors (Booth et al., 2003) are developed. Glass ceiling refers to invisible yet strong barriers that prevent women from accessing career advancement after a certain level in the corporate hierarchy. Glass cliff refers to how women are allowed to take on leadership roles when such roles become risky or unsafe, leaving women leaders exposed to greater levels of uncertainty and risk. Sticky floors refer to how women are kept in their position without opportunities for development and promotion (Booth et al., 2003). In addition to these global metaphors, some refer to a specific field, such as the cinematic world, in which the metaphors of the 'celluloid ceiling' and the 'celluloid hurdles' call attention to the hidden barriers that lead to masculine dominance that emerges the higher up the professional ladder one climbs and to the lost time of women's directors in the cinematic field apply to women's (Aharoni Lir and Ayalon, 2023). In terms of poor atypical leadership emergence, Özcan (2021) offered the bottleneck metaphor, alluding to the culture of self-selection bias among leadership elites that prevent atypical leader emergence. There are also metaphors that highlight unearned privileges afforded to dominant groups at work, such as the glass elevator that refers to invisible and often unearned support that some individuals get at work (Casini, 2016). All these metaphors explain the implicit and gendered mechanisms through which access to senior posts is delayed, rejected and rendered more precarious.

Numerical representation of gender diversity is important. However, it does not fully show the subjective experience of women and men in gendered jobs and organisations. Many constructs are used to describe gender diversity and gender equality in terms of lived experiences of women and men. For example, experiences of belonging and otherness at work are gendered (Özbilgin and Woodward, 2004a, 2004b) (i.e. women and men experience work in different ways in terms of cognition, affect and behaviours due to the entrenched differences in gender norms). Experiences of gender diversity can explain the mechanisms which encourage and discourage women, men and other gender identities from certain paths in careers, work and employment. Historically, there are significant gender differences in terms of opportunities afforded in life and work. Gender diversity is also studied in terms of access to opportunities. For example, women's access to certain forms of work, occupations and positions of power and privilege have been historically constrained by law, customs and cultures, leading to their exclusion and demarcation from careers of their choice and positions of power and influence (Witz, 2013; Karatas-Ozkan and Chell, 2015). History shows that the feminist women and organised and collective demands of women for equality have led to considerable gains internationally. Over the last 100 years, the push for gender equality has garnered significant gains for equal opportunity for women internationally. However, there remains wide gaps in our understanding of gender norms, gender diversity and gender equality demands if we broaden our focus from the traditional to emergent and contemporary needs for equality. For example, research shows that women were disproportionately affected by the Covid19 pandemic, and they were subjected to higher levels of redundancy when compared to their male peers and the highest levels of redundancy among all periods of recession in the UK (Topping, 2021; Simpson and Morgan, 2020).

Most of the gender diversity research that we have today focuses on contemporary organisations and numerical representation in positions of power, such as gender diversity in the boardroom (Reddy and Jadhav, 2019; Brown and Kelan, 2020; Wang and Kelan, 2013), as this is considered a contemporary challenge in the way of women's equality. However, there is also another major gender equality issue which is very pressing but remains relatively less regulated. That is the gender pay gap and gendered outcomes at work. The gender pay gap is the difference in hourly earnings between men and women. The gender pay gap may be caused by men and women doing different jobs which attract different wages by differences in productive characteristics, and it is a historical disadvantage that women suffer (Blau and Kahn, 2003). Yet the remedies for this gender inequality have been slow in progress due to the resilience of gendered care that penalises women and the impact this penalty has on earnings (Blau and Kahn, 2007). Chicha (2006), in her report to the International Labour Organisation, noted that weak gender pay equality legislation is largely responsible for the persistence of the gender pay gap over time. On a positive note, Iceland became the first country internationally to outlaw the gender pay gap by introducing equal pay certification (Wagner, 2022). Such coercive practices are likely to impact more than disclosure efforts to publicly shame companies in the UK (Healy and Ahamed, 2019).

Materiality, cultural construction and numerical representation of gender diversity in recent years are supplemented with gender diversity as discourse (Gill et al., 2017; Nentwich and Kelan, 2014). In such formulations of gender diversity, notions such as gendered discourses, sexist language and subtle forms of discrimination and gendered incivility are discussed. Nentwich et al. (2015) show that materiality and discourse-based aspects of gender diversity collude to generate gendered inequalities. In their work, they suggest that feminist struggles should also embrace material and discourse-based strategies to undo gendered hierarchies and gendered disadvantages in societies and organisations. Even in those contexts that support gender equality, Kelan (2009) argues that there is gender fatigue, as individuals and organisations have an increasing tendency to call themselves gender neutral or gender blind as if such a thing could be possible or desirable.

Gender diversity requires an intersectional understanding, as gender diversity is not a monolithic form of diversity. Gendered experience is shaped by other categories of diversity and difference, such as ethnicity, class, sexuality, religion and age. When gender diversity is considered without other categories of diversity and difference, it could become an instrument for discrimination and exclusion by ignoring unique forms of discrimination at the intersection of gender and other categories of diversity. Intersectional exploration could lead to a more refined understanding of gender diversity that reveals heterogeneity of gendered experiences across places, time and cultures.

Ethnic diversity

Ethnicity is a socio-cultural construct that refers to an identification with and belonging to a cultural background or descent (Van den Berghe, 1978). The meaning of ethnicity is specific to a particular geography and a historical point in time. Race is a construct which refers to so-called biological differences among individuals based on skin colour and other forms of appearance. Although racial differences and the role of such biological differences in shaping individual choices and chances have been largely discredited (April, 2021), race and ethnicity are often used interchangeably today. The primary reason for the continued use of the race category is that despite discredited biological evidence for differential treatment, individuals and groups are still subjected to racialisation, differential treatment based on their marked racial and ethnic differences. Research shows that there is considerable variation in terms of how ethnicity and race manifest across different places and in history (Nkomo, 2019; Chanlat and Ozbilgin, 2023 Taksa and Groutsis, 2010; Taksa and Groutsis, 2013a, 2013b; Groutsis et al., 2018a; Groutsis et al., 2018b; D'Almada Remedios et al., 2021; Groutsis et al., 2022). For example, what it means to be a black and minority ethnic in Britain today is markedly different to how that was in the early 1800s and how it is in other countries, such as South Africa, India or China, where ethnic minority and majority dynamics and histories are markedly different (Shahabuddin, 2016). Ethnic diversity relates to assumed, suggested and accepted differences based on ethnic identity (Phinney, 1996). Ethnic diversity often makes an uneasy topic as the ethnic lines in most countries despite decades of legal changes that support ethnic equality. Unprecedented levels of migration, improvements in transportation and communication technologies and the building of extensive virtual networks and connections of global teams make ethnic diversity an immediate reality and a future challenge that societies and organisations need to manage effectively (Castles, 1995). Movements such as the #blacklivesmatter and anti-racist, anti-slavery and decolonising interventions have raised awareness of ethnic diversity and entrenched and systemic forms of racism, ethnocentrism and xenophobia that haunt societies and institutions of significance, such as education, employment, law, security, employment and social welfare.

Ethnic diversity discourses emanate from long struggles for racial equality. Anti-slavery movements, anti-colonial struggles and efforts to decolonise social and work lives have given meaning and purpose to frames of ethnic diversity internationally (Avery et al., 2018). It is remarkable to note that the #blacklivesmatter movement has gained an international character beyond North America (Parker et al., 2020) and had a particular impact in the rest of the English-speaking world, providing new impetus for race equality and gender diversity efforts (Özbilgin and Erbil, 2021b). Yet the struggle for ethnic diversity has been bumpy, as ethnic diversity has also been framed by the ultra-right wing and nationalist parties as a threat to security and something that undermines national and religious identity. Unfortunately, populist and regressive messages were taken up as national policymaking. For example, in the UK, the national policy called the Hostile Environment Policy (HES), which Theresa May's government introduced, aimed to make the UK an unattractive proposition for ethnic minorities and migrants (Griffiths and Yeo, 2021). Similar discourses and practices were produced across Europe that challenged the possibilities of coexistence and multiculturalism. Stringent visa requirements that tie migration to economic contribution potential alone are inspired by a combination of nationalist and neoliberal logic, which valorise financial viability over social, political and humanitarian calls. The shift in migration policy that upholds economic rationales for migration and citizenship has become globally evident. Any analyses of ethnic relations at the point of migration, therefore, need to question the tensions between economic versus social and humanitarian choices.

Ethnic diversity has been the subject of national, organisational and individual-level framing. At the national level, different philosophies have informed how ethnic diversity is regulated. For example, countries such as Britain have pursued multiculturalism policies to make it possible for ethnic groups to coexist by retaining their cultural traditions and authenticity (Collier, 2001). However, in other countries, ethnic diversity is viewed as something that needs to be integrated into the corpus of the national culture. For example, in France and Germany, ethnic minorities are expected to adopt a national identity once they have citizenship. Until then, they are treated as outsiders within. Different paths that colonialism and the treatment of ethnic relations have taken in Britain, France and Germany generated different ways that ethnicity is framed in these countries. The discourse of assimilation is used in relation to ethnic minorities in France. This discourse would be inflammatory in the UK, as it is charged with the idea of a unified national identity to which the migrants and ethnic minorities are supposed to adhere (Vassilopoulou et al., 2019).

Differences between domestic ethnic diversity, migrants and refugees are often treated under ethnic diversity, even though the lived experiences of local and migrant ethnicities are markedly different (Uygur, 2022; Groutsis et al., 2023). Fine differences, such as pathways into the labour market, social integration, cohesion and participation of these groups, are lost in efforts to generate general theories of ethnic diversity. Accounting for and counting ethnicity complicates ethnic diversity. Karakas and Özbilgin (2019) explain that even among European countries, ethnic diversity is defined, regulated, counted and accounted for differently (Kyriakidou et al., 2016). For example, in countries such as Britain and Ireland, ethnic data is collected to understand if different ethnic communities are impacted similarly by social policy and workplace practices. However, in countries such as France, Germany and Italy, collecting ethnic diversity data and monitoring ethnic differences particularly by employers are subject to legal restrictions (Klarsfeld et al., 2014). These restrictions are historically anchored due to the shadow of the past fascist regimes that used ethnic data for ethnic cleansing.

Ethnic markers are based on ascription, affiliation and self-identification. In some countries, such as South Africa and the USA, ethnicity is predominantly marked by skin colour (April, 2021). Across Europe, cultural background and heritage mark manifestations of ethnicity (Simon, 2013). In other countries, such as Turkey, China and Iran, ethnic differences are marked by mother tongues, cultural differences and languages (Aktürk, 2012). However, in others, ethnic differences could manifest in citizenship and passport, such as the countries in the Gulf region (Akinci, 2020). Therefore, at a national level of analyses, manifestations of ethnicity appear to be highly context-dependent.

Similar to gender diversity, ethnic diversity is also rich in theoretical frames. Ethnic diversity is studied in terms of numerical and symbolic representations in positions of power and across different occupational and work groups (Oerlemans et al., 2008) and in terms of spatial patterns by which different ethnic groups cluster in space (Klaesson et al., 2021; Klaesson and Öner, 2021). Ethnicity is also studied at the level of individuals, teams and organisations. At the level of individual ethnic bias, stereotyping threats and notions, such as subconscious bias, are used to frame the psychological aspects of ethnicity (Watson, 2017). At the level of teams, ethnic diversity is studied to explore how teams manage ethnic differences in the short and longer terms (Watson et al., 2002). At the level of institutions, there are powerful theories of institutional racism and systemic racism, which push the emphasis on how institutions and systems, with their processes, practices and norms, could generate racist outcomes (Williams, 1985; Feagin, 2013). Concepts of institutional and systemic racism move the responsibility and guilt of racism from individuals to institutions. With such a shift, also interventions for ethnic equality would be differentiated. If ethnic diversity is framed as an issue of psychology, individual-level interventions could be offered. If it is framed as a systemic issue, institutional interventions could be offered. The politics of where the responsibility for ethnic diversity and equality resides has been the subject of much debate.

Studies on ethnic and racial diversity often focus on dominant local ethnic differences. Such focus means that studies on domestic forms of ethnic diversity do not often capture indigenous, migrant and refugee experiences. In recent years, there is a growing focus on indigenous experience as a diversity concern (Pio and Waddock, 2021). Studies on native American, native Canadian, Aboriginal Australian, New Zealand Maori and other indigenous populations have highlighted different ways of knowing and varied forms of repetition of historical injustice as emergent themes for indigenous diversity (Pringle, 2009; Konrad et al., 2005). Migration presents a global challenge, according to the UN. Migrants face unique challenges which are different to what local ethnic groups experience. Migrant diversity has led to multiple frames of migrant identity (Özbilgin et al., 2022). While migrants receive some degree of a welcome in countries which experience skills shortages (Groutsis et al., 2020), migrant populations have been subject to populist campaigns of hate and exclusion (Palalar Alkan et al., 2023; Groutsis et al., 2023). Xenophobia, racism and the legacy of colonial relations affect migrant populations differently. Even segregating migrants as skilled migrants, economic migrants, forced migrants, expatriates and self-initiated expatriates reflects the uneven nature of the naming practices (Al Ariss, 2010). As migrants, refugees and indigenous communities often fall outside the focus of workplace studies that explore local ethnic diversity, it would be a good idea to include these groups as separate diversity categories. Knappert et al. (2020) argue for the utility of including refugees in workplace diversity efforts as a unique concern.

Beyond these debates on the level of ethnic diversity, Britain is at the centre of an international controversy regarding ethnic diversity as I am writing this book. The ruling Conservative government in the UK has commissioned and published a report by the Commission on Race and Ethnic Disparities (CRED). The report suggested that Britain is now a model country in terms of ethnic diversity, and the institutional racism identified in the Stephen Lawrence Inquiry (1999) some decades back no longer exists. The CRED report (2021) received much criticism as the attainment levels of different ethnic groups have not changed nor has the severity of institutional racism on different groups (Gillborn et al., 2021). The period since the report on institutional racism was issued has not seen any radical progress regarding material and symbolic outcomes of ethnic diversity in the UK. Resultantly, heeding the criticisms in the UK, the UN has called the report an effort to whitewash ethnic and racial discrimination in the UK (Cumming-Bruce, 2021).

Whitewashing is a concept used to denote the pretence of race and ethnic neutrality of processes, systems and institutions, which in fact, generate racialised outcomes (Omhand et al., 2023). Whitewashing is a white privilege that renders white-dominated institutions and systems unaccountable for their racialised outcomes. The concept of whiteness is a political description, very similar to the notion of black, as it refers to the direct and indirect ways white supremacy is continued in organisations and societies (Al Ariss et al., 2014). One of the ways whiteness is protected is through white fragility in organisations when white-identified individuals take offence to the idea that racism and racist outcomes exist and that they could be complicit (Ng et al., 2021). White fragility also manifests in claims of race blindness, which suggests that the individual would decline to see race as relevant to a discussion. It is important to point out that racism exists beyond some people's claims of blindness to race, gender and sexuality (Holmes IV, 2020b), which merely serve to render mechanisms of discrimination tacit and implicit in shutting down any discussion of systemic and institutional forms of inequality (Apfelbaum et al., 2012; Pearce et al., 2014).

It is also important to discuss levels of desirability and pecking order among ethnic and racial groups. While some racial groups are highlighted and elevated by state policy as model ethnic groups, such as Asians in the USA and UK, other groups could be stereotyped and held in low regard. Chou and Feagin (2015) explain that even the model minority stereotype does not protect these groups from racism. Ethnic bias and stereotyping are commonly used to create hierarchies among ethnic groups, preventing solidarity among ethnic minorities. Pecking orders emerge not only between majority and minority ethnic groups. They are also evident among ethnic groups. Creating ethnic hierarchies was a key strategy in the colonisation project (e.g. Wanjiru-Mwita and Giraut, 2020). Certain ethnic groups were drawn in to run the administration, invited to join the armed forces and engage in trade, among others. Creating and sustaining functional divisions among ethnic minorities have historically helped the colonisers to manage these groups more effectively and without much collective resistance (Yalkin and Özbilgin, 2022; Özbilgin and Yalkin, 2019). In the neocolonial world order, creating levels of desirability among ethnic groups and questioning collective phraseology, such as BAME (black, Asian and minority ethnic), in the UK, as was done in the report of CRED (2021), are efforts which seek to weaken the solidarity among ethnic groups towards demanding and achieving social justice.

Manifestations of ethnic diversity are historically and geographically anchored. The path to reconcile ethnic diversity and establish positive frames of coexistence has been treacherous, with many setbacks due to the populist anti-immigration turns in national and international politics. What ethnic diversity lacked in terms of progress towards equality presented it with a rich set of concepts to frame manifestations of ethnic diversity in terms of disadvantage, inequality and exclusion at multiple levels of analyses.

Sexual orientation diversity

The term sexual orientation diversity refers to sexuality and gender identity differences in a particular social context at a particular historical moment (Lubensky et al., 2004). Sexual orientation and gender identity categories are social constructs. LGBT+ is an umbrella term which brings together gender identity and sexual orientation categories, such as lesbian, gay, bisexual, trans and plus (refers to other categories which include intersex, asexual, polyamorous, queer, sapiosexual and many other sexual and gender identities). While LGBT+ is used as an acronym to bring all minority gender identities and sexual orientations together, it is important to acknowledge that there are divergent concerns and complex demands for voice and equality within the LGBT+ community (Bell et al., 2011).

Research suggests that sexuality is a spectrum, and the complexity of social, biological and cultural factors and individual choices blurs the boundaries between sexual orientations. Some individuals identify themselves as heterosexual even though they have same-sex intercourse. Some individuals are homosexual without experiencing same-sex intercourse (Laumann et al., 1994; Tanriverdi, 2022, p. 161). Therefore, sexual orientation is broader than sexual experience alone, complicated by social identification and romantic relationships. In international studies, more than 20 per cent of the population identify themselves as non-heterosexual. Sexual orientation equality is a category of equality which is relatively recently legitimated and protected by law. More than half of the countries internationally provide protections against sexual orientation discrimination today, and across over 80 countries today, sexual orientation equality in employment is protected by law (ILGA, 2021). Usta and Ozbilgin (2022) show that toxic contexts for sexuality motivate individuals to migrate and seek refuge in countries that offer sexual freedom, safety and security. Due to the removal of the stigma on self-identification and protections afforded to individuals who come out as LGBT+, the number of individuals who self-identify as LGBTQ+ has increased considerably in recent years. The progress towards LGBT+ equality at the social level received some support at the national level. The president of the USA, Joe Biden (2022), has declared that the USA will enforce sexual orientation equality internationally through their international diplomatic and trade relations. Despite these recent developments, there are many countries where sexual orientation diversity is criminalised, stigmatised, unprotected or unacknowledged.

As a term, LGBT+ refers to the social movement that seeks to promote equality and inclusion for individuals of historically marginalised gender identities and sexual orientations. LGBT+ diversity and inclusion are often prevented by different forms of hate, discrimination and exclusion, such as homophobia, biphobia, transphobia and stigmatisation that LGBT+ individuals experience in their life course (Özbilgin et al., 2022a; Özbilgin and Erbil, 2023e). One of the challenging aspects of advancing LGBT+ diversity is the heteronormative and heterosexist (Pichler et al., 2010) construction of social and institutional arrangements. Heteronormativity is a hegemonic belief system that assumes the normalcy and superiority of heterosexuality over other sexual orientations and gender identities (Robinson, 2016). Heteronormativity is a pervasive hegemonic system which is not only upheld by cis-gender individuals but ubiquitous in most institutions and cultures (Holmes IV, 2019). Other frequently used terms in sexual orientation diversity are cis-gender and cis-sexual to refer to those individuals whose gender identity and sexual orientation match their biological sex and attributed sexuality (Cava, 2016). Sexual orientation and gender identity minorities constantly struggle with heteronormative and cis-gender, cis-sexual norms in organisations and social settings. For example, from birth to death, all significant life events, such as family practices, educational choices, healthcare arrangements, socialisation patterns and work and employment practices, are crafted to cater for heterosexual, cis-gender, cis-sexual individuals to the exclusion of LGBT+ (Öztürk and Özbilgin, 2014). Some of the key struggles for LGBT+ movements have been the legitimation of LGBT+ relationships, support for coming out and tackling harassment, bullying and hate crimes against LGBT+ individuals (Holmes IV, 2020b).

One of the key concerns of sexual orientation and gender identity diversity has been disclosing or concealing one's sexual orientation and gender identity (Özbilgin et al., 2022a). Due to ongoing historically entrenched forms of violence, bullying, harassment and discrimination that sexual orientation and gender identity minorities experience, coming out remains a central concern for LGBTQ+ individuals (Aydin and Ozeren, 2020). Organisations must recognise the right to privacy and facilitate coming out in a safe environment. Özbilgin et al. (2022a) identify that LGBTQ+ individuals could choose to pass as cis-gender and heterosexual for many reasons beyond the fear of violence alone. Coming out is also a lifelong process, as individuals may come out or pass depending on their encounters with other individuals and institutions (Trau et al., 2018).

Sexual orientation equality is often called a litmus test of diversity. Because those organisations which support sexual orientation diversity also tend to support other forms of diversity (Özbilgin et al., 2022a; Özbilgin and Erbil, 2023e). Sexual orientation diversity, as a recently legitimated form of diversity, can equip an organisation to achieve value-based and cultural changes, which could help them be inclusive to other categories of diversity. However, we need to make a cautionary note here. The LGBT+ movement is not strong and unified. On the contrary, the movement has divergent interests, as the conditions of work and life for lesbians, gay men, bisexuals and trans others are not always similar or aligned. For example, Beauregard et al. (2018) show that trans issues are severely underrepresented as diversity concerns in FTSE100 organisations. There are tensions and contradictions in the demands of these separate groups. For example, a group of trans-exclusionary lesbians protested trans inclusion in the 2018 London Pride, claiming that the trans participants are subverting the political message of the Pride with their glamorous participation (BBC, 2018). Similarly, there were discussions and tensions between gay and lesbian groups which would like to retain the radical sexual politics of the movement and those who wish to blend into society and its family and conservative values. Despite these tensions, sexual orientation diversity is likely to feature more prominently in the future thanks to the push of the LGBT+ movement internationally. Pichler et al. (2017) show that organisational support for LGBT+ workers lead to positive organisational and individual-level outcomes, as LGBT+ workers would return the favour in effort and performance.

Class diversity

Class is a term which refers to the socioeconomic standing of an individual or a group in a social context at a given time. Class diversity is about differences of socioeconomic standing and background among a group of individuals. Drawing on Bourdieu (1984), it is possible to locate class diversity in terms of the symbolic capital of individuals (i.e. the social standing that individuals accrue through transposition and deployment of economic, social and cultural capitals in a given field of relations). Although Bourdieusian theorisation of class (1987) based on dispositions, habitus and capital endowments has gained considerable currency internationally, manifestations and imagination of class diversity often remain specific to geography and societies. Class diversity is evident across all societies. Class may manifest across all aspects of life, including how one speaks and appears, in consumption patterns, choices, chances in life and work and engagement with family, healthcare, law and other significant institutions. Class status could be overtly or subtly situated in an individual's cultural, economic and social standing. Britain is often identified as a class-based society. Scholars such as Savage (2015) have noted that the British class structures have transformed yet retained their explanatory power at work and in social life. Kate Fox (2014) suggests that class status does not only shape an individual's ways of being, behaving and feeling but it also informs their boundary conditions with other individuals, as class positions are not often permeable in the UK.

Understanding class diversity could reveal different educational and career paths, choices and chances of individuals at work and in societies (see Simpson et al., 2021, 2022). Similarly, class could help us realise how certain professions, occupations, organisations and work sectors are classed (i.e. segregated by class inequalities and shaped by class diversity). Friedman and Laurison (2020) demonstrate that there is a class ceiling for working-class individuals, signifying a gap in their pay and conditions when they are compared to those of their middle- and upper-class counterparts. The authors identify a pay gap of 16 per cent between working and middle-class professionals doing the same job. Their findings suggest that class is, in fact, an important source of material inequality, particularly in the UK. Although class diversity is studied as a central concern of sociology, it is not commonly considered in the management and organisation literature as a category of workforce diversity, with some recent exceptions, which call for the theorisation of class in organisation studies (e.g. Romani et al., 2021; Zanoni, 2011). This inattention to class has been due to the absence of legislative support for class diversity and class-based equality. Class discrimination is not outlawed in the UK. As a result, class diversity is also not commonly monitored in social and employment systems (Ashley and Empson, 2012). Thus, class-based discrimination remains a silent killer in the UK and a taboo subject in discussions of diversity interventions.

In rare cases, when class diversity is considered to combat class-based discrimination, class mobility is used as the method of diversity intervention. In countries where class-based discrimination and diversity are pronounced, class mobility is supported through the democratisation of education and employment practices (Kurz and Muller, 1987). Class mobility has been at the centre of many struggles in social and economic fields. For example, the Beveridge Report (1942) in the UK is often cited as the turning point for welfare reforms and class mobility through education, as it opened up access to education for children from working-class families, among other sweeping welfare reforms in the UK. Due to a lack of an organised social movement, except for trade unions, which try to improve the conditions of their members at work, class diversity and mobility as its fundamental tool have not gained much traction in terms of legal protection and institutional practice. As a result, class discrimination in social and institutional settings remains widely unchallenged, and class hierarchies remain intact. Added to this has been the denial of the relevance of class in political and social policy circles which blocks social progress for class diversity and mobility. Scholars such as Friedman and Laurison (2020) and Romani et al. (2021) have argued that class is a significant category of diversity and has explanatory power in accounting for power and status in domains of work and life.

Class equality is often represented through trade unions and collective workers' movements, which highlight the plight of working-class individuals internationally. However, class diversity is broader than working-class issues alone. There are many different alternative categorisations of class offered by offices of social statistics, sociological surveys and national welfare systems. Broadly, there is an aristocracy, elite class, upper class, middle class, working class, precariat and unemployed, among many other terms and shades of class descriptions that are fit for specific purposes. However, the European socioeconomic categories include in common terms the higher salariat; lower salariat; higher grade white-collar workers; petit bourgeoisie, or independents; higher grade blue-collar workers; lower grade white-collar workers; skilled workers; semi- and unskilled workers; and unemployed (Rose and Harrison, 2007). Nevertheless, a plurality of classification of socioeconomic standing signals the contested terrain of class.

Class intersects with other categories of difference. There is nowhere more prominent than the take-up of certain social causes and social movements by individuals from different class positions. For example, the anti-capitalist movements seek to promote the plight of the working poor. In the same way, other social movements intersect with class issues. For example, the anti-slavery, post-colonial and #blacklivesmatter movements are often associated with middle- and working-class interests. In contrast, #extinctionrebellion (XR), which raises concerns about the extinction of species and broader environmental issues, is branded as an elite and upper-class movement. Bell and Bevan (2021), in their study of XR, note that the movement does not include black, Asian and minority ethnic (BAME) support and tend to lack working-class representation. The Yellow Vests movement (Mouvement des gilets jaunes) had a predominantly working-class character, as in many French social movements before (Adam-Troian et al., 2021). As the movement grew and tensions and different agendas emerged, different groups started wearing their vests in green for environmentalists, red for left-wing, pink for LGBT+ and feminists and black for anti-colonial and anti-racists (Kipfer, 2019). For example, the Black Vests (Gilets noirs) movement emerged out of Yellow Vests and collaborated with Black Lives Matter and protested for the rights of undocumented migrants and minority ethnic citizens in France. These cases highlight tensions, divisions and solidarities built across and within social movements. Ozbilgin (2018) explains that intersectionality is important for the sustainability of social movements, failing which they may become marginalised.

The class also manifests as different constructs across different countries. For example, the class could converge with education, occupations, proximity to aristocracy, dominant tribes, castes or political parties. The class could be signalled predominantly by educational attainment in some countries, such as Germany. Economic wealth could signal a higher class position in others, such as modern-day Russia and the Gulf region. What makes class a complex and difficult-to-identify diversity category is the often implicit nature of its markers of social standing and its ever-present prevalence across all aspects of education, life and work.

In the absence of legislative support, class diversity is left to the goodwill and voluntary efforts of organisations. For example, Tatli and Özbilgin (2012b) showed that arts and cultural studies students from working-class backgrounds fail to enter the labour market in their fields of study due to classed barriers of entry (i.e. one year of an unpaid internship). The absence of laws that prevent class-based discrimination has prevented the creative and cultural sectors from addressing class discrimination. If organisations take the challenge of promoting class diversity, they could broaden their definitions of talent and merit to eliminate class bias. For example, elite educational qualifications are often conflated with merit, and such elite qualifications often have a class bias (Reay, 2022; Özbilgin et al., 2016). Reay (2022) rightly calls the lack of attention to class bias in education the 'elephant in the room' for societies divided by arbitrary class boundaries and biases that limit their choices and chances in education and life.

Class diversity could also manifest in socialisation patterns, extracurricular activities and accents individuals have (Bourdieu, 1984; Savage, 2015). Because class interlaces occupational status and social standing, class diversity could also be a source of authenticity problems at work. For example, research shows that professional service firms have upper-class ethos and professionals within them often feel obliged to change their regional accents in favour of received pronunciation (Özbilgin et al., 2015). Manifestations of class diversity are manifold, and there is limited support for ending class discrimination without supportive laws. Organisations could make their cultures more inclusive of class diversity by identifying and eliminating class bias in their institution-making practices, extracurricular arrangements, cultural practices and artefacts, policies and practices. However, creating such a climate and culture of inclusion for class diversity will not be easy, as class permeates and biases all aspects of merit, talent and competence in the same way that these constructs are gendered, ethnicised and sexualised.

Physical, mental and sensory diversity

The physical, mental and sensory abilities of individuals display considerable variation. Disability is a condition which prevents an individual from performing a life skill. Disabilities could be physical as well as mental, intellectual and sensory. Some disabilities are visible, and some are invisible (Muyia Nafukho et al., 2010). Disability is defined individually, socially, legally, culturally, medically and biologically in different terms (Siebers, 2008). The disability rights movement has been pushing for the recognition and accommodation of disabilities. The United Nations Convention on the Rights of Persons with Disabilities (CRPD, 2008) has four levels of ratification by nation-states. The CRPD encourages recognition of rights, protection against discrimination and accommodation of individuals with a disability. Lang (2009) cautioned that despite its significant impact, the legal enforcement of the CRPD would not be sufficient to dismantle deeper structural disability discrimination internationally. The legal and rights-based models of disability describe what conditions are considered a disability and how this access and accommodation could be provided. However, there is variation in definitions of disability across national legislations and its transformative power (Minkowitz, 2017) despite the relatively unifying force of the CRPD.

The medical models of disability focus on the diagnosis and treatment of disabilities and the limitations of the body. Degener (2016) argues that the medical model of disability promotes formal equality. However, it is challenged by the CPRD, which promotes a human rights model of discrimination that focuses on substantive equality claims for individuals with disabilities.

Areheart (2008) explains that the medical model of disability presents a goldilocks dilemma, by which individuals are marked as too disabled or not disabled enough. The author argues that this type of stereotyping and stigmatisation is not helpful for individuals with disabilities. The medical model of disability locks individuals with disabilities to fixed positions in relation to the provision of the state, employers and society.

The individual model of disability focuses on the individual's lived experience and their self-definitions of disability. The social model of disability takes such individual definitions and frames them as culturally and socially specific structures and practices which give particular meaning to disability in a given context. As such, the social model of disability posits disability as a social construct that changes over time and across locations and frames disability as a form of disadvantage imposed by society on individuals with disabilities. The social model, therefore, considers disability as a construct which is based on what resources, such as technology, enable mobility and access the society affords to offer or withdraw from people with disabilities (Shakespear, 2006). The social model of disability frames disability as social choices and resource allocation decisions that enable and disable individuals. For example, according to Oliver (2013), society affords some individuals transportation technologies which enable them to fly, some individuals are facilitated to travel by trains and cars and internet technologies facilitate their communication. However, the same societies may not afford disabled individuals access to technology, resources and accommodations that could help them overcome their disabilities. The social model of disability shows how disability is an outcome of social choices which enable or disable individuals.

While the social model of disability is instrumental in explaining the social construction of disability, it is criticised for dismissing the lived experience of disability by reducing such embodied experiences to social choices and structures. The embodied model of disability acknowledges that disability is not merely a social construct. It is also an embodied physical and psychological experience that social frames cannot simply explain. The embodied model of diversity focuses on how disability is experienced as a bodily phenomenon and returns legitimacy to the voice of individuals with disabilities in shaping their own choices and chances. Some authors have considered the social and embodied models of disability as irreconcilable poles in studies of disability, as the former focuses on the advancement of disability rights and access/accommodation, drawing on the transformative power of social change and the latter focusing on the embodied experience of disability beyond the social construction. However, scholars like Lang (2007) consider varied models of disability could be considered together under the banner of the social model of disability, as they all serve to progress the rights and improve the experiences of individuals with disabilities, who invariably face discrimination and oppression in societies which are structured around needs of able-bodied and non-disabled individuals.

The progressive model of disability suggests a focus on the abilities and potentials of the individuals, inviting a focus on the potentiality of individuals with disabilities. A study of labour market inclusion of individuals with mental illness (Hennekam et al., 2023) showed that individuals with mental disabilities have largely internalised and accepted the structural biases in the labour market system. Resultantly, individuals with mental illness rarely demand accommodation and the development of inclusive structures. Therefore, progressive efforts to transform labour market structures should focus on systemic change rather than a focus on what individuals with mental illness or neurodivergence should or could do (Kirby and Smith, 2021). Removing barriers to labour market participation of individuals with disabilities requires changing, for example, largely redundant and ableist requirements based on assumptions of an able-bodied and able-minded workforce (Jammaers et al., 2021). Similarly, Valsecchi et al. (2021) assert that employers, to manage the health and well-being of their employees, including those with disabilities, should consider both the tenants of the social model of health and well-being a re-elaboration of the social model of disability (Foster, 2018) and the business case argument (Bleijenbergh et al., 2010; Noon, 2007)

Adopting a progressive lens, April et al. (2023) offer the term *diversability* to disability diversity and to make it inclusive, as other terms in the field of diversity underpin its socially constructed nature. Diversability as a term offers to contest the negative connotations that disability has in understanding how individuals are differently abled. How disability emerges depends on its social, medical and cultural framing. The inclusion of people in the labour markets and social structures by diversability presents an ongoing challenge internationally. There is a need to move from a deficit model to one that captures the potentiality of a diverse range of abilities. Further, it is also important to retain a strong sense of the embodied experience of disability and the resultant suffering, exclusion and discrimination that they face. Only through progressive framing and embodied understanding of disability could it be possible to craft social and organisational designs that tackle exclusion and promote inclusion.

Interspecies diversity (Biodiversity)

Among etic categories of diversity, interspecies diversity and biodiversity are relatively new yet growing categories. The Anthropocene is the historical period marked by human impact on ecology. It is common to see depictions of species with humans placed firmly at the top of an assumed hierarchy between species in biology textbooks. The UN Convention on Biological Diversity (2023) recognises the adverse impact humans have on the physical environment and interspecies diversity. Growing international recognition of the destructive impact of humans on biodiversity has led to this convention. The international recognition of the significance of biodiversity and its regulation underlines that all life is interdependent in the world and that human impact needs to be better regulated to protect life on earth.

In the long history of the world, the domination of humans over other life forms and natural resources is a relatively recent period of the Anthropocene, marked by the disproportionate and hierarchical treatment of nonhuman species. In this period, humans have not only placed themselves at the top of the interspecies diversity but also narrated the relationship between themselves and other species along the lines of utility/disutility, sentience/insentience, labourer/threat, aesthetics/disgust and compassion/hatred. The polarised, divisive and hierarchical treatment of life forms based on human needs, feelings and behaviours require further critical scrutiny. Humans have prioritised life forms based on their utility/disutility for humans. While some animals, plants and fungi have been used for their potential as food, clothing and energy source, others have been ignored or destroyed because of their disutility to humans as vultures, pests, weeds or toxic.

As per the focus of this book on workforces, biodiversity is of particular importance, as humans are not the only labourers. Other species have always been put to work for humans, often without pay and decent conditions of work. Examples include horses for transporting; dogs for policing and as guides; seabirds for catching fish; rats, rabbits and monkeys in medical tests; cattle, sheep and goats for dairy products and meat; and dogs, cats, fish and other animals and plants as human companions.

Humans are capable of caring for their health and longevity through medical science. Similarly, they extend their care and compassion to some life forms through veterinary science, ecological interventions and the preservation of critical natural resources. However, their impact on biodiversity, ecology and the natural environment has been devastating. Developments in human and veterinary medicine and biotechnology offer new possibilities for protecting and supporting biodiversity and using natural resources more effectively. Supported by international conventions, national interventions, social movements and voluntary organisational actions, there are some attempts to consider the effective management of biodiversity.

Social movements, such as #extinctionrebellion and #climateaction, have converging agendas that seek to protect and preserve life on earth and natural resources. Similarly, inspired by the needs of species facing extinction or in need of advocacy to fight the depletion of natural resources, several charitable and state organisations, such as Greenpeace, have been formed. Similar movements from the Global South have also galvanised support for the environment. For example, the Gezi Park uprising in Turkey originally started to protect trees in Gezi Park from city development plans. The movement, then, acquired an intersecting character and expanded into other progressive movements and strengthened. The threat to interspecies diversity is real. Humans have the strongest adverse impact on this diversity with their assumed superiority and dominion over other life forms.

As the focus of this text is mainly on workforce diversity, it would be important to explore interspecies diversity at work. Many species of animals work for humans. Similarly, other life forms are used at work for their utility as food and clothing, insulation and a source of energy and heat. It is only in recent years that workforce diversity scholarship has started, including aspects of interspecies diversity and interspecies labour in its research efforts. In particular, animal labour is drawing considerable attention from scholars who highlight animal labour (Blattner et al., 2019), animal welfare (Donaldson and Kymlicka, 2019), animal labour rights (Cochrane, 2016) and interspecies justice (Pepper, 2022) concerns as part of organisational efforts to manage diversity.

The hierarchical model of interspecies diversity resembles other forms of diversity we explored in this book. The relations of power and dominance that humans have with other species and the hierarchies that humans have imposed on other life forms have created an uneven field of interspecies relations, where care, compassion, labour, aesthetics, hate and ecocide are disproportionately levelled at different species. So the struggle to repair uneven and destructive relationships at work and beyond requires consideration of interspecies diversity and labour as an etic concern of diversity management. Effective international regulation is required to address the corrosive impact of humans on the natural environment. Although such efforts are often criticised for being too slow and ineffective, there is recent evidence to the contrary. The Montreal Protocol to protect the ozone layer by limiting the production and use of substances that cause ozone depletion has worked well. The ozone layer is showing signs of repair (World Meteorological Organization, 2022). International protocols and conventions such as this can have a significant impact on repairing the uneven relations between humans and biodiversity.

One of the key tenets of this new diversity management category is the representation and legal recognition of the rights of species and nature. Nonhuman species cannot represent their interests in human-oriented systems and institutions. As such, nonhuman species require representation and legal recognition for their rights to be honoured and their existence to be protected. In some countries, nonhuman species are protected by law and nature is recognised as a legal entity, the integrity of which could be defended with the force of law. Besides these legal regulations, organisations take variable voluntary and compliance-driven approaches to managing interspecies diversity, mainly by regulating their impact on the natural environment.

Techno diversity (Cyborg diversity)

Techno diversity is how a diverse range of technologies are becoming essential, natural, relational and inseparable parts of organisms, including humans. Techno diversity manifests in four different forms: First, technology for human use, which is in line with the traditional way technology has evolved. Second, technology with the organic interface leads to cyborg life and hybridity, evident in life-enhancing biotechnology products and prosthetic technological parts. Third, the technology works as a relational conduit between people, taking the form of digital platforms that facilitate economic, social and even romantic exchange between people. Fourth, technology as an autonomous entity emerges as complex robotic, algorithmic and artificial intelligence systems that evade human governance and create other digital and augmented realities. Promulgation of new forms of technology and human engagement has taken a radical and disruptive path that shapes how we view diversity. Technological innovations are increasingly interfacing technology with humans in education, healthcare, communication and daily activities, such as eating, exercising, working and sleeping. The platform economy has brought technology to all aspects of life. Biotechnological advances in healthcare make it possible for humans to overcome disabilities through biotechnological body parts and technological devices. Cyborg refers to the interface of a biological organism and technology in the same body (Clynes and Kline, 1960). There is a remarkable range of technological implants and prosthetic organs to support movement, senses, life and cognition, as well as other functions in cyborg forms for humans, animals and other forms. Haraway's (2006) cyborg manifesto highlights the disappearing boundaries between fact and fiction of cyborgs, the hybrid of organisms and technologies and how cyborgs have gendered and material aspects which need to be considered as part of feminist and socialist progressive agendas. Cyborg diversity is now in every part of our lives, including the regulation of time, place and our cultural and symbolic relations, deepening the interdependence of humans and technology in daily lives.

Not only advances in biotechnology but also algorithmic systems, artificial intelligence and augmented reality technologies have transformed how life is enhanced, sensed and experienced. In the world of work, technology has facilitated a radical transformation of the meaning, processes and contexts of work. In terms of the meaning of work, there are sectors of work where algorithms are fast replacing human labour (Ozkazanc-Pan, 2021). Chui et al. (2016) explain that algorithms will replace people in predictable physical work, data collection and assessment activities. However, algorithms are less likely to take over human labour in relational aspects, such as engagement, management and leadership. Work processes are transforming through techno diversity, as the process of shopping, eating, ordering food and transportation has changed radically with AI-led platforms and gig economies. Similarly, the meaning of workplace, working time and work arrangements have changed radically with the introduction of disruptive technological innovations, which have rendered the boundaries between work, home, working time and holiday rather porous and arbitrary (Choroszewicz and Kay, 2020). However, techno diversity does create disproportionate outcomes. For example, in a study of techno diversity in healthcare settings, Lepkowsky (2017) identified a disproportionality of impact on technologically savvy and technologically illiterate populations. Similarly, Husain et al. (2022) identified intersectional disadvantages in using digital consultation in healthcare during the Covid19 pandemic. Older age, lower socioeconomic status and limited language proficiency patients have been more disadvantaged in using techno diversity, the digital system, in medical consultation. There is also a Global North and Global South divide in access to and literacy of techno diversity. While the Global North reportedly suffers from digital dependency, an inability to withdraw from digital engagement in work and life (Jarzombek, 2016), the Global South lacks digital literacy and suffers from the cybaltern (Tuzcu, 2021) (i.e. the extension of uneven colonial hierarchies of power and knowledge in the field of high technology use). Advances in techno diversity, if left unregulated, do not offer a level playing ground but deepen the inequalities within the framework of the West-East dichotomy.

With the disruptive development of techno diversity, the assumption that humans can effectively govern the impact of techno diversity is severely undermined. In many sectors of work, algorithmic systems evade governance. One of the problems in the field of education and techno diversity in electronic platform applications has been the domination of a limited number of companies in this sector and the divisions that these platform companies cause in terms of the Global North and Global South divide (Al Dahdah, 2021). Techno diversity also causes scientism among human users. Scientism is a misguided belief that decisions made by machines and algorithmic systems are less biased than human decisions (Vassilopoulou et al., 2022). Algorithms have implicit emotions, as humans with emotions have created these algorithms, and these emotions have been tacitly inscribed in algorithmic systems. Further, Bach and Dayan (2017) show that human emotions have algorithms. Although the assumption of bias and emotion-free techno diversity is now widely contested, there are still wide regulatory and governance gaps in negating the adverse impact of techno diversity. Not only the biases of techno diversity but also people's prejudices about techno diversity shape their relationship with technology. One of these biases is technophobia (Khasawneh, 2018)., which is the fear of technology, and algorithm aversion (Jussupow et al., 2020), which is the dislike and avoidance of algorithms. Akin to other forms of phobia and aversion, progressive approaches to techno diversity suffer setbacks due to human fears, phobias and aversion.

Human governance of techno diversity becomes challenging also in terms of ownership, value chains and stakeholder value of techno diversity. Techno diversity–led organisations now have ownership and value chain systems which generate profits only for owners and investors, pushing out other stakeholders who design, manufacture and deliver services and goods through technology-led platform firms. Techno diversity in a governance vacuum creates uneven economic outcomes and warps social and economic systems of distributive justice. One of the radical suggestions for remedying the ownership and governance structures of techno diversity is to give technological products, including robots and artificial intelligence, a legal entity status. This will help algorithmic systems to assume responsibility for their impact and for these systems to be taxed appropriately so that the wealth generated could be redistributed.

At the organisational level, techno diversity and its impact must be recognised as an institutional entity that requires effective and equitable management and governance. One small step towards achieving this is to include techno diversity as a category of diversity in management efforts as techno diversity interfaces. It has differential impacts across all other categories of diversity. Organisational interventions for managing techno diversity should focus on eliminating the uneven impact that techno diversity could have. Management interventions could also focus on eliminating bias inherent in techno diversity and combat human fears, phobias and hate that can prevent the progressive use of technology.

Other forms of etic diversity

There are other categories of diversity with universal recognition. For example, there is greater age diversity in organisations. In countries like the UK, age diversity is protected by laws against ageism. Age diversity has increased internationally in the workplace, as it is now possible for older workers to have second or third careers and return to work after retirement, as life expectancy has increased internationally (Boehm et al., 2011). Resultantly, work teams now have higher levels of age diversity. The cohort (generational), age (biological) and seniority (duration of service at work) diversity as different constructs of age diversity (Djabi and Shimada, 2017) because social, biological and organisational manifestations of age have different implications. Meliou and Mallett's (2022) study extended intersectional research on gender and age in self-employment by illustrating how individuals seek to transcend disadvantage by drawing on their intersectional reflexivity, extending research on intersectional analyses of otherness (Özbilgin and Woodward, 2004b).

Relationship status diversity manifests as a universal diversity category. Whether individuals are single, in relationships, cohabiting or married have different social meanings. Workplace implications of having or not having relationships cuts across all other aspects of diversity, such as sexual orientation diversity (Hammack et al., 2019), gender, ethnicity and disability. Marital status has been used as a justification to discriminate against single individuals or in other forms of relationships (Weichselbaumer, 2015; Beattie, 1990). Work-life balance needs of single individuals and individuals from atypical backgrounds have also been ignored in organisational policies in favour of white, middle-class, heterosexual women in matrimonial relationships (Özbilgin et al., 2011). In recent years, work-life balance policies have started giving individuals in other forms of relationships, such as LGBT+ families and single individuals, access.

Religion and belief diversity is one of the challenging aspects of diversity, as religion and belief differences and diversity have been the source of many diversity conflicts (Uygur and Aydin, 2019). Syed et al. (2018) distinguish between negative conflict and positive qualities of religious performance. Religion and belief diversity today are protected in progressive organisations to ensure that people from different faiths and beliefs, religions or none, could work together effectively. Religion is a source of much moral energy and motivation in business history, which shapes the way entrepreneurial and business norms are formed today (Uygur et al., 2017; Karakas et al., 2017). Some scholars include spiritual diversity in the equation to capture the demands for bringing the whole self to work beyond religious diversity (Hicks, 2002; King and Holmes IV, 2012). Religious, spiritual and belief diversity can clash, collide and have tensions with other progressive categories of diversity (Ozturk, 2017). For example, religious doctrines may clash against the human rights of women, ethnic minorities, LGBT+ individuals and individuals with disabilities, among others. Many renewed tensions and roadblocks on the way of progressive diversity agendas emanate from religious dogma. In recognition of the conflicting nature of religious beliefs and the new normal in emergent equalities, legislators consider demands for religious rights, freedoms and identity, often in light of fundamental human rights (Vickers, 2017; Hennekam et al., 2018). For example, religious dogma sometimes clashes with women's right to education, employment, safety and reproductive integrity and LGBT+ rights to relationships, education, employment and dignified life, among other tensions with other progressive agendas of equality, diversity and inclusion.

There are many other etic forms of diversity, most of which are not protected by legal or social arrangements. Nevertheless, categories such as cultural diversity (Fine, 1973; Ozgen et al., 2017) and functional diversity (Bunderson and Sutcliffe, 2002) are some categories which are universally recognised with locally different meanings. The next section focuses on locally meaningful categories of diversity, the meaning of which does not travel universally.

EMIC FORMS OF DIVERSITY

The categories of diversity that we discussed earlier (i.e. gender, ethnicity, class, sexual orientation and disability) are etic categories of diversity. Etic categories of diversity are the ones which have universal currency and are widely studied internationally. There are also emic categories of diversity, which are limited to certain geographies. Emic diversity categories emerge at specific times, places and cultural contexts (Tatli and Özbilgin, 2012a, 2012b). To flesh out emic categories of diversity, it is important to study how power, resources and relationships in a local setting are accumulated by certain groups when others are disallowed to have access to these resources. For example, confessional differences in religious diversity is an emic diversity category for Lebanon (Al Ariss and Ozbilgin, 2010), where confessional groups compete for resources, power and social connectivity across domains of work and life. In the case of the

UK, Traczyk (2020) explains how class-based accent discrimination is an emic legal category not protected by law. In contrast, some accents intersecting with class could be covered by race discrimination legislation. In particular, in the UK, working-class accents would be subject to educational and employment discrimination. Turkmenoglu (2020) explores appearance-based discrimination as an emic category of diversity, which is recognised as salient in some local cultural settings. Özbilgin et al. (2023a) explain that appearance diversity intersects with other forms of diversity, leading to locally meaningful outcomes. As part of appearance, body shape, body paintings and body weight (Roehling et al., 2007) are considered as salient diversity categories in some contexts.

Postcode discrimination, which marks the ethnic origin and religious difference by geography and leads to the discrimination of job applications from certain neighbourhoods in France, could also be considered an emic category of diversity. In France, postcode discrimination is the ethnic and racial disadvantage individuals face in deprived and disadvantaged neighbourhoods marked by postcodes. Although Kiwan (2011) cautions that terms such as postcode discrimination may euphemise racism, which remains a taboo subject in some contexts. Similarly, Özbilgin and Yalkin (2019) show that *biat* (i.e. subservience to authority) presents a condition colouring how merit and talent are constructed along biased lines of proximity to political authority in Turkey with its neo-Ottoman transformation of workplace values. In their study of the ingratiation behaviour of Turkish academics, Özbilgin et al. (2019) show that ingratiation and flattery present emic diversity criteria, providing privileges to those who engage with it and affording punitive measures against those who decline to engage in flattery at work, informing one of the ways that power and privilege are shaped in Turkish academia.

Tribal ties in African countries and the Middle East and familial ties and lineage in Asia are also emic categories of diversity, which do not apply to other locations in the world but shape an individual's access to resources and power based on different kinds of belonging and affiliation (Zhou and April, 2020; Hecan and Farhaoui, 2021). Minbaeva and Muratbekova-Touron (2013) highlight clanism as an emic category concern in some cultural settings. Similarly, Babacan (2019) states that hemseri, which roughly translates as 'townsfellowship', is an emic category of diversity in Turkey. The answer to one of the first questions that you will be asked in Turkey, 'Where are you from?' will determine the degree of proximity of your birthplace to the other person and the possibility of your cooperation with them. Finally, the caste system in India is an emic category of diversity, as this specific social stratification system delineates the fault lines between social, economic and institutional positionalities of individuals based on their backgrounds in different castes (Mahalingam, 1998). One of the problems with the emic categories of diversity is that their treatment of outsiders often does not provide an in-depth understanding of these concepts. Therefore, there is a need for insider theorisation of emic categories of diversity for them to be understood better.

MULTIPLE CATEGORIES OF DIVERSITY AND INTERSECTIONALITY

Most diversity studies either use diversity as a generic term, as in the case of diversity management or focus on a single category of diversity (e.g. gender diversity). This tendency in the literature has two limitations. First, treating diversity as a generic term subsumes categories of diversity together, failing to attend to differences in agendas and priorities of diversity categories. Second, single-category studies of diversity suffer from blind spots, hierarchies and power imbalances within that single category. For example, studies of gender alone may implicitly endorse and entrench ethnic, class and other forms of inequality (Özbilgin et al., 2011). If we choose a particular example of gender diversity in the boardroom, single-category studies of gender diversity in the boardroom have largely neglected the complexity of multiple forms of diversity and inequality. For example, disability and sexual orientation diversity in the board-room has been neglected not only in scholarly circles but also in organisational policy and regulation efforts (Özbilgin et al., 2022a; Özbilgin and Erbil, 2023e). In recognition of how single-category framing of diversity failed to reflect the complexity of the lived experience and undermined the efforts to combat a wider range of inequalities at work and in life, some schol-ars have advocated that multiple forms of diversity should be considered together and not in isolation. Such studies are often labelled as intersectional diversity works.

Intersectionality is a term which was originally introduced by Kimberley Crenshaw (1991) to signify the fact that individuals have and belong to multiple categories of identity and diver-sity. All individuals have gender, ethnicity, class, sexual orientation and other socio-demographic backgrounds. Thinking of multiple diversity categories together provides a more realistic eval-uation of an individual's choices and chances. Crenshaw argued that the experience of black women cannot be explained by race or gender alone. More than an accumulation of different forms of discrimination (COE, 2022), it is their unique combination that accounts for the inter-sectional experience. While some scholars show that considering multiple categories of diver-sity helps us understand the cumulative effects of multiple forms of disadvantage (Bağlama, 2020; Chicha, 2012; Woodhams et al., 2015), some scholars demonstrate that intersectional analyses do not always generate cumulative but often interesting outcomes (Modood et al., 1997; Tatli and Özbilgin, 2012b; Kelan, 2014).

McCall (2005) argues that there are three types of intersectional analysis. Intercategorical, intracategorical and anticategorical complexity inform the intersectional analysis. Intercate-gorical complexity, which is also referred to as categorical complexity, is the way multiple and intersecting diversity categories are used as analytical tools to account for inequalities and dis-crimination. Intracategorical complexity uses multiple and intersecting categories of difference but accepts them as dynamically changing social constructs which explain the experience of individuals and societies at a given point in time. Anticategorical complexity takes the form of deconstruction and rejection of categories as performative constructs. The anticategorical complexity has a postmodern take on intersectional analyses, which engages with the discourses rather than the materiality of intersectional experience.

One of the challenges of studying intersectionality has been that intersectionality is often studied from the perspective of individual experiences with intersectional experience (i.e. black or white women's experiences in North America) (Smith and Nkomo, 2021), reflecting on their divergent choices and chances. However, intersectionality is also a quality of institutions and societies. Similar to individuals, institutions and societies have intersectional character. For example, institutions such as family, education, employment, law and healthcare and societies have intersectional qualities, as they have ethnicised, gendered, classed, sexual and age-based characteristics, as their intersectional processes and outcomes could lead to differential out-comes across many categories of difference and fault lines (Kamasak et al., 2020a, 2020b, 2020c). Discussions of systemic bias, institutional discrimination and inequality regimes could benefit intersectional exploration.

Intersectionality also emerges with certain intersectional tensions, intersectional hostilities, intersectional possibilities and intersectional solidarities (Karakas and Özbilgin, 2019; Özbil-gin and Syed, 2019). For example, there are marked tensions between demands for tradition and progress at the intersection of religion/belief and sexual orientation diversity (Kamasak et al., 2019). Similar tensions exist across most intersections of diversity categories. Sometimes, different groups of disadvantage are pitted against each other by populist policies (Uygur and Aydin, 2019). For example, migrants and minority ethnic groups could be pitted against the working class or religious minorities against women's rights. A pecking order (Yamak et al., 2016) often emerges among diversity categories. International research shows, for example, that gender diversity is the most regulated category of diversity. Resultantly, gender diversity takes precedence over other categories of diversity in policy and practice.

Intersectional hostilities and tensions could cut across levels. Intersectional hostilities exist in the macro context as regulatory tensions. For example, certain forms of diversity, such as gender and ethnicity, are protected by law, and others are not afforded legal protection, such as class diversity in the UK. Intersectional hostility and tensions also manifest at the group level. Different diversity claims within the group could be contradictory, even within the same category. For example, what blind people want and what people with hearing impairments and what individuals with mental illness want to make workplaces more accessible could conflict. Kusters (2017) refers to competing hierarchies in the use of space in accounting for deaf access to space negotiated with sexism, classism and audism. Similarly, there are intersectional hostilities among the LGBT+ movement in Britain. For example, a group of feminists and lesbians protested the trans movement in the 2018 London Pride, highlighting tensions among the LGBT+ movement (BBC, 2018). Organisers of the Pride march later apologised for including this divisive group. At the micro-individual level, intersectional hostility may exist across intersectional identities of individuals. While devoutly religious, individuals may support equality and inclusion for groups devalued by their religious beliefs. Such cases of individual intersections could cause internal intersectional and identity tensions. Yip (1999) explores the relationship between gay Christians and the church and coins the phrase of counter-rejection that gay Christians are forced to experience to combat the chasm between their sexual orientation and the gay exclusionary doctrines of the church. Another less talked about aspect of intersectionality is 'collisional intersectionality', which occurs when social signifiers of dominance are intermixed with those of perceived weakness. Aharoni Lir and Ayalon (2022) capture the collisional intersection between hegemonic masculinity and ageism when they examine the loss of power attributed to men in the film industry as they reach the second half of their lives.

Alongside intersectional tensions, there are also intersectional solidarities (Kamasak et al., 2019). Many single-category social movements are gaining intersectional character to benefit from intersectional solidarities. When examined on their single issue and single category, social movements may be easily marginalised by dominant groups. Nevertheless, when they receive intersectional solidarity from other groups, they gain strength and support. Opie and Livingston (2022) refer to shared sisterhood as a way to garner intersectional support for dismantling bias and inequalities in organisations and society. At the organisation and group level, dealing with single categories of diversity strains the limited resources afforded for diversity policy and interventions. Therefore, finding common possibilities of solidarity among disadvantaged groups could help them make stronger claims for equality. At the micro level, individuals could draw strength and energy from synergies of their intersectional identities (Tsouroufli, 2023). For example, black women may turn their intersectional disadvantage to draw solidarity from feminist and anti-racist movements.

Questioning where diversity intersections reside offers possibilities for the extension theory of intersectionality, which in the main remains in the domain of individuals. Viewing intersectionality at multiple levels of individuals, groups, systems, institutions and national/international structures (Kamasak et al., 2019, 2020c) offers a possibility of transforming those levels of structures and institutions to make them more welcoming for intersecting identities (see Karatas-Ozkan et al., 2022, for an empirical example). Encounters of individuals, groups and institutional structures could be viewed as encounters of intersecting identities at these micro, meso and macro levels. Tensions, possibilities and solidarities could emerge in these intersectional encounters.

ILLUSTRATIVE CASE: MIGRATION OF DIVERSITY

Since its introduction in the late 1980s in the North American context as an alternative way of framing social differences in the workforce, diversity has become a globally recognised concept (Mor Barak, 2016). However, in its travel, diversity has gained new meanings and categories, bent and shifted focus depending on the new social and symbolic contexts it travelled to. When the concept of diversity travelled to the UK, it was embraced as part of the neoliberal turn that the country was going through. Diversity was received as an instrumental discourse that focused on individual differences rather than collectivist and solidaristic notions, such as equal opportunities. While the class was a diversity category in North America, when the concept travelled to the UK, gender, ethnicity, sexual orientation, disability, religion and belief are considered more salient than the class as a category. Diversity was embraced in Britain due to its multicultural policy, which allowed for the coexistence of ethnic communities. When the concept travelled to France, diversity was viewed through the lens of the French revolution and its founding principles of equality, freedom, secularism, solidarity and fraternity. Taboos in the case of France were religious and ethnic diversity, the former owing to the French principle of secularism and the latter based on a post-Second World War law that disallowed the collection of ethnic data. Diversity discourse travelled to Germany, and it was considered through the lens of instrumental benefits to the business. As Germany and France did not have a multicultural social policy, their approach to diversity was through the lens of integration and assimilation of diversity to the dominant identities (Tatli et al., 2012). The intersectional character of diversity practices also changed over travel. Depending on the national priorities, some categories of diversity are emphasised. Gender diversity is the strongest category of diversity internationally in terms of theory and practice. However, when race duty was introduced to the public sector in the UK, ethnic diversity became a central concern temporarily, changing the pecking order of diversity categories. Similarly, in France, Germany and Italy, while gender diversity was the most significant concern for the diversity scholarship, the integration of migrants and refugees is now considered under the banner of diversity and drives social policy on diversity. Regarding intersectional hierarchies of theory and practice, it would be a good idea to explore the tensions and possibilities of solidarity between gender diversity and ethnic diversity scholarship and practice across Europe.

Diversity also travelled to destinations beyond the Global North. For example, in Turkey, it was mainly adopted by global organisations and their local branch networks. However, this adoption was only ceremonial, as Turkey lacks supportive equality legislation, and it has an antagonistic socio-political context for diversity policies and discourses. In such an adversarial context, diversity is widely ignored by policymakers and organisational leaders (Küskü et al., 2021, 2022). The Turkish case of intersectional diversity has complications. Turkey has a significant investment in integrating refugees and migrants, serving as a holding territory for refugees who mainly wish to travel to Europe. However, the country has a poor track record for gender, ethnic (indigenous), disability and sexual orientation diversity fronts because of religiously inspired populist and antagonistic stances that its political elite adopts against diversity. Knappert et al. (2018) show the intersectional complexities of the exclusion of refugees and gender diversity in Turkey. The Gezi Park movement, the largest uprising in Turkish history, has shown support for intersectional solidarity between environmental activists, feminists, anti-racists, anti-capitalists, the LGBT+ movement and the heterodox religious movement (Özbilgin and Erbil, 2021b). The force of the state suppresses the legacy of the Gezi Park movement. However, the taste for social justice remains an unfulfilled promise in a country dominated by liberal market logic and libertarian ideology that pushes the responsibility to individuals, abdicating the state and the market of duty of care for diversity.

How diversity manifests across countries is context-dependent. A complex set of historical influences and path dependencies and recent national priorities and social movements shape the context of diversity and the hierarchies of manifestation among multiple diversity categories. This case illustrates how diversity gains shape with the socio-cultural and symbolic context it travels.

CONCLUSION

Diversity manifests in multiple forms. There are etic and emic forms of diversity. Etic categories of diversity are generic, and they are universally recognised. Gender, ethnicity, class and sexual orientation are some examples of etic diversity categories. Although they can be interpreted differently across national borders, these categories now have wide international recognition. Emic categories of diversity exist as local forms of diversity. The caste system in India, the tribal structures in some African countries and indigeneity in countries like Australia, New Zealand and Canada present unique and emic categories of diversity. In this chapter, we also reviewed multiple forms of diversity across etic and emic categories. We explored intersections between these multiple categories. The chapter concludes with an illustrative case that examines the travel of diversity and its manifestations across different countries in Europe and wider.

CHAPTER 3

DISCIPLINARY INFLUENCES
ON DIVERSITY SCIENCE

There are only very few disciplines of science which do not use the term diversity in different contexts. In social sciences, diversity often refers to socio-demographic differences. In formal sciences, there are mathematical and statistical techniques developed to measure distributive differences among certain phenomena, such as matter or life forms. Natural sciences, which have sub-divisions of physical and life sciences, use diversity as a way to explore different qualities that exist in matter and life forms. Beyond disciplines of science, in fields of humanities and arts, diversity could manifest as differences in style, form, aesthetics, expressions or as cultural constructs that relate to values, beliefs and ideologies. Diversity science is multidisciplinary, and it draws on insights, methods and frames from across disciplines to study diversity more intimately in varied contexts. It is impossible to do justice to the multidisciplinary influences on how diversity is received across fields of sciences, humanities and arts in this book. Instead, we examine the influence of varied disciplines of study and science on the multidisciplinary framing of diversity in social sciences. In this chapter, we explore and trace how the development of the notion of diversity in other disciplines has helped to frame diversity in social sciences. First, we attend to the formal sciences and explore how mathematical measurements and logical approaches developed for diversity are mobilised in social sciences to measure diversity. Second, we turn to natural sciences and examine how they approached the essential qualities of difference in material and natural phenomena and how these influenced the development of the social science approach to diversity at work and in life. Third, we examine manifestations of diversity in humanities, arts and other disciplines of study to understand how their frames impact how diversity is understood in social sciences. Finally, we explore how across disciplines of social sciences, such as sociology, psychology, politics and economics, diversity is defined and operationalised.

Rich pickings of diverse definitions and frames from different science disciplines is not a value-free process. Each discipline has contributed unique perspectives to the study of diversity. While disciplinary influences from formal and natural sciences have been for the measurement of diversity and identification of its concrete manifestations, humanities and art fields have contributed to an understanding of diversity as discourses and aesthetics, performances and expressions that challenge the status quo and the established order. Similarly, across sub-fields of social sciences, how diversity is defined, framed and operationalised presents a rich yet methodologically, theoretically and ideologically fragmented picture.

FORMAL SCIENCES AND DIVERSITY: EMERGENCE OF DIVERSITY MEASUREMENTS IN SOCIAL SCIENCES

Mathematics and logic, which are considered part of formal sciences, had a considerable impact on the way diversity is measured. The diversity index is a metric measure that mathematicians have developed in formal sciences to ascertain the level of difference across contexts. The diversity index has been adopted in natural sciences and social sciences to measure the diversity of materials, biodiversity and human diversity. The diversity index is widely used in quantitative studies of diversity in social sciences in subdisciplines of psychology, sociology and business and management. The Gini-Simpson index is widely used among economists, for example, to calculate income and other forms of inequality across different populations. Blau

DOI: 10.4324/9780367824044-4

index is the most common diversity index used by scholars in the field of equality, diversity and inclusion at work to measure the dispersion of certain groups in the population (Richard et al., 2004; Wellalage et al., 2013; Yoo et al., 2023). Blau index helps researchers quantify different forms of diversity, such as gender and race in populations, and examine such diversity in relation to other social and economic phenomena, such as pay, work conditions, performance and psycho-social dynamics. Authors such as Rushton (2008) warn that the use of diversity indices such as the Blau index should come with an interpretation of the particular context as diversity indexes themselves are not sensitive to the context of the relations of power that exist where diversity is measured.

The public view of mathematics and logic is that these disciplines offer undisputed calculations and arrive at objective results. However, these disciplines also have an inside track i.e. orthodox and an outside track, i.e. heterodox strands. The public view of mathematics and logic fails to capture the intrafield struggles for legitimacy among scientists and their struggles for recognition in other science disciplines. Nevertheless, thanks to the influence of formal sciences, diversity science has been using mathematical and statistical techniques to examine diversity in social and workplace settings. The use of diversity statistics has been influential in identifying patterns such as proportionate representation and critical statistics around treatment and material, psychometric, affective and symbolic outcomes of diverse communities. Such quantitative and statistical-driven approaches legitimated diversity science as an evidence-based approach in policy and academic circles, which values formal science data above other forms of scientific knowledge. This is why formal sciences have significantly contributed to diversity science, where the dominant methodological approaches drive statistical data. One of the concerns about the domination of positivistic and quantitative methods is methodolatry, which fetishises quantitative methods that treat individuals as numbers and omit unique individual experiences as error margins. While diversity and struggles for equality are intricately connected, subjective individual experiences of uneven relations of power may not be fully captured in statistically oriented research methods that are borrowed from formal sciences. Some scholars call for a broader approach to evidence in social policy, highlighting the warped emphasis on formal scientific methods in framing evidence that ignored the importance of narrative and other methods (Greenhalgh and Russell, 2009; Greenhalgh, 1999; Kelly et al., 2015). Despite these cautionary notes, mathematics, reasoning, and logic offer crucial frames and methodological tools of diversity science.

NATURAL SCIENCES AND DIVERSITY: BIODIVERSITY, NEURODIVERSITY AND SOCIAL SCIENCES

Subdisciplines of natural sciences have been using the concept of diversity to measure dispersion in materials (Atatüre et al., 2018) and among life forms (Russell et al., 2004). Social sciences adopt many diversity constructs developed in natural sciences to frame their diversity concepts. For example, biodiversity is fundamental to understanding diversity among all life forms. Biology, as a subdiscipline of natural sciences, has contributed to understanding the diversity among all life forms and the relationships between them, including humans and nonhuman life forms. Human biology has also explored the biological foundations of diversity among human beings, such as sex, age, sexuality, disability, and race, among others. Biodiversity refers to the diversity of life forms on earth and, as such, includes not only human diversity but also diversity among animals, plants and fungi. Biodiversity research informs efforts to conserve biodiversity, which has been under considerable threat mainly due to human activity. Research on biodiversity has contributed to our understanding of diversity and the importance of protecting and conserving diversity for the sustainability of life on earth, as all life on earth is interdependent in inextricably complex ways. However, the frames we borrow from natural sciences tend to focus on fixed and essential qualities that constitute dispersion among groups. In terms of human diversity, the discipline of biology continues to offer insights into fields such as neurodiversity (McGee, 2012), and how human neural networks are differently structured, leading to different forms of ability and talent to emerge. In earlier adoptions of natural science frames to social science definitions and descriptions of diversity, there is a sense of essentialism, viewing such differences as fixed and unchanging. Essentialist tendencies in direct adoptions of diversity frames from natural sciences to social sciences have been subject to considerable scrutiny. Haslam (2011) explains that essentialism in framing human diversity has negative social consequences as individuals, unlike inanimate objects and other life forms, are uniquely capable of choice, change and strategic manipulation of their qualities. The complexity of human chances and choices renders essentialist frames of diversity naive in accounting for the complexity of human diversity.

Many of the biological differences among people are used historically to uphold value judgments about the social choices that people make. For example, gender differences in reproductive systems and bodily qualities are measured to account for the choices that individuals make. It is only later in history that social scientists contested such biological approximations. For example, Eisenberg (1995) critiques the biologically deterministic accounts of the human brain, revealing how these supposedly scientific fictions are ill-founded. The nature-nurture debate questions whether biology or socialisation has an explanatory power over the choices and chances of individuals. Beyond the dichotomous thinking around the constitutive power of biology and social environment, there is the interplay between these disciplines of biology and social sciences and how this interplay could provide us with more sophisticated explanations of humans and biodiversity than each discipline could.

Natural science perspectives, which often come with essentialist and deterministic ideas about diversity, are sometimes usurped and misused to give meaning and legitimacy to diversity beliefs. The use of biological constructs to refer to diversity could also be done to justify discrimination and stigmatisation and reduce it to biological and innate qualities. A common example of such misuse is attributing certain positive and negative qualities to women and men, different ethnic groups, and age cohorts based on a biologically deterministic approach. The upsurge of populist discourses in the Global North around minoritised groups, migrants, refugees and ethnic others harming the economic, social and political well-being of nation-states draws on essentialist notions of diversity, which lacks an appreciation of such diversity in context. Vassilopoulou et al. (2022) show that essentialist arguments around Turks in the right-wing populist discourses in Germany undermine the symbolic worth of this group and prevent them from reaching their full potential in the labour market.

Although biology offers social sciences great insights into human diversity, much of the diversity in human physiology, psychology, and social behaviour cannot be explained by the discipline of biology alone. Other scientific disciplines have alternative forms of evidence that can help us understand human diversity.

HUMANITIES, ARTS AND DIVERSITY: CULTURAL DE/CONSTRUCTIONS AND AESTHETICS OF DIVERSITY

Disciplines of humanities and arts also have rich frames of diversity. It is possible to distinguish between hard and soft variants of diversity science. While hard diversity science uses counting, representation and proportionality, soft diversity science has become the domain of values, virtues, critique, construction and deconstruction of ideas. The formal and natural sciences have contributed to the development of quantitative, statistical and deterministic theorisation and methods, which formed the 'hard' diversity science. However, the humanities and the arts have contributed qualitative, critical, narrative, expressive, aesthetic theorisation and methods, which informed the 'soft' diversity of science. Much of the humanities field focuses on human diversity from the perspective of varieties of narrations, stories, creativity, choice, agency, and potentiality that human beings bring with them. Humanities disciplines also offer rich insights into values and virtues such as freedom, equality, inclusion, cohesion, liberty, and solidarity that shape how we frame diversity in social sciences. The humanities is the domain of language, literature, culture, history, and philosophy. Most of the human values, philosophies, ideas and frames that we use today in social sciences on diversity come from the discipline of humanities.

In the arts, diversity is viewed as human performances, expressions, and aesthetics, which overcome the spurious Cartesian duality between mind and body through embodied expressions of thought and aesthetics (Özbilgin and Bell, 2008). What humanities and arts contribute to the field of diversity sits in some contrast to the contribution of formal and natural sciences with their focus on exploring essential values, virtues and qualities of diversity. Humanities and arts also bring diverse perspectives and methods to diversity, such as narrative, discourse, aesthetics, expressive and reflexive and embodied perspectives/methods. In this context, it is important to acknowledge a broader international convention: the Convention on the Protection and Promotion of the Diversity of Cultural Expressions, promoted by UNESCO (2005). The convention considers diversity in terms of cultural expressions and seeks to promote an inclusive environment in the international creative and cultural industry. The convention has been a bridge between humanities, the arts and social sciences that shaped diversity.

Critical studies of diversity owe much to the contribution of the field of humanities (Ahonen et al., 2014; Zanoni et al., 2010). The narrative, textual and critical analysis tradition in humanities has fostered interpretive and critical traditions of diversity science that explore hidden relations of power beyond numbers. Scholars in this critical interpretive approach have contributed to cultural and aesthetic constructions of diversity. Humanities and the arts inspire and condition the idea of hope and progress towards equality, diversity and inclusion in social movements and social sciences, as humanities and arts scholarship can point out the detrimental, unfinished and incomplete nature of social and institutional transformation from perspectives that speak truth to power.

SOCIAL SCIENCES AND DIVERSITY

Social sciences are where human diversity has found a critical conceptual home. All subfields of social science have a considerable emphasis on human diversity. Subdisciplines of social sciences have explored diversity and its social constructions, drawing on other science disciplines. Later, we examine the subdisciplines of psychology, sociology, political science, economics and management and organisation studies. How subdisciplines of social sciences approach diversity is in line with their central focus. For example, the individual-level analysis is typically conducted in psychology, societal-level analysis of diversity is common in sociology, and macro national- and international-level analysis borrows elements from politics and economics. Business, management and organisation studies borrow elements from other subdisciplines of social sciences and a broader range of scientific disciplines to tackle questions of diversity.

Psychology

The discipline of psychology examines the cognition, behaviour and affect in individuals and groups (Stockdale and Crosby, 2004). By exploring these differences, psychology has contributed to understanding workforce diversity by examining cognitive biases, such as unconscious bias; discriminatory behaviours, such as microaggressions; and affective disorders, such as incivility. The explicit focus on the individual ways of thinking, acting and feeling about diversity has caused psychological studies to overlook systemic forms of inequality, discrimination and exclusion that individuals could face. Further, the American Psychological Association (APA, 2021) issued a recent apology to people of colour for its complicity in perpetuating racism and eugenics. APA offers remedial courses of action, which suggests a progressive turn in the discipline of psychology.

Nevertheless, the discipline of psychology has made some important contributions to the development of our understanding of diversity. Social identity theory helps us understand how individuals treat differences and similarities within and outside their reference groups. Social comparison theory helps us understand collaborative and competitive behaviours that individuals could display in and outside their groups (Tejfel and Turner, 1986, 2004). Similarly, psychology has focused on individual-level biases, which lead to differential and prejudicial treatment of in-group and out-group members. Psychology has also explained the cognitive processes people use to eliminate guilt and shame when discriminating or showing aggressive behaviour towards others, such as moral disengagement (Bandura et al., 1996). Similarly, the concept of dehumanisation (Haslam, 2006) refers to the failure to attribute human traits to outgroup members (e.g. based on race and ethnicity [Jahoda, 2015], gender and sexual orientation [Tanriverdi and Gezici Yalçın, 2022]). Villesèche et al. (2018) explore the connections between diversity and identity from multilevel and critical lenses. One of the central concepts that psychology contributed to the diversity interventions in organisations has been the concept of unconscious bias (i.e. implicit bias or implicit stereotype in social identity theory), a set of internalised biases and prejudices that individuals hold as natural and normal beliefs, which evade conscious criticism (Oberai and Anand, 2018). The field of psychology has also contributed to the development of diversity science with concepts that refer to the dark and bright sides of human psychology. On the dark side of the psychology of diversity, there are the concepts of stereotyping, otherness, prejudice, bias, aggression, violence, harassment, mobbing and bullying. On the bright side, psychology explores inclusion, equal treatment, belonging and personal security and safety as orienting concepts. April et al. (2012) use a range of psychological constructs, such as identity, inclusion, intention and expectations, to frame new ways of capturing diversity in organisational settings.

One prominent emphasis in the field of psychology has been on coping mechanisms (Lambert and Taylor, 1990) and coping strategies (Coleman et al., 2001) and resilience (Romero et al., 2014; Hardlovsky et al., 2018) for individuals who face antagonistic contexts and traumatic experiences. Although it is important to understand how individuals cope with and develop resilience against bias, discrimination and inequality, psychological approaches often fail to recognise that coping and resilience are signs of systemic problems that prevent individuals from underprivileged backgrounds from thriving, experiencing joys of life, reaching their full potential and bringing their authentic selves to work. The focus on solving problems of individual trauma induced by discrimination, inequality and incivility cannot be overcome by improving individual strength, coping and resilience alone because coping and resilience are still less than thriving.

In recent years, many of the constructs that psychologists have developed are used as dominant frames for diversity interventions in organisations. For example, unconscious bias training, harassment and bullying training, coaching and mentoring and allyship are some contemporary and popular diversity interventions. For example, allyship gained currency among practitioners of diversity in recent years. Allyship refers to the support that individuals in positions of power give to individuals and groups which are disenfranchised. Allyship programmes in organisations seek to promote intra-organisational awareness and support for diversity interventions (Özbilgin et al., 2023a). In line with the psychological research traditions, Dharani and April (2021) show that at the encounter of individuals and their environment, the individual locus of control has more predictive power than environmental conditions. However, one of the criticisms levelled at psychological frames of diversity has been their strong focus on the individual levels of analyses at the expense of team, organisational and wider structural conditions which shape individual experiences at work. For example, some psychological concepts (e.g. psychological capital, see Doci et al., 2023) have been harnessed by the neo-liberal ideal of individual responsibility, pushing structural causes and macro-national and organisational responsibility for addressing inequalities to the margins.

Sociology

Sociological approaches to diversity have focused on the issue of power, status and representation in numbers (DiTomaso et al., 2007). Power manifests in multiple forms as access to resources. Developing the notion of human capital, Becker (2009) suggested that individuals could achieve their life goals if they trade their human capital, which he framed as education, experience and knowledge, for access to positions of power and influence. Yet later research identified that even when individuals from atypical backgrounds (i.e. women, minority ethnic, LGBT+ and disabled) have human capital, they face barriers to entering positions of power and influence. For example, Küskü et al. (2007) show that despite numerical advancements towards equal representation of women in engineering in Turkey, gender stereotypes and biases remained resistant. Bourdieu (2020) expanded the notion of capital to social, cultural and symbolic capital. Social capital is the totality of an individual's connectedness and connectivity in a social field. Individuals could mobilise their social capital for other forms of capital and influence. Cultural capital refers to an individual's education, experience and knowledge in a particular context. Cultural capital could also be transformed into other forms of capital and influence, as individuals try to negotiate their chances and choices in social and economic fields. Finally, symbolic capital is an individual's respectability and symbolic worth in a particular setting. All forms of capital accumulation lead to the enhancement of an individual's symbolic capital and vice versa. Individuals in different fields of symbolic relations have different volumes and kinds of capital at their disposal. There are inter- and intrafield struggles for power and influence. What holds fields intact is the habitus, the taken-for-granted assumptions and internalised intersubjectivities in a particular field of relations (Wacquant and Bourdieu, 1992). Individuals assume that their routines and behaviours and positionalities in any given field are natural. For example, academics in social sciences tend to be left-leaning, consuming similar products and valuing and producing similar work. Drawing on sociological frames, Tatli (2011) explained the agency of diversity managers in the structural conditions of the interfield struggles for power and influence in organisations. To understand the position and influence of actors in the field of diversity, it is important to appreciate relative fields and the symbolic significance they are afforded in each field in which they are located.

Adherence to the rules of the game, when internalised, is called an illusio, which refers to how individuals are drawn to the allure of a game, such as employment in a particular sector of work with established routines, and how the allure of the game renders them insensitive to the harm that the game induces on them and other players. Through the illusio of a field, individuals may lose their ability to criticise their own game, even when the game hurts them (Greenhalgh et al., 2021). Bourdieusian analyses could help us understand how diversity manifests along the lines of capital allocations and access to different forms of capital. In the same way, feminist and postfeminist arguments and struggles could be understood as a difference between capital-poor and capital-rich women. The concept of habitus accounts for why individuals may be under the impression that what they experience at work and in life is natural, not a consequence of a series of multilevel choices. For example, Fenech et al. (2021) show how habitus is gendered, naturalising higher performance evaluation scores for men than women. Habitus is the taken-for-granted assumptions and routinised behaviours of individuals at work. An individual may only be able to break with habitus and achieve reflection if they come out of their context or develop insights into other fields which have varied choices of fields.

Hardin (1968), in his sociological work on the tragedy of commons, explained that the use of collective resources requires optimum regulation. Failing to regulate the use of the common good, the common ground collapses. Meyer (2020) explores the idea of commons in the field of entrepreneurship and identifies collective interest and action as fundamental to forming entrepreneurial commons. Meliou et al. (2021) show that responsible leadership emerges from shared interests. Therefore, it is essential to understand diversity as a shared value, concern or interest so that it can be taken up as a leadership responsibility. Scholars such as Adler and Aycan (2018) highlighted the need to move away from the divisive treatment of diversity towards recognising diversity as an asset. The theory of the tragedy of commons is particularly important for studying diversity as a resource. Jonsen et al. (2013) explain that if diversity is a resource, its effective management is the only means by which diversity could be protected.

Sociological constructs, such as the interplay of structure and agency; capital endowments; habitus; and commons account for the social construction of discourses and practices of diversity. The meso-level contribution of sociology to studies of diversity has been to explore power relations among different actors and interventions of diversity.

Political science and law

Political scientists and law scholars study diversity as a set of rights and inter-communal relations. Political science and law are two disciplines which continue to be dominated by power elites, such as white, upper-class men (Mershon and Walsh, 2016). As such, the theorisation of diversity has been through the perspective of the power elite. These disciplines need to embrace diversity to remain relevant, as Sinclair-Chapman (2015) argues. Nevertheless, scholars have explored the politics of diversity and how diversity interventions are crafted. In the discipline of law, the need for legal reforms to support diversity, equality and inclusion is also extensively studied (Ripstein, 2001; Gowder, 2013). We also examine the role of legal regulation in shaping the organisational landscape of diversity interventions later in this book.

Mayes and Allen (1977) brought political science to organisation studies to define organisational politics as the intention and desire to influence outcomes. The politics of diversity in organisations has two distinct approaches and ideologies of change enshrined in conservative and progressive politics of difference. The liberal approach is enshrined in the equality of opportunity perspective. It assumes, in the same vein as the human capital theory which we discussed earlier, that individuals should be afforded the same standards and chances to overcome inequalities. Although the liberal approach has been instrumental in eliminating overtly discriminatory statements from discourses and policies in social and economic fields, it has proven rather ineffective in garnering deep-level addressing of historical and entrenched forms of inequalities. The liberal approach is also problematic because it places the responsibility for change on individuals. It implicitly suggests that as individuals from disadvantaged groups attain the same level of knowledge, skills and abilities as the dominant groups in society, they could overcome inequalities. Thus, the liberal approach has pushed the responsibility of change to individuals, where diversity efforts focused on positive action (i.e. offering training and education to disadvantaged groups with the assumption that they had a deficit in these regards, even when the dominant groups are not better qualified).

The radical approach suggests that the historical forms of disadvantage could not be attained through such a deficit model and by trying to fix individuals from atypical backgrounds. To attain a deeper level of change, the radical approach suggests affirmative action and positive discrimination against historically disadvantaged groups. The radical approach opposes the deficit model of the liberal approach. It locates the problem with the unearned privileges of the dominant group, offering strategies for combating arbitrary privileges afforded to dominant groups. Although the radical approach promises deep-level changes to relations of power and diversity, it is often met with resistance and backlash when implemented.

Recognising the ineffective nature of the liberal perspective and the socially unacceptable nature of the radical perspective, Cockburn (1991) offered a third-way approach. The transformational approach comes with two agendas. The short-term agenda engages in liberal change and tackles discriminatory practices. The short-term agenda is soft and ineffective. It prevents backlash against the change interventions. But the long-term agenda involves transforming organisations and societies into more welcoming sites for atypical individuals. The transformational change agenda offers small gains in the short term and wider transformations in the longer term. The liberal, radical and transformational change agendas inspired by conservative and progressive political ideologies coexist in social and organisational policy depending on the micro and macro politics of the context. Political science has contributed more than just how diversity-led change is envisioned at the macro level. It also highlights how macro-level actors, such as states, social movements and organised unions, affect choices and chances for human diversity.

Cockburn (2010), in her later work, has demonstrated that gender relations and politics are not limited to the organisational field but are interlaced with the macro-political phenomenon, such as peace and war, emphasising the role of the feminist movement to support the former to avoid the latter. In addition to these feminist frames of reference, there are also ethnic diversity concepts, such as multiculturalism, interculturalism and cosmopolitanism. These concepts by scholars who support ethnic diversity (Modood, 2013) organise ethnic and community relations and inform social policy frameworks. Similarly, a political reading of progressive social movements and their interplay with the law and organisational changes (Özbilgin and Erbil, 2021b) contributes to the development of diversity research beyond the confines of workforces and micro-individual level experiences.

Economics

Studies of diversity with economic perspectives include a wide range of diversity measures, such as based on wealth and poverty, often beyond the socio-demographic diversity categories based on historical disadvantage that we focus in this book. Bartlett (1996) suggests that the economics curriculum would benefit from expanding towards more critical issues of gender and ethnic diversity data in its main curriculum. Economics could help frame economic utility and disutility of equality, diversity and inclusion for different communities, organisations and nation-states. For example, women experience gender penalties in access to jobs, pay and conditions (Blau, 1996). Similar penalties are cited for ethnicity, sexual orientation and disability (Woodhams et al., 2015). In particular, the gender pay gap is merely reported in some countries but remains unchallenged in most countries. It is only Iceland which passed legislation to criminalise the gender pay gap (Olafsdottir, 2018). Despite over 70 years of gender equality legislation in Europe, the gender pay gap remains resistant to change in the UK. When UK organisations started disclosing the gender pay gap, it became clear that in key industries, such as finance, the gender pay gap in some organisations remains incredibly high, at over 50 per cent in its global financial firms (Healy and Ahamed, 2019).

Mainstream economists had an interest in the nexus of education and employment. Nobel Prize–winning economist Gary Becker's (2009) human capital theory is often cited as a way in which individuals from diverse socio-demographic backgrounds could achieve labour market participation through education and training. The human capital theory posits that labour market participation and career success are contingent upon education, training and skills. However, this theorisation does not account for disparate outcomes that women and men, majority and minority ethnic groups and higher and lower socioeconomic backgrounds achieve at the same level of education and skill. It is based on an old paradigm where labour market participation of disadvantaged groups could be explained through their educational and training deficit. Recent studies show that sexism, racism and other discriminatory practices may account for low labour market participation and success rates of individuals from disadvantaged backgrounds. Revealing the dark side of access to the labour market, economists such as Robert William Fogel (1994, 2003) have shown that racial exploitation and slavery have served generously to capitalist interests and that immorality made economic sense. More critical economists such as Joseph E. Stiglitz (2000, 2012, 2016) have problematised the expansion of the neoliberal market logic's uneven impact on human rights and equality at work. Stiglitz (2012) argues that developed countries have introduced regulations to hold their labour markets accountable for human rights and equality for workers. However, in developing countries, where protective measures are not taken, neoliberal expansion has brought about more exploitation and discrimination, which remained unchecked (Erbil and Özbilgin, 2023).

Among more critical economists, Robert H. Frank (2008, 2011) has shown that the rich become richer through the growth of the capitalist system. European scholar Thomas Piketty (2013) has demonstrated that capitalism, which has widened the middle class to date, is likely to end up concentrating wealth in the hands of the political elite and the richest through ownership of technology and the decline of population growth. The contribution of the economics discipline to the field of diversity is remarkable in showing the intricate interplay between demography, education, wealth and labour market outcomes. While neoclassical economic theories largely ignored the dark side of the capitalist system on diverse communities, critical realist and institutional economic theories showed the disparate and uneven impact of dominant economic systems on disadvantaged communities.

Business and management

Business, management and organisation scholars are interested in how diversity is measured, monitored and regulated in business and organisational settings. Diversity is defined as division, difference, variety, disparity and separation in business and management (Harrison and Klein, 2007). Accounting for diversity in the field of management and organisation emanates from the promise in earlier diversity management scholarship that diversity is likely to contribute to the competitiveness of organisations in terms of performance, innovation and talent acquisition gains (Kamasak et al., 2020b; Küçükaltan, 2018). This instrumental approach has meant that the earlier focus of workforce diversity research has been on the antecedents, correlates and multilevel consequences of workforce diversity in terms of individual, team and organisational outcomes. This meant that workforce diversity scholarship has drifted slightly away from human rights and equality demands-based agendas of the equality, diversity and inclusion work. However, the growing evidence on the consequences of workforce diversity suggested that the relationship between workforce diversity and performance outcomes is complex, multidimensional and contingent rather than simplistic and unidirectional and generalisable. First, workforce diversity scholars have identified many negative consequences of diversity, such as industrial conflicts, miscommunication and reduced speed of action, among others. Second, the research also demonstrated that the supposed benefits of diversity, evident in one strand of diversity, did not apply equally to all. Third, and more recently, scholars have shown that it is not the workforce diversity that generates the organisational value but the effective management of diversity. Furthermore, several antecedents, such as leadership support (Ng and Sears, 2018), a climate of inclusion (Nishi, 2013), a supportive organisational culture, availability of resources at the disposal of diversity and the legitimacy and support afforded to diversity in the external and internal political context have been identified as significant antecedents of workforce diversity which could help with the effective and deep-level implementation of diversity interventions.

In recent years, there has been a cynical turn in assessing the impact of diversity interventions. Some scholars have identified that diversity interventions, which are based on training and education of staff alone, such as equal opportunities training and unconscious bias training, had a poor scientific basis for use (Taksa and Thornthwaite, 2023) and negative consequences (Noon, 2018), such as ineffectiveness. Recent evidence suggests that diversity interventions which remain at the shallow level and aim at fixing people at work are not likely to generate the desired positive outcomes. Diversity interventions which target changing the system, the culture of the organisation and structures and routines to make them more welcoming and accommodating to diversity are found to be more effective in garnering positive outcomes at work.

ILLUSTRATIVE CASE: INTERDISCIPLINARITY AND THE CASE OF COVID19 PANDEMIC RESPONSE

The WHO (World Health Organization) declared Covid19 a global pandemic on March 11, 2020. Tackling Covid19 as a global pandemic required a global and transnational response. Earlier days of the pandemic received different responses from politicians. Some national representatives speculated that the virus was only affecting certain racial groups and there was no reason for worry. Covid19 received much media attention and policy analysis, mainly without partial scientific evidence. From its early days, the scientific orthodoxy of the WHO and national health policy groups, dominated by clinical scientists, adopted a line which rejected the evidence that Covid19 coronavirus was airborne. The WHO, in particular, pursued an orthodox line, suggesting the best way of protection to be frequently washing hands, keeping social distance and cleaning surfaces. Most Western countries have quickly adopted this stance based on particle transmission of Covid19. Accepting airborne transmission would require using N95 masks, improving ventilation in public places and keeping away from crowded places. The reasons for adopting particle transmission in Western countries were manifold but largely based on the scientific orthodoxy that clinicians uphold. Clinical scientists often rejected evidence that physicists provided of airborne transmission of Covid19. Clinical scientists that dominated health policy committees dismissed such evidence as weak or anecdotal (Greenhalgh et al., 2021).

Asian countries such as Japan and Taiwan have adopted different lines. Instead of outright rejecting airborne transmission, they embraced evidence provided by heterodox science, (i.e. physics). By doing so, they went against the advice of the WHO and healthcare policy in Western countries. Orthodoxy and heterodoxy are classifications of approaching scientific knowledge. The orthodox view is the inside track, established approaches to science. Heterodox science is still legitimate but presents marginal access to the inside track of a particular discipline. Disciplinary knowledge in science often develops inside and outside tracks and hierarchies. Such hierarchies of knowledge are detrimental to the sustainability and innovative potential of science which thrives in interdisciplinary and democratic settings. In this case, aerosol-transmission science was considered heterodoxy, as it was pushed to the margins of the evidence building by scientific orthodoxy in Western countries. The purist approach adopted by the inside track of clinical scientists to dismiss evidence from physicists has led to many ill-informed decisions and healthcare policies that ultimately led to avoidable deaths. The interfield struggles between aerosol-transmission scientists (heterodoxy) and particle-transmission science (orthodoxy) could be averted if scientific orthodoxy and hegemony recognised the value of scientific pluralism and interdisciplinarity. Instead, the inside scientific track has led to methodolatry (Chamberlain, 2000), a term for the fetishisation of a narrow spectrum of methods (i.e. clinical trials in this case) and rejection of heterodox methods (i.e. evidence of airborne transmission from physicists).

Besides the general devastating effects of the pandemic, there are also differential consequences by diversity categories. The gender impact of the pandemic is studied. While some scholars demonstrated that women, young and old people were more adversely affected in terms of exposure to transmission (Cotofan et al., 2021) and negotiation of domestic workspace, others have highlighted that the pandemic has created a space for gendered renegotiation of space in the domestic sphere (Elfira et al., 2021). Similarly, minority ethnic groups, due to their high concentration in certain industries with a higher risk of exposure, have been more adversely impacted (Patel et al., 2020; Census, 2021). Disability, LGBTQ+ and religious minority groups have also reported negative impacts on their community health in access to healthcare (Armitage and Nellums, 2020; Halkitis and Krause, 2021; Taragin-Zeller et al., 2020). So the global pandemic did not have a universal and even impact across communities and socio-demographic fault lines. In fact, today, one of the most significant challenges remains vaccine equity/equality across nations, regions, communities and other fault lines. Thus, the impact of the Covid19 pandemic was felt more adversely among already vulnerable communities across the fault lines.

Exploring why and how the pandemic response failed in the UK, Greenhalgh et al. (2022) identified that a lack of interdisciplinarity in the policy circles has led to the failure to recognise that Covid19 virus is airborne. The authors show that evidence provided by physicists advised airborne transmission. UK's healthcare policy authorities are dominated by clinical scientists who unjustly dismiss evidence from physicists as anecdotal. Whereas in Japan, the healthcare policy accepted aerosol transmission and inclusion of heterodox science led to the development of effective preventative measures, particularly making organisations and the national healthcare system responsible and resourced to take action. In the case of the UK, one of the main reasons for the failure of the healthcare policy has been the individualisation of responsibility. While the Japanese government has taken full responsibility for ventilating buildings better and creating safe spaces that can prevent transmissions, the UK government pushed for individual responsibility, failing to acknowledge and accept institutional and national responsibility. The transnational and interdisciplinary collaboration did not happen during the pandemic. Transnational collaborations among scientists could have prevented national-level policy failures. The poor pandemic response emerged due to a failure of disciplinary silos, interfield struggles among scientists and national-level policymaking based on knowledge hierarchies. The Covid19 pandemic has shown that national-level policymaking remains limited and ineffective in addressing global challenges. As a total social fact (Chanlat, 2020, 2022) and a civilisational challenge (Bruna, 2022), the Covid19 pandemic calls for a transdisciplinary dialogue, transnational coordination, transversal multilevel cooperation and, in a word, increased *pluralistic social regulation* (Bruna, 2021, 2022; Rouine et al., 2022).

Healthcare systems are strained further due to Covid19 and years of neoliberal and libertarian policies, which undermined the public commons ethos of the healthcare systems. The neoliberal take on healthcare has served private sector interests well and pushed up the cost of healthcare internationally. The publicly funded healthcare systems are put under strain to demand privatisation. The neoliberal turn in healthcare has implications for workforce diversity, as disadvantaged communities and marginalised social identity groups are exposed to higher levels of health risk and cost as the Covid19 crisis and uneven death rates by demographic diversity show. As a solution, there is a need to return to interdisciplinary, transnational and pluralist, evidence-based policymaking in healthcare and the public sector ethos and public commons ideas in healthcare to provide safety nets that can improve the quality of care and eliminate the uneven healthcare provision that faced the public during the Covid19 pandemic. Diversity-led innovative solutions could have overcome interfield struggles and meaningless hierarchies of knowledge across scientific disciplines and prevented major healthcare failures by adopting pluralist, interdisciplinary and transnational approaches to create safety nets for vulnerable groups internationally.

CONCLUSION

This chapter focused on different science disciplines and how they contributed to diversity science in the social science field. From formal sciences to pure sciences and social sciences, diversity science has borrowed elements of methods and analysis techniques to study the multifaceted nature of human diversity across different settings and levels of study. What appears interesting, though, is that not one single method or approach can reveal the complex nature of human diversity. Interdisciplinarity and cross-national knowledge exchange provide rich insights for developing our understanding of human diversity. Therefore, diversity science today adopts plural approaches to address its complex challenges. An illustrative case shows how the Covid19 pandemic had an uneven impact on diverse groups. The case also illustrates the significance of interdisciplinary and transnational diversity research and collaboration in diversity-led responses to global crises.

CHAPTER 4

WORKFORCE DIVERSITY AND ITS CONSEQUENCES

Earlier research in the field of diversity has focused on the consequences of workforce diversity. For example, studies have explored the correlation of workforce diversity with a set of organisational outcomes, such as engagement, innovation, creativity, innovation and performance. Studies focusing on the positive consequences of workforce diversity contributed to the development of the business case for diversity, which brings together evidence for the utility of workforce diversity for individuals, teams and organisations. The business case for diversity has become popular in the 1990s, as organisational actors (i.e. diversity officers) were asked to provide evidence to show that diversity and inclusion interventions would contribute to the bottom line. To an extent, the requirement to achieve buy-in from corporate gatekeepers suggests a lack of trust in the possible positive consequences of workforce diversity.

While equality, diversity and inclusion concerns have remained largely social and moral until the 1990s (Köllen et al., 2018), the shift to diversity management has generated a more instrumental and strategic interest (McDonald, 2003) in the effective management of workforce diversity, as diversity is presented as a growing trend in the workforce internationally. However, the business case for diversity has been criticised for lacking a strong evidence base, as the connection between organisational outcomes and workforce diversity was complicated by a large set of factors, such as the categories of diversity that were examined, the size of organisations that are considered and the national context which is explored (Buche et al., 2013).

In a study on accounting for diversity in global organisations, Özbilgin et al. (2016) found that the earlier studies on workforce diversity and organisational outcomes were misleading, considering that workforce diversity is often framed as an organisational resource, and what matters is the effective use of a resource rather than the existence of a resource that leads to positive organisational outcomes. Therefore, the authors suggest that it is not workforce diversity as a resource that contributes to organisational performance but the effective management and regulation of workforce diversity that generates positive organisational outcomes. If left to its natural course, workforce diversity may even lead to negative organisational outcomes, as endemic forms of inequality, uneven power relations and social injustice may result in negative outcomes, industrial conflicts and toxic employment relations at work. Therefore, exploring the consequences of workforce diversity alone would generate a mixed set of outcomes. Instead, research should consider the link between diversity interventions and organisational-, team- and individual-level outcomes. With this awareness, the link between diversity and causal links in terms of performance, innovation, the bottom line, social responsibility and sustainability have been explored regarding workforce diversity and appropriate diversity management interventions.

DIVERSITY AND PERFORMANCE

In its introduction as a strategic management concept in the North American context in the late 1980s, workforce diversity was associated with a positive contribution to organisational performance and competitiveness. The original framing of workforce diversity considered it as a competitive organisational resource. Pitts and Recascino Wise (2010) explained that much diversity research lacked evidence on its consequences in organisations. In over ten years, much of the research work in the field of workforce diversity has focused on the consequences of diversity

DOI: 10.4324/9780367824044-5

on organisational outcomes (Fitzsimmons et al., 2022). While the mainstream work focused on the top management team gender diversity, recently, Joo et al. (2018, 2022) revealed that managerial-level diversity leads to higher levels of organisational performance provided that there is gender diversity among subordinates. Hundschell et al. (2019) identified that workplace diversity leads to higher performance and team resilience. Studies which examined the organisational-, team- and individual-level consequences of diversity have highlighted that diversity leads to dual outcomes: while diversity could cause industrial disputes, lead to problems in communication and reduce workplace harmony and integration (Gong et al., 2011; Wolff et al., 2010; Stahl et al., 2010; Shachaf, 2008), it can at the same time improve an organisation's financial and business performance (Herring, 2009; Kochan et al., 2003), innovation potential, employee engagement and commitment (Gonzalez and Denisi, 2009; Leslie and Gelfand, 2008; Mckay et al., 2007). The duality of the impact of workforce diversity on organisational-, team- and individual-level outcomes rendered outcomes of research on the performance of diversity inconclusive and complex.

More recent studies have pointed out that the relationship between workforce diversity and workplace outcomes is complicated by how diversity is managed in organisations (Özbilgin et al., 2016). It would, instead, be a better idea to query the relationship between diversity interventions and workplace outcomes. Polzer et al. (2002) identified among workgroups that interpersonal congruence (i.e. how similar individuals feel toward their workgroup members) could positively impact their group effectiveness. Studies such as these suggest that beyond diversity, how it is regulated and how individuals are made to feel in diverse settings matter to how they approach life and work. However, more recent research demonstrates that interpersonal cultural diversity (i.e. individuals coming from different cultural backgrounds) and intrapersonal cultural diversity (i.e. an individual having multiple cultural repertoires) lead to different outcomes in terms of creativity and performance in organisations. Diversity alone may not lead to positive performance outcomes without individuals having diverse cultural repertoires (Corritore et al., 2020). Understanding diversity requires a multilevel, multifaceted and relational investigation, exploring its different manifestations from multiple perspectives.

Akron et al. (2016) show that team diversity leads to positive organisational outcomes and that organisations should build atypical work arrangements to accommodate workforce diversity at the team level to garner such performance benefits. However, Brennan (2022) distinguishes diversity interventions for justice and diversity interventions for the bottom line and explains that these two types of workforce diversity should not be conflated. The former kind of diversity intervention that connects with social justice is there to level the playing field of individuals from disadvantaged backgrounds. The kinds of diversity interventions that promote performance, however, may relate to practices of group cohesion and improved communication among team members. While the social justice and equality based on diversity interventions focus on improving equality outcomes for historically disadvantaged groups, the latter categories of workforce diversity that connect with performance tend to focus on other kinds of diversity based on skills, abilities and knowledge, for example. Moon and Christensen (2020) provide evidence to contest this dichotomous thinking between workforce diversity and social justice and performance rationales, showing that diversity climate could moderate the effect of workforce diversity based on social inequalities on organisational performance. Diversity climate, the preparedness and maturity of an organisation to accommodate and support diversity, could help improve organisational performance in diverse organisations, even though the relationship is complicated by a large number of moderating factors, such as measurement type and source, outcome type, demographic diversity and climate strength (Holmes IV et al., 2021). An early study by the Chartered Institute of Personnel and Development (Özbilgin et al., 2008) showed that progressive organisations tend to focus on multiple rationales and draw support from a wide range of antecedent conditions for implementing and motivating their diversity interventions, then polarised arguments, such as maturity of diversity, social justice, performance drive, legal support or voluntaristic engagement on their own.

While exploring the interrelationship between workforce diversity, organisational outcomes and diversity management, it is important to understand also the complexity of beliefs and practices. Cho et al. (2017), in their study of social enterprises, show that while social entrepreneurs believe in the way diversity contributes to performance, they report that they are not likely to take up interventions that promote diversity. Their findings present a cautionary note that highlights the subtle disconnect between diversity and equality beliefs and diversity practices and outcomes. Benschop (2001) suggests that workforce diversity and its management in organisations could lead to affective, cognitive, symbolic and communicative changes and outcomes. Therefore, exploring outcomes should also consider a range of outcome measures.

Despite extensive research on workforce diversity and performance in organisations, the evidence does not present a conclusive picture due to the complexity of diversity categories and measures and moderators of performance in organisations. We know that some forms of workforce diversity may lead to positive performance outcomes in some contexts and under certain conditions. Roberson et al. (2020) suggest that workforce diversity would yield positive outcomes, such as reducing inequalities, if managed effectively. Similarly, other researchers suggest that diversity interventions should target organisational development if it is to make a positive contribution (Dobbin and Kalev, 2022). Some diversity interventions focus on fixing the disadvantaged groups (i.e. offering women, minority ethnic people and other atypical candidates opportunities for development when it is the institutions which discriminate against atypical candidates that should change and develop). So in terms of the contribution of workforce diversity to performance, what matters is the organisational development, cultural, systemic and institutional change interventions rather than interventions which seek to offer training and education that do not connect with organisational development efforts.

DIVERSITY AND INNOVATION

Innovation is defined as the amalgamation of two or more fields of knowledge to contribute to a development of an idea in another field. Organisations need innovation for longevity, sustainability and growth. Many scholars have explored whether workforce diversity contributes to innovative potential and innovation outcomes in organisations. Sung and Choi (2021) show that contingencies complicate the interplay between workforce diversity and innovation at the organisational level. Furthermore, the type of diversity also matters (i.e. gender or age) and the organisational environment (e.g. turbulent or stable) in predicting the impact on organisational innovation. Earlier research has highlighted that diverse teams have greater innovative potential. Thus, innovation, in essence, is the practice of effectively managing the diversity of ideas to develop existing ideas further. Wikhamn and Wikhamn (2020) identify a nonlinear, U-shaped relationship between gender diversity and employee innovation, showing that high levels of gender diversity lead to innovation. Guerrero (2022) also identifies that women and migrant workers contribute to venture potential and innovation in organisations. Similarly, Ellis and Keys (2015) found that racial diversity contributes to organisational innovation. In contrast, Maré et al. (2014) report that when other control variables are introduced, such as size and sector, they do not find any positive correlation between local workforce diversity and innovation.

At a philosophical level, workforce diversity is possible only when there are proportionately high numbers of individuals from atypical backgrounds, such as women, minority ethnic and other marginalised and underrepresented groups in positions of power and privilege. The innovative potential of disadvantaged communities is often ignored in the extant literature (April and Dharani, 2021). Increasing representation of atypical individuals in the workforce brings to the organisational stage the conflicts and interfield struggles between organisational orthodoxy (i.e. the inside track), which is made up of the traditional demography and those heterodox newcomers (i.e. outsiders within and atypical track). The struggle between atypical members of a workforce and the established members is between orthodoxy and heterodoxy. It is a struggle for legitimacy, access to power, rules and resources. Heterodoxy brings innovation to organisations through dissent, difference and opposition to the normative routines of the inside track (Greenhalgh et al., 2022). Samdanis and Özbilgin (2020) suggest that atypical individuals are innovators from the margins, as they bring insights from different socio-demographic backgrounds and contribute to the pool of perspectives in organisations. What is often considered an atypical workforce in organisations makes up more than 80 per cent of any talent pool (Özbilgin and Erbil, 2023e). However, the innovative potential of an atypical workforce remains untapped due to a complex set of historical reasons, including entrenched forms of exclusion and discrimination that bar atypical candidates from positions of power, influence and innovation. There is a need for deliberate action by organisations to cultivate the innovative potential of diversity. Mohammadi et al. (2017) report that increasing ethnic and disciplinary diversity would help organisations innovate.

One of the barriers to innovation in organisations is the groupthinking that homogeneous teams suffer. Social identity theory shows that teams with similar knowledge, skills and expertise could, on the one hand, develop heuristic methods to act fast with improved communication speed. On the other hand, such homogeneous teams could have shared assumptions they take for granted. In time, they may lose their ability to have healthy views about their work processes and develop blind spots about their processes and outcomes. Workforce diversity offers a solution to groupthink, as diversity brings different opinions, dispositions, aspirations and needs in organisations and opens up possibilities of dissent, difference and opposition, which break the impasse of groupthink.

Heterogeneous workforces may suffer from illusio (i.e. blindness) due to the allure of the game (Bourdieu and Wacquant, 1992). Individuals start suffering from illusio and become insensitive to the negative consequences of the games that they play when they experience little contestation or opposition. Only when individuals receive external views may they develop cognitive dissonance sufficient to mobilise innovative solutions (Mergen and Ozbilgin, 2021a). Organisations which lack diversity are blinded by the games of their power elite, who, over time, lose their ability to have a healthy and critical view of organisational routines. Such groupthink and illusio could prevent the innovative potential of teams and organisations. To foster innovation, organisations in sectors which thrive on innovation have deliberate strategies to bring in ideas and views of a diverse range of customers and employees from different backgrounds (Bjögvinsson, 2012). For example, the most popular technology products you find in the global market owe their success to diversity-led innovation as they use design thinking that translates the needs of a diverse range of individuals to design and final products and services (Liedtka, 2015). Design thinking works with the principle that diversity in end users' needs could be mobilised to find innovative design solutions for products and services. In the case of workplace diversity, design thinking could garner such a transformation.

Some organisations use workforce and social diversity to co-design and co-innovate products and services. Design thinking is widely used to develop products and services in innovative ways. Groups of individuals from different demographic backgrounds are engaged in the design process and encouraged to state their needs for particular services and products for which co-innovation is sought. Once these diverse needs are gathered, product innovation seeks to accommodate and satisfy these diverse needs. The purpose of the co-design is often to make products appealing and accessible to as wide and diverse a market as possible. Most organisations today would engage in user experience to co-design their products. Christensen et al. (2021) suggest that design thinking is also possible for diversity scholars and practitioners to disrupt organisational designs and routines through diversity-led innovation.

Although design thinking practices serve organisations well to capture diverse markets, they rarely bring more equality and inclusion, as the diverse cohorts of customers and users involved in co-design and participative design do not ultimately have co-ownership of the products and services which they help to co-innovate. Co-ownership, if socially or legally demanded, could potentially transform the uneven power relations that current practices of diversity-led co-design interventions suffer. Bringing users as owners of design and innovation ideas could address, to some extent, the uneven relations of power and resources between markets and consumers through diversity-led innovation practices. One way that diversity-led innovation through co-design could be used is in the design and delivery of diversity training in organisations. In their current form, diversity and inclusion training is often offered with the needs of diverse communities in mind. However, these training programmes rarely combine with organisational transformation efforts that capture the spirit of diversity-led innovation in organisations. Co-ownership with design thinking would lead to organisations considering the demands of diverse communities beyond the design of their training programmes and embedding these requirements into the design of their systems and structures.

The relationship between workforce diversity and innovation is complex. While the evidence on the relationship between workforce diversity and innovation suggests that workforce diversity could be a prerequisite for innovation, diversity-led innovation could also help organisations transform in sustainable and lasting ways. To enhance the relationship between diversity and innovations, organisations need to foster a diverse climate and improve the organisation's preparedness to a diverse workforce.

WORKPLACE DEMOCRACY, EQUALITY AND HUMANISATION

From birth to late life, individuals are exposed to varied forms of systemic and institutional bias, inequality and discrimination in their life cycles (Hoffman, 1977). By the time an individual joins the workforce, they will have encountered many institutions with varied forms of bias. Sociologically, the family, education, healthcare, law, police and employment are all institutions that individuals encounter from birth to old age. Organisational efforts to manage diversity should be considered a small but significant part of efforts to tackle the life cycle of discrimination and inequality that individuals experience in their encounters from an early age. Kamasak et al. (2020a) explain that when the individual intersections of difference and diversity meet with institutional intersections, the intersectional encounter may have hostile or positive outcomes. For example, an institution marked with a white male-dominant culture may not provide a positive context for a migrant female worker. As it is impossible to change individual intersections, organisations could transform their intersections to make their cultures and structures accommodating to atypical and non-traditional workers. Thus, the purpose of workforce diversity interventions is also to provide democracy, tackle inequalities and foster humanisation in institutions of significance so that coexistence is possible among members. Roberson et al. (2020) suggest that diversity interventions could be specifically designed to reduce workplace inequalities.

Education provides a significant institutional setting in which diversity concerns are addressed. Social and cultural diversity is a reality in education as well as workplaces today and into the future. If we take the field of education as the waiting room for the workforce, the education sector has experienced unprecedented growth in numbers and diversity in recent years (Resnik, 2007). Futuristic research predicts that the higher education sector will continue to grow over the next decade, with over 300 million students entering higher education in 2030 (Choudaha and Van Rest, 2018). These are signs that diversity is not only a contemporary issue but also a future challenge for higher education and employment sectors. Marketisation of higher education limited equality of access (Gibbs, 2018). Further, the democratisation of education has not been matched by the democratisation of workplaces at the same speed. While the new talent emerges as diverse cohorts, the nexus between education and employment still offers a hostile context for new graduates from atypical and non-traditional backgrounds (Tchibozo, 2012). Inequalities in the world of work remain broadly resistant to change. Further down the line in careers, individuals from atypical and diverse backgrounds face greater degrees of inequality and discrimination if we consider the cumulative effects over their life course and the myriad of new challenges they face as newcomers to positions of power and influence as they advance in their careers. International research on equality, diversity and inclusion at work shows that the pace of change is slow, and the systemic and institutional forms of inequality are deeply entrenched (Bartels-Ellis et al., 2019). This context provides a strong impetus for organisations to manage workforce diversity to eliminate bias, inequality and discrimination.

What provides the normative push for organisations to engage with workforce diversity interventions is social movements. Many social movements have gained international momentum highlighting sexism, racism, xenophobia and other forms of social injustice and inequality in the early 2020s. Social movements are good predictors of what is to come in the social and legal regulation of workplaces and other domains of life. We can predict that there will be a turn to social justice agendas in the treatment of equality and diversity at work, as a larger number of organisations will start engaging with social movements to improve the conditions of work for their workers. We can also predict that the human rights and equality demands will become more international in the future, culminating in efforts to regulate diversity through international, cross-border and global interventions. Social movements such as Black Lives Matter, MeToo, Women's Marches, LGBTQ+ Pride Marches, Gezi Park, Arab Spring, Tiananmen Square protests and, more recently, the Women, Life, Freedom movement have transformed the moral landscape internationally for national governments and global organisations in particular (Özbilgin and Erbil, 2021b; Turkmenoglu, 2016). However, there are many modes of moral entrepreneurship (Greenhalgh, 2019) pushing for divergent moral approaches to diversity. Therefore, in this fragmented moral landscape, there is a need for leadership, allyship and championship that can translate the demands of social movements into practical and pragmatic ideas and actions.

Humanisation at work is defined as a process by which work becomes less unpleasant and more accommodating of human needs. Workforce diversity interventions could be used to foster humanisation at work. Discourses of workforce diversity often refer to high-road practices of human resource management that increase flexibility at work to make workplaces more welcoming for newcomers (Nishii and Özbilgin, 2007). In countries where human rights are not legally or socially protected, diversity interventions may lack focus on humanisation as drivers (Özbilgin and Yalkin, 2019; Küskü et al., 2021, 2022). Prati et al. (2021) suggest that one way to tackle dehumanisation in diverse groups is to move from single identity categorisation based on gender, ethnicity, class and so on towards complex and multiple-identity categorisation. Authors suggest that multiple-identity categorisation offers possibilities of tackling dehumanisation for outgroup members at work that can transcend social identity-based conflicts.

Ely and Thomas's (2001) earlier work on workforce diversity suggests three alternative rationales for implementing diversity interventions in organisations. These are the performance, institutional and moral rationales. We explored the performance arguments rationales earlier. What Ely and Thomas refer to as moral rationales fit well with the equality, democracy and humanisation rationales that we explored in this section. Despite some cynical assessments of the moral intentions of organisations to pursue diversity interventions to whitewash, woke wash, gender wash and pinkwash, organisations report engaging with moral rationales, such as democracy, equality and humanisation, along with performance and institutional rationales. A recent OECD (2020) study shows that organisations report multiple rationales, including moral and social justice motives, for pursuing workforce diversity interventions.

THE BOTTOM LINE FOR DIVERSITY

The term, the bottom line, refers to the net result in the balance sheet of an organisation. Organisations tend to demand their activities to contribute to the bottom line (i.e. the shareholder value of an organisation). However, under the leadership of Kofi Annan, the Secretary General of the United Nations has led efforts at redefining and upgrading the bottom line from shareholder value/profitability towards a broader focus on people, planet and profits, emphasising the newly assigned responsibilities of organisations to their employees, communities and environment (Jennifer Ho and Taylor, 2007). As bottom-line arguments broadened, so did the rationales that motivate workforce diversity interventions in organisations, from a shareholder focus to a focus on people and the planet. Broadening of the bottom-line arguments resulted in a focus on workforce diversity and diversity management efforts to adopt broader stakeholder approaches which include internal partners, such as shareholders, employees and managers, and external partners, such as customers and local communities. Broadening the focus of diversity management from shareholder to stakeholder approach liberates workforce diversity interventions from a compulsion to make a financial contribution to the balance sheets of organisations and brings back human rights and moral concerns of workforce diversity.

However, the triple bottom-line rationales on their own may not be compelling enough for organisations to act on stakeholder demands. Unlike shareholders, who can legally hold management accountable, broader stakeholders have less power to impact the decisions of organisational actors. The stakeholder approach remains a voluntary consideration for most organisations. The voluntarism of the stakeholder approach leads to reduced voice for stakeholders. Organisational actors may listen to the voices of stakeholders, yet most stakeholder demands could be considered noise and ignored, and few demands may be incorporated. The stakeholder approach retains the uneven power relations regarding the legitimacy of different stakeholder voices. Therefore, it is important to regulate stakeholder demands so that organisations can consider different demands on an equal footing. Thus, the triple bottom-line arguments for workforce diversity are important yet insufficient means through which to regulate workforce diversity effectively. For effective regulation of workforce diversity, there is a need for stakeholders to be supported through coercive regulation of the state or normative pressure of social movements or customer groups (Kamasak et al., 2023). While triple bottom-line arguments may be adopted in organisations, their impact on workers is yet to be established. April and Blass (2010) have developed a psychometric measurement of the broader bottom-line impact of diversity interventions across ten dimensions: senior managers, immediate managers, values, recruitment, promotion/progression and development, fitting in, bullying/harassment, dialogue, organisational belonging and emotional well-being. The impact and veracity of triple bottom-line business case commitments need to be checked for different stakeholder interests.

One of the major criticisms of bottom-line-based business case arguments is that they are symptomatic of a trust deficit in workforce diversity. Since its introduction to the corporate world in the 1980s, the discourse of diversity management has suffered a trust deficit. When diversity interventions are presented to the corporate boards, which are predominantly made up of white, heterosexual men, it comes with a message of changing power relations at work across social demographic lines. The shift from equal opportunities to diversity management was partly to free demands for equality from corporate trust deficit by aligning such demands with strategic and bottom-line goals of corporations. This shift has reduced the backlash by corporate leaders who come from typical backgrounds. They were less threatened by diversity management interventions which promised consideration for all forms of difference, removing the personal threat to white, middle-class, able-bodied men. Yet diversity management has been received with partial welcome in corporate circles, which continued to demand evidence for its viability, contribution, sustainability and moral basis for implementation. This trust deficit was felt by practitioners and led to research studies on causal links between workforce diversity and its team-, workplace- and organisational-level outcomes. It is possible to transcend this trust deficit by heeding Jung's (2010) notion of synchronicity, which suggests going beyond causal links as acausal connections and possibilities of acausal coexistence could also lead to positive outcomes.

One of the manifestations of such a trust deficit was that diversity professionals had to present their demands for resources for workforce diversity interventions as a contribution to the bottom line. Practitioners had to turn to academic research, often from business schools, which are aligned with the performative and neoliberal agenda of the market for evidence. Thus, the mainstream research in the field of diversity management in the early years took the form of providing evidence of a contribution to the bottom line (i.e. profitability and shareholder value of organisations). Earlier works in the 1990s and 2000s have explored how diversity in general, and gender diversity in particular, contributes to the bottom line of organisations. Early findings showed some support for the expectation that gender diversity contributed to the organisational bottom line, provided that the conditions are right for such diversity in the organisation (Dwyer et al., 2003). However, more studies have demonstrated that such research generated only tenuous evidence for the contribution to the bottom line unless organisations take measures to accrue benefits of diversity through planned interventions (Roberson et al., 2017b). Further, some scholars (e.g. Kucukaltan and Ozbilgin, 2019a) questioned whether organisations which performed better would recruit more diverse talent and if the relationship was not as straightforward as once suggested.

When aspects of diversity which emanate from human rights and civil liberties movements were originally used in diversity research in pursuit of bottom-line contributions, in later years, there was a depoliticisation of diversity research with the introduction of a wider range of 'diversity' criteria which does not connect with social justice, such as diversity of skills, diversity of functions and cognitive diversity. Critical diversity management scholars have criticised the performance and bottom-line-based rationales for diversity research and suggested that such efforts diverted attention from the moral and human rights agendas which should inform diversity. In recent years, the single bottom-line arguments are contested, with the United Nations endorsing triple bottom-line rationales from corporations. The UN called for a move away from the single bottom line, which focused merely on the economic performance of the firm, to the triple bottom line, which includes a focus on economic, social and environmental performance for corporations. This shift is particularly important, as it is a step towards greater responsibilisation of corporations and management beyond their single-minded responsibility to their shareholders. The expansion from shareholder to stakeholder arguments in corporate responsibility marks a new perspective for workforce diversity. It now allows diversity professionals a greater range of rationales of performance through which to negotiate their resources. However, as we cautioned earlier, stakeholder approaches are not fully enforced, except for voluntary take-up by organisations, and they often lack effective drive and impact for transforming organisational structures, systems and cultures that retain uneven relations of power among socio-demographic groups.

DIVERSITY AND SOCIAL RESPONSIBILITY: COMPLEMENTARITY VERSUS COMPETITION

In neoliberal political contexts, where the state aligns much of its interests with those of the market, organisations are increasingly expected to take on the role of the state in responding to social demands. Responsibilisation of organisations, according to Stiglitz (2000, 2012, 2016), is one way that nation-states could mitigate the negative impact of liberalisation and capitalism on human rights and equality at work. Thus, in neoliberal countries, advanced democracies often delegate social responsibility to organisations. This is observable in the introduction of equality and human rights laws in Britain, where neoliberalism remains a dominant and uncontested dominant ideology with individualism, voluntarism and market competition as regulating forces. In particular, with the introduction of 'reasonable adjustments' in the disability discrimination legislation, the responsibility of the state to offer disability benefits is eased with the introduction of organisational responsibility to accommodate workers with disabilities. In countries where untamed versions of neoliberal ideology operate, workers with disabilities are exposed to the forces of the market and fall out of safety nets (Özbilgin et al., 2022b). Thus, at the nexus of market ideology and workforce diversity, social responsibility could moderate the chances and choices of atypical workers if organisations are responsibilised through law and normative pressure from social movements and community/customer groups. However, in the case of France, Brabet (2010) questions the boundary conditions of the power and utility of social responsibility as a regulatory framework contingent upon the resources, power and intentions of the critical individual and institutional actors that promote it.

With the introduction of the triple bottom-line arguments, diversity management has gained considerable expansion beyond demands for an economic contribution. With this expansion, the line between diversity management and organisational efforts to manage social responsibility became rather blurred (Hansen and Seierstad, 2017; Galizzi et al., 2021). For example, the organisation's support for social movements such as #blacklivesmatter is framed as social responsibility and diversity interventions (Yang et al., 2021). The rapprochement between corporate social responsibility and workforce diversity could be viewed as complementarity, which can help organisations coordinate their interventions. Carroll's (1991) corporate social responsibility pyramid includes diversity as an aspect. Similarly, social responsibility is also widely adopted as a rationale for promoting workforce diversity in organisations. The complementarity of social responsibility and diversity agendas may foster interventions that translate the demands of social movements into organisational change interventions. April and Peters (2011) explain that individual and communal modalities of work have some overlaps and fundamental differences, which can inform why diversity and social responsibility discourses are shaped differently, even if they have complementarity. On a more critical note, complementarity between diversity management and social responsibility may also derail diversity management from its legal support, enshrined in human rights and equality laws. Social responsibility interventions are broadly driven by voluntary efforts of organisations, while diversity interventions garner considerable strength from legal pressure from equality laws.

In fact, the voluntaristic and charitable ethos of social responsibility efforts in organisations contrasts with the solidaristic social movements that supported and legitimated diversity demands in organisations. Most of these demands are now part of human rights and equality laws in nation-states. For example, more than 150 countries now have gender equality legislation, which legitimate demands for gender diversity in organisations. However, social responsibility efforts largely operate with the goodwill of corporations, with some normative pressure from customers and communities. A voluntaristic stance of social responsibility, when combined with similar tendencies in diversity, could lead to ineffective measures for both fields. For example, Özbilgin and Tatli (2011) point to voluntarism as one of the main causes for the failure to close the gender pay gap in the UK.

There is a contextual arbitrariness associated with workforce diversity as a social responsibility. Contextual arbitrariness emanates from how social responsibility is shaped across time, place, institutions and cultural and symbolic domains. History gives meaning to the social responsibility of organisations. Several categories of workforce diversity, such as by sexual orientation and religion, are protected by law only in the last two decades. Thus, there is a temporal dimension to the legitimation of the social responsibility of organisations to consider workforce diversity. Social mores change, followed by legal and corporate responsibility changes. Chapman et al. (2022) show that a long commitment to diversity charters reduced collective turnover in higher education institutions in the UK. However, the same effect could not be identified in organisations which recently joined diversity charters.

Geography also gives meaning to social responsibility. Different countries and sectors have different levels of affinity with social responsibility arguments. Social responsibility is shaped by the degrees of demands that society could levy on organisations across different national and cultural settings. Social responsibility arguments for workforce diversity are common in countries such as France, which frames diversity management in line with the equality principle of the French revolution (Tatli et al., 2012). In the case of the UK, the connection of diversity with performative arguments and single bottom-line arguments earlier in its introduction to the UK has meant that the diversity discourses diverted away from social justice and responsibility arguments. While in the public service sector and the not-for-profit sector social responsibility arguments could hold value, they are unlikely to have the same weight in supporting diversity interventions in sectors which operate with neoliberal values of individualisation, competition and financialisation, such as the financial services sector (Özbilgin and Slutskaya, 2017).

There is also a cultural and symbolic meaning attributed to workforce diversity as social responsibility. Depending on the systems of values and meanings that govern business-society relations, different configurations of workforce diversity for social responsibility emerge (Yamak et al., 2016). Thus, when framing diversity management arguments, it is important to consider to what extent social responsibility arguments and outcomes would be legitimate in that specific organisational, sectoral or national context. However, there is an intricate interplay and complementarity between workforce diversity and social responsibility as their agendas for organisational change overlap in certain dimensions.

DIVERSITY AND SUSTAINABILITY

Sustainability is often defined as an ability to satisfy needs over time without jeopardising how future generations may satisfy their needs. Sustainability has dimensions of the longevity of need fulfilment, inter-generational accountability and impact across spheres of economic, social and environmental context. The United Nations Brundtland Commission report by Brundtland (1987) frames sustainability as taking responsibility for our common future, which takes the practice of meeting present needs without sacrificing the way future generations fulfil their own needs. Contrary to the dominant logic on accepting the earth as the natural heritage of the human species, here and now, equality among all species of life should be guaranteed by organisations and governments without compromising life. The general strategic goal at the core of corporate sustainability definition is a multilayered approach to value creation, which satisfies all the stakeholders with dignity and inclusively (Bakoğlu, 2010, 2014). Sustainability is a prized outcome for organisations in turbulent environments, as their existence over time could be challenged due to changes in their internal and external environment. The relationship between workforce diversity and the sustainability of organisations is worth exploring (Williams et al., 2017). Scholars such as Maj (2018) have been calling for integrating workforce diversity measures in sustainability reporting in organisations. As diversity management efforts seek to end inequalities and foster possibilities and productive coexistence of individuals from diverse backgrounds, workforce diversity, if managed well, could contribute to the sustainability of organisations.

The relationship between workforce diversity and sustainability is not unidirectional. Sustainability is no longer a new term for the corporate world. Neither is the management of diversity and its varied consequences. Some scholars consider diversity as part of sustainability, or that these two concepts are inextricably connected. Similarly, some diversity scholars consider sustainability as a significant outcome of effective management of diversity. Workforce diversity reportedly contributes to the sustainability of organisations (Galletta et al., 2022; Goc and Kusku, 2020). However, workforce diversity does not always lead to positive and sustainable outcomes. If not managed well, it can lead to failures. It is also important to discuss when workforce diversity leads to adverse organisational and environmental outcomes. The availability of evidence on the impact of workforce diversity interventions suggests that when a diversity intervention fails, the legitimacy of diversity may come under question. This phenomenon is called diversity on trial (Samdanis and Özbilgin, 2020). When other forms of interventions in functions, such as marketing or finance, succeed or fail, organisations rarely question the legitimacy of their marketing or finance function. Instead, they would focus on how to improve the effectiveness of these functional areas. Yet when a diversity intervention fails, the organisation may question the legitimacy of the diversity management function. Resultantly, diversity management suffers a blow to its sustainability and possible positive impact on the organisation. Further, some critiques of diversity call it a fad or a flavour of the month and something to go out of fashion, sustainability of diversity interventions could become shaky and tenuous.

The research shows that effective management of diversity when it targets organisational changes could contribute to organisational sustainability. One particular evidence of that is the competition for talent between the financial services sector and the high-technology sector in the UK. The finance sector was the destination for the top talent in the UK, with attractive pay packages and ideal terms and conditions of work. The sector traditionally recruited graduates from elite universities for the management and leadership route and offered rather rigid and competitive work patterns and long hours of work culture. Although the sector was numerically female-dominated in staff, it remained male dominated in the corporate boardroom and across positions of power and influence because of its masculine-dominated work ethos (Özbilgin and Woodward, 2004a). The sector needs to be explored further regarding its paternalistic culture, which may complicate its gender representation and culture (Aycan et al., 2013). The financial services sector enjoyed relative stability and growth and employee trust before the financial crises, which shook the confidence in the sector's ability to retain staff and offer job security. The financial services sector is currently suffering from recruitment and retention problems in recent years and fails to attract diverse talent. Digitalisation in the financial services sector is creating a renewed need for different talent and causing major shortages (Fletcher, 2022). At the same time, the high-technology sector offers both high wages and plenty of flexibility which accommodates the needs of a diverse workforce (Mashiah, 2021). It is evident that the high-tech industry is drawing away the traditional labour pool of the financial services sector, which is ill-prepared to cater for the changing needs of the diverse population, unlike its competitor, the high-tech sector. Returning to our argument around the contribution of workforce diversity to the sustainability of organisations and sectors, it is evident from the example of these two sectors that the preparedness and accommodation of diversity help organisations attract, recruit and retain the best talent, which is fundamental for their sustainability in a world economic system, where talented staff are the most important resource. Workforce diversity could support sustainability if workforce diversity is managed effectively and if workforce diversity interventions are sustainable over time and with recognition of the common good of future generations. Thus, there is a mutually enhancing relationship between workforce diversity and sustainability.

ILLUSTRATIVE CASE: FROM WORKFORCE DIVERSITY TO POSTHUMANIST DIVERSITY AND ITS CONSEQUENCES

In this chapter, we focused on the causal links between workforce diversity and a number of organisational outcomes. However, recent studies show that our narrow focus on human diversity when we are exploring workforce diversity may be too narrow. Workforce diversity has a human-centric approach, as it focuses on differences among human populations in the workforce with a view to ensuring peaceful, productive and safe coexistence. This human-centric approach has been recently contested, as human diversity does not exist in isolation from global environmental challenges, such as global warming, extinction of species and uneven development of technology that evades governance and disrupts global welfare arrangements. The assumption of superiority and dominion of humans over their environment and technology has brought the world and its natural resources to the brink of collapse. In this turbulent context, it is time to broaden the focus on workforce diversity towards posthumanist diversity (Park, 2014; Offor, 2022) which allows us to question the relationship between humans, the natural environment and technology.

Feminist scholars have called for attention to how feminist scholarship should engage with ecological and environmental concerns (Gaard, 2011). Eco-feminists have shown how environmental concerns and the rights of animals and the environment intersect with feminist agendas (Shiva and Mies, 2014). Similarly, techno-feminist scholars have highlighted that technological advances have uneven gendered impacts (Wajcman, 2006, 2011), calling for critical assessment of the relationship between gender differences and technological change. Adding to this complex relationship between gender diversity, technology and nature, other categories of diversity, such as differential impacts of human diversity on the natural environment and technology in the Global North and Global South, make it possible for us to go beyond human-centric approaches to diversity.

The assumption that humans have dominion over nature and technology proves increasingly challenged with the decline of natural resources due to human consumption and abuse and the unprecedented complexity that algorithmic systems have gained that defeat human governance. As the dominion of human diversity over nature and technology fails, we are stepping into an era of posthumanist diversity. What would be new forms of diversity that come with this phase? While animal labour (Cochrane, 2016; Blattner et al., 2019) and animal rights (Köybaşi, 2018; Regan, 2013) are studied extensively in different national academies, new themes are emerging, such as legal rights for nature (Sheber, 2020) and robot labour rights and responsibilities (Birhane and van Dijk, 2020). This phase is similar to the historical period in which the idea of the corporation was introduced. Although corporations are not human beings, they are given legal rights and responsibilities. Incorporating the environment and robots will allow the environment to be defended as a legal entity and robots to assume some rights and show responsibility towards the environment and humans. Similarly, better recognition of animal labour and robot labour will allow effective protection of animal labour and the responsibilisation and taxing of robot labour.

There are two illustrative examples of this posthumanist turn in diversity. First is recognising the environment as a legal entity with rights in Ecuador and Bolivia (Berros, 2021). Concerns for biodiversity and protection of the environment converge with diversity agendas, such as indigenous rights movements, anti-capitalist movements and anti-racist movements in meaningful ways. This legal change is exemplary in that it allows nature, the silent stakeholder in our lives, to be defended against exploitation and unfair use. As such, it creates possibilities for feminist, anti-racist, LGBTQ+ and other social justice movements to build solidarity with environmental movements, showing intersectional solidarity towards the protection of biodiversity. Of course, there remains the challenge of operationalising the legal rights of nature in different national settings and legal systems. Further, early reports from Ecuador suggest that the financial problems have prevented Ecuador to stop encroachment of corporate interests (i.e. drilling) in the country (Einhorn and Andreoni, 2023). Therefore, there is a need for a concerted international effort instead of disparate measures at the national or organisational level.

The second illustrative example is the European regulation of algorithmic systems. The proposal for a regulation laying down harmonised rules on artificial intelligence by the European Union is a departure from the approach of the Silicon Valley to leave the economic and social consequences of AI technologies to the operation of the market (Ebers et al., 2021). The proposed EU regulation brings possibilities of considering the impact of AI technology and robot labour as levels of risk on social, economic, political and environmental life. This legislation opens pathways for future recognition of robot labour as a legal entity (Fink, 2021) in the future could help nation-states address how the value generated through robot labour is accrued only by the owners of those technologies. Taxing robots, which sounds like a radical and futuristic idea, could provide possibilities for rebalancing income distribution which is devastated by the AI-led gig economy. Giving robots and nature legal rights and responsibilities could help human diversity to gain new allies in social movements that focus on ecology and technology.

Posthuman diversity emerges if we break with the dominion of human diversity over biodiversity and techno diversity. Posthuman diversity will be based on a sustainable and even relationship based on a new deal between humans, the environment and technology. Consequences of posthuman diversity would be the intersectional consideration of human diversity with biodiversity and techno diversity concerns. We provided multiple examples of such co-regulation and future crafting for a fairer deal for posthuman diversity. Humans will continue to be the main actors with agency in the posthuman diversity era. However, human agency can be used for creating sustainable futures if movements that support human diversity, such as feminist, anti-racist, LGBT+ and disability movements among others, connect with challenges posed by global warming, destruction of the natural environment and poor governance of technology. In support of this normative change, we are seeing some early signs of intersectional solidarity between feminist, anti-racist, LGBT+ and anti-colonial movements and movements that support the rights of the environment and effective governance of technology.

CONCLUSION

This chapter explored the intended and real consequences of diversity. Studies on diversity and its consequences show that diversity on its own leads to complex outcomes and the evidence on consequences of diversity is complicated by levels of analyses, types of diversity and environmental contingencies, such as preparedness of the cultural and national context (cf. Aycan et al., 2014). Workforce diversity in its unmanaged form may cause negative outcomes, such as miscommunication, disharmony, conflicts and disputes among groups, as much as it leads to the previously discussed positive outcomes. Thus, workforce diversity also has significant potential to foster innovation, creativity and high performance. Research shows that the negative consequences of diversity could be mitigated and positive consequences fostered if organisations manage diversity effectively and if there is a positive diversity climate. Yet our illustrative case in this chapter shows that our focus on workforce diversity could be expanded if we refocus our attention on the deteriorating relationship between human diversity, the natural environment and technology. In subsequent chapters, we will revisit the emergence of such a posthumanist new deal in workforce diversity.

CHAPTER 5

AGAINST WORKFORCE DIVERSITY

Diversity is not always framed as a positive construct. There is an ideological divide in treating diversity as a positive or a negative construct. There are also marked differences in how different categories of diversity are received in different contexts and over time. For example, gender equality may be supported but not class equality in one context. Sexual orientation diversity may be legitimated over time in one context but remain a criminalised taboo in another. Much of the negative framing of diversity comes from historically anchored forms of populism which tend to polarise diversity and differences, pitting social groups against one another. Morelock (2018) explains how the new insecurities of the 21st century have fuelled new forms of authoritarian populism that often frame social diversity as a negative construct.

While the academic attention has been on the potentiality of workforce diversity, populist discourses have been fuelling social tensions and moral panics that social and workforce diversity poses threats to the traditional ways of life, social and economic well-being and political stability and sustainability. In the previous chapter, we considered the evidence of the positive consequences of workforce diversity and its effective management. In this section, we turn to arguments developed in recent years against workforce diversity and the evidence provided to support these claims.

THE DARK SIDE OF DIVERSITY

Research shows that workforce diversity, if not managed well, has negative consequences and a dark side (Özbilgin et al., 2016). Workplace diversity could have negative consequences if left unsupported. For example, gender diversity could lower the value of a profession or category of management (Reskin and Roos, 1990) if men's control over professions and leadership roles remains unchecked (Witz, 2013). Ethnic diversity could exacerbate harassment, divisions and tensions if the workplaces do not take effective measures to combat harassment and bullying (Fox and Stallworth, 2005). Sexual orientation and gender identity diversity could also lead to hate crimes related to homophobia, biphobia and transphobia if hate crimes are not outlawed or addressed by organisations (Kamasak et al., 2020a). Class diversity could lead to divisions and industrial disputes if social class hierarchies are not tackled or eradicated in the workplace (Shih et al., 2013). Linguistic diversity could lead to communication and cultural conflicts unless organisations take effective actions to eradicate uneven treatment of linguistic diversity (Erbil et al., 2023). Religion and belief diversity could also lead to confessional divisions and conflicts if these divisions and appropriate ways to approach such diversity are not properly regulated (Uygur and Aydin, 2019). Home Office statistics in England and Wales show a substantial increase in hate crimes reported to police from 2020 to 2021. There was a 19 per cent increase in hate crimes by race, a 37 per cent increase in religious hate crimes, a 41 per cent increase in hate crimes by sexual orientation, a 43 per cent increase by disability and a 56 per cent increase in hate crimes by transgender identity (Home Office, 2022). In England and Wales, hate crimes against diversity are on the rise. It is important to explore the role of context in shaping adversarial and hostile treatment of diversity.

There is a dark side to diversity and how diversity is treated in different contexts. Context brings meaning to the extent to which a form of difference or diversity is valued or devalued. Context is a multidimensional phenomenon, which has temporal (i.e. past, present and future),

DOI: 10.4324/9780367824044-6

spatial (i.e. place, geography, local and global), cultural (i.e. beliefs, artefacts, assumptions and ways of being and doing) and symbolic (i.e. language, action and communication) dimensions (Chanlat and Ozbilgin, 2023). Context gives meaning and value to codes and forms of diversity. For example, sexual orientation and gender identity diversity were largely denigrated, criminalised or ignored in the past (Zuckerman and Simons, 1995). Today, in most democratic countries, LGBTQ+ rights are protected by law. Within 30 years, there has been major progress towards the legal protection of sexual orientation diversity. However, this progress was not even across countries, where resistance and setbacks are also prevalent (Hill, 2009). International Lesbian and Gay Association (ILGA) report that internationally, 11 countries provided constitutional protection to LGBTQ+ individuals, 57 countries provided broad protection and 81 countries offered employment protection. Seven countries offered limited or uneven protection. On the dark side, two countries had de facto criminalisation of LGBTQ+, up to eight years imprisonment was given in 30 countries, 27 countries have ten years to life imprisonment, five countries punished with the possible death penalty and six countries have an effective death penalty for LGBTQ+ individuals in 2020. Sexual orientation and gender identity diversity present a polarised picture across history and place.

Cultural context could shape the positive and negative treatment of diversity. Some diversity categories are valorised and legitimated culturally, and other forms of diversity are considered illegitimate and denigrated. For example, with the rise of xenophobia, racism and anti-immigration and anti-refugee sentiments, there is an emergent clash between those who defend multiculturalism and those who support monoculturalism and ethnonationalism. In the next section, we explore further how in the context of populism and totalitarianism, cultural constructions of diversity turn toxic. Symbolic context is also important in shaping frames of diversity. Language presents a significant symbolic tool for framing differences (Chanlat, 2014; Kamasak and Ozbilgin, 2021). If we take the example of language as a measure of diversity, speaking certain languages of the Global North, such as English, French, Spanish and German, presents the native speakers and learners' privileges at work, knowledge of other languages from the Global South may not have the same desirability for employers as proxies of merit or talent. Thus, the neocolonial hierarchies of knowledge (Yalkin and Özbilgin, 2022) continue through the symbolic order of languages to shape language diversity (Erbil et al., 2023) in uneven ways.

The temporal, spatial, cultural and symbolic context are determinants of positive and negative frames of workforce diversity. Küskü et al. (2021 and 2022) explain that when the macro-level equality legislation is ceremonial, meso-level organisational practices are weak and micro-level individual awareness is limited, there is a toxic triangle context for workforce diversity. The toxic triangle of diversity leads to diversity concerns being ignored and left unattended. The toxic triangle of diversity could be transformed only through multilevel efforts and opposition to the negative framing of workforce diversity. Thanks to social movements and progressive political and economic policies, there has been extensive legitimation to protect forms of workforce diversity which were previously treated with suspicion, lack of trust, contempt and bias.

A comparative OECD survey on workforce diversity (2020) highlights that disinterest is one of the main barriers and setbacks to effective regulation and management of diversity. The survey highlights that despite a leadership-level commitment to diversity and inclusion, there is a disconnect between leadership commitment and organisational experiences of workforce diversity. Ng and Sears (2018) find that supportive leadership discourses and actions are important antecedents for launching effective diversity interventions. Saba et al. (2021 and 2022) show that the assumption of continuous progress towards legitimation and support for workforce diversity is unfounded, as there are forms of backlash, setbacks and entrenchment to effective and positive treatment of workforce diversity. Most of the literature on diversity focuses on the legitimation of diversity beliefs (Samdanis and Özbilgin, 2020). However, there is also an extensive backlash against diversity and the resultant delegitimation of diversity categories. For example, the Trump administration has undermined gender and ethnic diversity in the USA (Silva, 2019; Mushaben, 2017), resulting in Black Lives Matter, MeToo movements and Women's Marches. Similarly, the conservative governments in the UK and Turkey have undermined LGBTQ+ rights, culminating in Stonewall protesting the UK government's efforts to undermine progress when other countries were making progress across Europe (Aydin and Ozbilgin, 2019; Kamasak et al., 2020a; Ozeren and Aydin, 2016). These are just three examples where setbacks were experienced in the legitimation of diversity and the responses from. Legitimation of forms of diversity and eradication of negative treatment of diversity have been long marches, conditioned by normative pressures from social movements, progressive social-political groups and diffusion of progressive social innovation through global and international organisations. Such normative pressures combat the dark side of diversity by fostering the adoption of diversity interventions at international, national, sectoral and organisational levels.

Woke is a term which refers to strong beliefs in social justice. Individuals and organisations are considered woke if they are committed to social justice. Individuals and organisations committed to social justice, equality, diversity and inclusion agendas are often branded as woke. There is a strong backlash against woke individuals and organisations in the UK and internationally. Woke beliefs demand the transformation of dated institutions with inequitable practices. Woke beliefs are under attack from conservative and traditional segments of society which are committed to traditional and national values. For example, Suella Braverman, the UK Home Secretary from the Conservative Party, launched an attack on woke individuals who carry out acts of civil disobedience, calling them 'the coalition of chaos, the Guardian-reading, tofu-eating wokerati and, dare I say, the anti-growth coalition that we have to thank for the disruption we are seeing on our roads today' (YouTube, 2022). Such attacks on woke values of equality, diversity and inclusion are not uncommon among conservative, traditional and illiberal groups today. Some scholars have investigated the authenticity of woke claims in organisations, highlighting how organisations may engage with more authentic forms of woke (Mirzaei et al., 2022). There is also growing critical scholarship (Rhodes, 2021) which questions the intentions of woke organisations as corrosion of democracy or usurpation of effect by capitalism (Kanai and Gill, 2020). Diversity beliefs, part of the woke culture, are subject to political and scholarly scepticism in their corporate use. This approach frames engagement with woke ideas as a sinister ideological turn, although the evidence suggests gaps between corporate commitment and delivery. Critique of corporate engagement with woke as woke washing (Foss and Klein, 2022) is essential but insufficient without mechanisms of accountability, regulation and governance in the industry.

Woke bashing is becoming common among not only alt-right movements but also scholars (e.g. Waldman and Sparr, 2022; Wright, 2022) who commit to purist ideals of scientific and methodological normativity, unjustly undermining committed scholarship as unscientific. As woke is an inclusive term of intersectional solidarity, it gets attacked by scholars who believe in hierarchies of equality, such as the priority of labour rights above all else or feminist demands over other kinds of equality. Woke beliefs are public demands for social justice across all categories of diversity. This backlash signifies that public demands for social justice are increasing. There is also resistance against woke bashing among scholars (Thomason et al., 2023). The normative pressure on legislators, regulators and policymakers to hear the demands of the woke turn is high. The woke turn in public opinion and the emergent wokerati to subvert a term of abuse could provide cathartic changes to how social, economic and political systems and institutions have so far failed to cater for equality, diversity and inclusion.

Workforce diversity leads to several negative consequences in contexts hostile to diversity and difference. The dark side of diversity could be mitigated if the context becomes more accommodating of difference and diversity. The expectation that spatial, temporal, cultural and symbolic contexts could become more accommodating of all categories of diversity is naive, as contexts change in irregular, uneven and interrupted ways. There is not always progress. Backlash, setbacks, entrenchment, resistance and opposition to diversity are common occurrences. However, the emergence of a strong backlash is also a sign of strong demands for progress.

BACKLASH, RESISTANCE AND OPPOSITION TO DIVERSITY

Resistance and opposition to change are common phenomena in life and work. A backlash is a form of resistance against demands for social justice and equality at work. There are reported cases of backlash and resistance against feminism (Faludi, 2009), anti-racism (Steven and Wessendorf, 2010), LGBTQ+ (Hill, 2009) and disability rights demands (Krieger, 2010) for equality at work. A backlash could take different forms. Backlash can be a reaction to the proposed diversity-related activities, such as training or proposed changes at work (Mobley and Payne, 1992). Backlash may also be a reaction due to ignorance about diversity, disinterest in changes or fears of losing their established power and privileges with diversity interventions at work (Saba et al., 2021). Increased diversity at work regarding headcounts and cultural diversity may also lead to anxieties among dominant group members who show backlash against workforce diversity.

Workforce diversity was introduced as a concept which could draw less backlash than alternative concepts, such as anti-discriminatory, affirmative and equal opportunities interventions (Nishii and Özbilgin, 2007). Despite its soft approach to promising a welcoming environment for individuals from all backgrounds, workforce diversity is now subject to considerable backlash in workplaces and macro-political contexts. At the macro level, there is a considerable backlash against diversity. We explore these in the latter sections of this chapter. In this section, we focus on the individual forms of backlash in the main. Kidder et al. (2004) highlight that backlash against diversity interventions could take affective, cognitive and behavioural forms.

The case against diversity comes from two distinct routes. First, there are tendencies in human nature such as homophily (McPherson et al., 2001) and homosociality (Bird, 1996), which means that individuals are attracted to those who are similar to themselves (homophily). They wish to socialise with like-minded individuals from similar socio-demographic backgrounds (homosociality). Resultantly, individuals from atypical backgrounds could be perceived as undesirable both socially and as work colleagues. There are organisational-level interventions which try to improve individuals' levels of comfort with out-group members and individuals with distinctly different characteristics. Without such interventions, we can predict that diversity could lead to divisions and conflicts among people. The second reason there is a growing case against diversity is the backlash and setbacks that have been developing against the long march toward equality, diversity and inclusion. The backlash and resistance to diversity culminate into discourses, highlighting the detrimental consequences of diversity among different groups.

With the democratisation of education, talented individuals now come from diverse backgrounds. Yet there remains a route to positions of power and privilege in societies based on traditional values (i.e. based on demographic privilege, for example, white, male and upper-class privilege). Societies and workplaces are becoming sites of contestation between earned and unearned privileges. Individuals with prototypical and traditional backgrounds (e.g. upper-class white men) feel threatened, as they need to compete for work and careers with talented individuals from diverse backgrounds. The notion of white male fragility (Gross et al., 2022) partly underpins the fears associated with workforce diversity, which signals an end to the tie between power and socio-demographic privilege of the white, heterosexual, upper-class men.

Certain social, economic and political ideologies and values that they underpin may also foster contexts of antagonism against diversity. Stiglitz (2012) explains that the expansion of the neoliberal ideology in particular had a significant adverse impact on the way human rights and diversity are framed and regulated, particularly, in countries where social welfare regimes are underdeveloped and legal protections for diversity and equality remain ceremonial or limited. Thus, untamed forms of neoliberalism foster cultures of backlash, resistance, insensitivity and antagonism against workforce diversity (Kuskü et al., 2021, 2022)

Not all backlash, resistance and opposition to diversity are unhealthy. There is a growing body of research showing evidence that when workforce diversity interventions are ineffective, they lead to negative outcomes and backlash. For example, Dobbin and Kalev (2022) show when diversity interventions work and when they fail, drawing on the US data. Similarly, in the UK, Noon (2007 and 2018) shows the failures of workforce diversity and diversity training. Research which is critical of the way diversity interventions are framed suggests the use of evidence-based approaches and calls for interventions which change institutions beyond a narrow focus on individual cognition, affect and behaviours at work. A reflexive approach to the design and delivery of diversity interventions could help organisations and policymakers to learn from backlash and resistance to diversity.

TOTALITARIAN AND POPULIST OBJECTIONS TO DIVERSITY

Totalitarianism refers to the regime of a government or a state that expects complete subservience from the public. Totalitarian regimes emerge in fascist, nationalist and communist forms. They tend to erase diversity and differences to secure unanimous obedience to the state's power. Friedrich (2013) identifies three characteristics of totalitarianism: a close tie between a party and the police force, a totalitarian ideology and absolute political control of the economy and society. Totalitarian attacks on diversity are historical. For example, the totalitarian regime of Nazi Germany attempted to eliminate Jews, homosexuals and people with disabilities, considering diversity a threat to the power of the Nazi party. Today, totalitarian ideologies are emerging and gaining visibility as violent responses to liberal demands of feminist, anti-racist, post-colonial and LGBTQ+ movements (Graff et al., 2019). Most recent bombings of gay clubs, school shootings and attacks on minority ethnic and religious groups are inspired by totalitarian ideologies. Socio-political setbacks against diversity range from retrenchment in gender equality gain to setbacks internationally (Saba et al., 2022; Özsoy et al., 2022). Totalitarian ideology feeds on and attempts to shape the basic beliefs of the public and uses populism as a mechanism to retain rigid control over the public.

Populism is a way of appealing to the majority (i.e. common people), suggesting that they have a bad deal due to the poor choices made by the established order. Brubaker (2017) defined the last decade as a 'populist moment' in which leaders appealed to the popular fears, hopes and expectations of common people to serve their own ends. Populist views may undermine diversity, presenting diversity as a conspiracy against the common people, a threat to social and economic life and a culturally corrosive phenomenon. Diversity has been under considerable populist attack in recent years. Populism has been the main medium of communication by ultra-right wing, ultra-left wing and ultra-nationalist groups that pit common people against social and cultural others (i.e. diversity). Populism causes societal polarisation and fault lines in societies.

Varshney (2021) shows the similarity between populism and nationalism, as both appeals to sovereignty and the majority. Therefore, it is not surprising to see nationalist and racist alt-right groups adopt populist discourses. Using populist arguments, alt-right groups have been attacking the value of social and workplace diversity internationally, positioning diversity as a challenge to the freedoms and sovereignty of common people (Chatterjee, 2021). Alt-right groups are ultra-right wing and white supremacist groups which consider equality, diversity and inclusion as impositions on their freedom of speech. For example, the invasion of the Capitol in the USA by alt-right groups and many other transgressions by such groups against gender, race and LGBT+ equality have been widely tolerated in recent years under the guise of freedom of speech. Freedom of speech is often used as discourse to attack and silence social justice demands (Sultana, 2018). Alt-right individuals engage in racist, sexist and homophobic and other forms of insulting and intimidating speech against atypical individuals, claiming that doing so is part of their right to freedom of speech.

Waisbord (2018) explains that populism also presents a challenge to the way diversity is communicated. Populism often contradicts liberalism and democracy associated with communication in societies. Populism leads to censorship and rejection of diverse perspectives and undermines opposition and possibilities of dissent. For example, the populist views on women's reproductive rights appeal to the traditional majority that holds religiously inspired views to ban abortion and curb women's reproductive integrity in the USA and Poland (Gwiazda, 2021; Lowndes, 2017). Similarly, populist objections to the Black Lives Matter movement manifested as All Lives Matter, appealing to and conflating common people's denial of involvement in racism and their need for equality internationally (Özbilgin and Erbil, 2021b). Holmes IV (2020a) explains that police brutality that led to the Black Lives Matter movement has systemic and relational dynamics that denigrate the symbolic value and inclusion of Black people in the US. The populist backlash against equality demands is not unique to the US context. Populism in British politics pits LGBT+ groups towards internal divisions, notably the LGB aspect against the trans movement (Armitage, 2020), and exposes the human rights of LGBT+ individuals to renewed contestation. Eatwell and Goodwin (2018) note that the populist backlash against diversity is part of a revolt against liberal democracy, which allowed diversity and inclusion agendas to flourish in the Global North.

The expectation that diversity should be treated with dignity is often unfounded and misguided when we examine how different forms of diversity are subjected to symbolic, material and social denigration. One of the ways diversity is denigrated is through populist beliefs, which are misguided yet with strong world views (Mergen and Ozbilgin, 2021a) that undermine the potentiality of already vulnerable groups, such as refugees and migrants, trans and working class. Populism is an approach which overplays the misguided and unfounded beliefs, fears and stereotypes about certain vulnerable groups in society. Populist policies and practices of diversity devalue diversity and present it as a threat to communities.

Populism is fast becoming the modus operandi of national politics across a wide international geography. Populism is used widely to contest civil liberties and human rights (Morelock, 2018). Lopez Areu (2018) distinguishes between forms of populism. On the one hand, inclusive populism could bring people together towards common goals. On the other hand, all diversity categories receive populist backlash to different degrees. There is an important role that social movements, progressive politicians and leaders could play in addressing the populist responses to diversity. The populist backlash against diversity also requires responses and resistance by diversity researchers and practitioners. Populism is here to stay in the near future. The damage it has done to the discourses and practices of diversity is evident in the legal, social and economic challenges posed. Designing effective diversity interventions will require organisations to identify, understand and combat populist reactions to legitimate demands for equality and diversity. As a practical solution to political populism around refugee integration, Knappert et al. (2021) show that politicians' contact with refugees influences how they think about refugee integration. Therefore, the authors propose to not only include politicians' attitudes in thinking about and researching diversity and integration but to also invest in programs that facilitate positive contact between politicians, refugees and the general public.

WORKFORCE DIVERSITY AS A THREAT

When we consider that workforce diversity is changing the socio-demographic and moral landscape with the introduction of atypical workers in organisations, it is not surprising that there are fears, anxieties and concerns emerging around the change that workforce diversity may inculcate at work. As we outlined earlier, the conservative, traditional and orthodox groups in organisations may frame their fears of change associated with workforce diversity as a threat to their established routines, processes and cultures. Thus, workforce diversity may be framed as a threat to security, social cohesion, communication and trust in organisations. Differences and divisions that diversity brings to any social or work group may divide the group and diminish its social cohesion.

Workforce diversity sometimes leads to discourses of job destruction and a decline in national and job security. Dystopian, militaristic and alarmist language is often used in the media to fuel anxieties about the advancement of diversity in organisations. For example, emotive terms such as 'waves of migrants' to play with populist fears of nationalists (Sakellari, 2021), 'empty cradles' to lament greater gender equality (Krause, 2001) and 'gay mafia' (Hicks, 2003) to imply a conspiratorial assault on cis-gender (i.e. an individual whose gender identity and biological sex are in line, which means not trans) and heterosexual norms in the corporate world. The use of conspiratorial and alarmist language exacerbates the worries that members of dominant groups have about the march of diversity, which is likely to lead to the demise of the system that benefited the dominant groups. At the heart of these discourses is a perceived threat to security. Not all discourses that treat diversity as a threat are antagonistic. There are new ways of resisting diversity, which appeals to a duty of care for diversity. There are benevolent forms of discriminatory and exclusionary frames, which are subtle in forms, that denigrate the agency and potentiality of atypical individuals and diverse workforces (Romani et al., 2019). Benevolent forms of sexism, racism, classism, homophobia, biphobia, transphobia and ableism implicitly undermine the contribution of diversity and covertly present diversity as a risk, a threat and a burden (Holmes IV et al., 2016).

Anxieties around diversity in the macro-political context in terms of refugees, migrants, sexual orientation minorities and women's rights impact on negative framing of diversity as a threat to national and social security. Among these categories of diversity, migrants and refugees are framed as threats to security in two different ways. First, migrants and refugees are often ignored or rejected in discussions of ethnic diversity, as local and emic ethnic differences are given priority (Aras et al., 2021). Most studies of ethnic diversity focus on locally established ethnic groups and exclude first-generation migrants and refugees (Özbilgin et al., 2022c). Second, migrant and refugee diversity is increasingly treated as a national security threat and a threat to social welfare and job security for the national labour markets. In this latter case, migrants and refugees are not protected by laws that govern human rights and equality that barely protect local ethnic groups (Lesińska, 2014). The negative framing of migrant and refugee diversity as a threat to security receives is fuelled by the decline of economic growth due to austerity being attributed to migrants (Vassilopoulou et al., 2018), climate migration worries (Baldwin, 2017), the rise of nationalism, xenophobia and racism internationally (Goodman et al., 2017). Building a wall on the Mexican border of the USA to prevent LatinX migration

(Massey and Riosmena, 2010), Fortress Europe (Kaytaz, 2015) that forces Syrian and Afghan refugees who try to move to the European Union to stay in Turkey and tightening anti-immigration measures and hostility in post-Brexit Britain with the Hostile Environment Policy (Webber, 2019) are three recent examples of growing macro-political-level framing of migrants and refugees as a threat to security across North America and Europe. Countries in the Global South are not immune to the deficit and antagonistic framing of diversity. For example, April (2021a) explains that Asian African refugees and migrants in South Africa were subjected to harsher discourses of xenophobia, racism and ethnic exclusion when compared to migrants from the Global North.

At the most-organisational level, some forms of workforce diversity are perceived as a threat to security. For example, when an occupation becomes diverse, sometimes the symbolic value of the profession declines. This has been witnessed in some professions, which lost their high-earning potential as they gained greater gender equality. Reskin and Roos (1990) argue that there are job and gender queues where men leave professions when women join their ranks for more lucrative male-dominated alternatives. Thus, feminisation leads to fears among workers that a job role is becoming less secure and lucrative. An increase in diversity in a job category, profession or leadership role could lead to a decline in the safety associated with that role. We explained the notion of glass cliffs (Ryan et al., 2016), which suggests the interplay of workforce diversity, insecurity and precarity. Increased levels of workforce diversity, if left unattended, could have negative and positive consequences. Some of the negative outcomes of workforce diversity are the likelihood of industrial conflicts, an increase in cases of harassment and bullying and toxic workplace relations due to different forms of discrimination, inequality and exclusion behaviours (Özbilgin et al., 2016). When diversity is not regulated, and the organisational climate, cultures and structures are not prepared for greater diversity, diversity could pose a threat to the security and sustainability of organisations.

Social cohesion is the glue that holds society together (Soroka et al., 2006). Societies with traditions of social cohesion benefit from stability in their economic, social and political systems and show resilience in times of crises and turbulence. One of the taken-for-granted assumptions of social cohesion is that homogenous societies would be more cohesive. Diversity brings complexity to social cohesion, as people from diverse backgrounds introduce new economic, social and political values and rationales to the organisation of societies and institutions. Diversity could lead to divisions, which proponents of social cohesion try to overcome by proposing varied strategies of multiculturalism (Modood, 2013), interculturalism (Cantle, 2012), integration and assimilation (Alba et al., 2012). While the former terms, multiculturalism and interculturalism, refer to a coexistence paradigm among different groups, integration and assimilation suggest a superior national culture, which needs to be adopted by newcomers. For example, in their study of cultural integration of young people, Stamou et al. (2022) show that young people who identified as part of the majority ethnic group appeared to be less engaged with issues of culture and belonging. For young people from ethnic minority backgrounds, issues of culture and identity appeared to be a lot more relevant and guided their overall account of schooling – as well as wider life experiences. Young people from minority ethnic backgrounds discussed their cultural identities as predominantly performed in the private sphere. In this respect, we observed learning experiences being underpinned by limited, superficial or partial notions of culture, which subsume it to religious belonging. Inclusion and integration were focused on accommodating pupils' rights to diverse religious practices rather than being driven by a dynamic understanding of the multiple aspects of cultural diversity. Tatli et al. (2012) termed the hierarchical tone in the integration and assimilation discourses as integracism (i.e. the implicit racist assumptions in discourses of integration and assimilation of migrants and refugees). Workforce diversity discourses could be seen as a threat to social cohesion if social policies are based on the integration and assimilation of diverse communities towards a national norm. However, discourses of multiculturalism and interculturalism view workforce diversity as complementary to the notion of social cohesion as they assume positive ties with minority and majority populations and view the coexistence of diverse communities as desirable and possible.

Solidarity is an important mechanism through which workers could retain power and influence at work (Morgan and Pulignano, 2020). Solidarity could be experienced in formal ways through trade unions and work councils and other workplace arrangements or in informal ways through social networks and resource and community groups at work (Meliou, 2020). Increased levels of diversity could threaten industrial solidarity, as solidaristic formations, such as trade unions and social networks, may not immediately catch up with the demographic changes in the workplace. Atypical workers may remain outside the solidarity networks which were not structured with them in mind. For example, white men continue to dominate the leadership structures of trade unions in industries with increased workforce diversity. Ledwith and Colgan (2003) identify a gender democratic deficit in how trade unions reflect on gender equality concerns, despite progress in recent years. Further, minority ethnic women end up experiencing the double burden of representing gender and ethnic diversity concerns in union structures (Bradley et al., 2005). Emergent forms of workforce diversity (i.e. by sexual orientation) may be viewed as a threat to the solidarity structures, as workers from traditional backgrounds dominate these structures. However, if solidarity structures could capture the changing nature of workforce demography and address the shared concerns of workers from diverse backgrounds, diversity could bring transformation and strength to the collective organisation and solidarity structures at work. However, to achieve such a transformation, solidaristic structures in the workplace need to overcome their implicit biases and trust deficit to diversity at work. Revised interest in workforce diversity in solidaristic structures may help build trust in emergent and established categories of workforce diversity (Kirton and Greene, 2021).

Trust is a cultural construct which could be tainted with many forms of bias and prejudice. Individuals are more likely to trust in-group members (Uslaner, 2006). As such, atypical individuals who come from non-traditional backgrounds may lack the trust of their coworkers and may fail to receive their cooperation and goodwill (Meliou et al., 2019). This leads to a trust deficit (Bruna et al., 2021; Kamasak et al., 2019) to workforce diversity among dominant groups. Trust deficit to atypical workers and workforce diversity manifest in how atypical workers are less likely to be considered fit for certain lucrative career paths, positions of power and authority. Trust deficit may emerge as a symbolic denigration of the potentiality of atypical candidates in terms of pay and conditions at work. Trust deficit in diversity keeps atypical individuals at lower echelons of organisations and in low-status and low-pay jobs. The trust deficit is not only espoused by dominant and majority groups towards minorities and atypical individuals at work. The trust deficit is also prevalent among communities that represent different categories of workforce diversity. For example, there are trust deficits between trans-exclusionary radical feminists (TERFs) and trans individuals. Gender diversity scholars and activists may not show support or trust towards the demands of ethnic diversity scholars and practitioners. There are intrafield struggles among diversity actors, who consider certain forms of diversity a threat to equality gains. Tatli and Özbilgin (2012b) refer to a pecking order between strands of workforce diversity, where gender, ethnicity and disability diversity take greater material and symbolic support due to the strength of the legal and social support that these categories receive. Villesèche and Sinani (2021) show that multiple categories of diversity, when used together, generate broader support for diversity from a network theoretical perspective, providing evidence that there is strength in intersectional solidarity. Kamasak et al. (2021) note intersectional hostilities and solidarity emerging in workforce diversity. Authors argue that the social and organisational policy should address the negative framing of diversity intersections and trust deficits to build possibilities of coexistence based on trust and solidarity.

Overall, the case against diversity is multifaceted and multilayered in terms of its temporality, geographic specificity and connectivity between political, social, scientific and organisational discourses. It is important to put the case against diversity in the temporal context and understand whether the case against diversity exists in the short or the longer term. Whether it is about a particular point in history (i.e. historically specific) or shaped by the macro-political, economic and social context in which it is located, the way to move from the case against diversity toward recognising diversity as a healthy and constructive phenomenon requires an understanding and tackling the underlying conditions which have caused the negative framing of diversity.

ILLUSTRATIVE CASE: DENIAL OF INSTITUTIONAL RACISM IN BRITAIN

Stephen Lawrence was a young black British teenager. A group of white men murdered him in a racially motivated attack in 1993. British police failed to bring the murderers to justice because the Crown Prosecution Service failed to prosecute. Only after a long struggle with the support of trade unions and an appeal to the government was the case reopened, following which prosecutions were made. An independent enquiry was launched by Lord McPherson, which led to a report that introduced the term institutional racism in British police and public service. McPherson's report (1999) and the identification of institutional racism have led to the development of several subsequent equality duties to public sector organisations to end systemic and institutional discrimination. The Stephen Lawrence case and the subsequent McPherson inquiry had a far-reaching impact on research, public policy and politics of equality and diversity in Britain.

However, approximately two decades later, the Conservative government commissioned a report to CRED to explore race relations in Britain. The CRED report (Sewell et al., 2021) announced that Britain no longer had institutional racism and that there were 'complex' reasons for the ethnic attainment gap across British institutions. The CRED report pushed the agenda for fairness and equity and individual responsibilisation as opposed to institutional change. The CRED report was received with much scepticism by professional bodies and academic researchers because it failed to frame inequalities as systemic, even though the identified inequalities signal institutional racism. CIPD (2021) wrote an official response to the report criticising the failure of the CRED report to demand more transparency and measures to combat the ethnic pay gap as a missed opportunity. The CRED report was condemned at the UN (2021) level as a whitewashing exercise without credibility. The CRED report is one of many efforts to derail diversity at the national and institutional level in the UK by removing critical frames, such as institutional racism, that has been used to enforce institutional change towards equality.

As this short illustrative case highlights, equality and diversity are highly politicised, with recent ideological shifts undermining the critical scholarly work that points to the significance of institutional responsibilisation for racial equality. It is important to understand how such a warped turn in public policy happened in Britain. Özbilgin and Slutskaya (2017) warned earlier that neoliberal politics in Britain have been pushing responsibility for equality, diversity and inclusion to the individual level, ignoring the role that organisations, systems and institutions play in perpetuating inequalities.

CONCLUSION

The unprecedented growth of demands for equality, diversity and inclusion at work have not been received with open arms by all actors in the world of work worldwide. There has been growing resistance and backlash against all categories of workforce diversity. In this chapter, we explored how diversity is framed at macro, meso and micro levels as a threat, resisted and denigrated across different contexts and regulatory and governance systems. Saba et al. (2021, 2022) argue that overcoming backlash to workforce diversity requires action at the macro, meso and micro levels. In the international field, there is a need to strengthen the legal backing of diversity interventions. Social movements play a significant role in responding to the backlash against workforce diversity. At the organisational level, diversity interventions may receive backlash. It is important to design interventions with participant needs in mind and coupled with organisational change initiatives. At the micro level, individuals have a role in responding to the backlash against workforce diversity along affective, cognitive and behavioural dimensions. The next chapter focuses on organisational interventions and the management of workforce diversity.

CHAPTER 6

THE MANAGEMENT OF DIVERSITY

All societies and organisations have always managed diversity, sometimes with contempt, caution and scepticism and sometimes with interest, curiosity, support and solidarity. In the last 30 years, diversity has become a management and leadership concept that is widely recognised and used internationally. The move from equal opportunities, human rights and employee welfare programmes to diversity management has been considered a paradigmatic shift by some scholars, while others attributed this shift to changes in the macro socio-political and socio-demographic context and liberalisation of difference in the context of the workforce. Whatever the reasons for it may be, diversity management is now an established field of professional work. In many global and national organisations across all sectors of work and industry, there are units or individuals responsible for diversity and inclusion. In this chapter, we explore the professional practice of diversity management.

THE STRATEGIC APPROACH TO MANAGING DIVERSITY

Diversity management is reportedly a strategic concern for organisations today (Thomas, 2016). This shift is because demographic diversity had meteoric growth due to several global changes. First, the advent of communication and transportation technologies made heterogenous encounters possible among people from different parts of the world. Expansion and democratisation of education internationally contributed to the growth of diversity in available talent. Further, the growth of the reach of global organisations and the expansion of their value chains worldwide have facilitated people from diverse backgrounds to work together. Similarly, the rapid expansion of knowledge and service sectors has highlighted the significance of human interaction and teamwork and diversity within this interaction, particularly for the sustainability of these sectors. In this context, diversity management emerged as a series of management interventions to better use diversity among people at work, both as workers and as customers. From product and service design to management of people to delivery and consumption of products and services, diversity management approaches made significant contributions to the way we manage modern organisations. However, Alcázar et al. (2013) explored whether human resource management strategies adequately consider workforce diversity. Their findings show that strategic human resource management does not capture diversity requirements. OECD's (2020) survey shows that organisational leaders show strategic interest in workforce diversity. Yet this interest does not adequately translate into concrete actions and interventions across management functions and individual practices.

Diversity management has become a strategic concern (Jackson and Alvarez, 1992) as effective management of human resources and acquisition and effective deployment of talent have become central issues for the field of strategy. In response, global and national organisations started considering the impact of human diversity on their strategic decision-making. One of the complications in the strategic treatment of diversity was the realisation that diversity management required shaping corporate strategy to accommodate the divergent needs and expectations of different cohorts of workers across diversity categories (Thomas, 2016). The key strategic shift in introducing a diversity approach to strategy was to understand the divergent needs of communities at work and to translate these needs into organisational design and future practices.

DOI: 10.4324/9780367824044-7

Universal and standardised strategy practices are challenged by exposure to workforce diversity, which requires a deeper understanding of divergent needs by gender, age, ethnicity, sexual orientation and disability, among other categories. Resources and rules should be recrafted to ensure that individuals from different backgrounds could be accommodated and could coexist in the same workplace with equal opportunity and outcomes. The strategic challenge of truly understanding the needs of a diverse workforce to transform organisational systems, policies, routines, processes and practices remains today. Many corporations, despite the explicit statements of their leaders, fail to welcome diversity with open arms or to implement deep-level changes to their strategy-making and practices. One of the challenges is that organisations that use outdated modes of strategy-making based on the top-down pursuit of a global strategy find that their plans are met with collective and individual resistance by certain groups of workers and in different regions/countries due to clashes with local customs, laws and traditions of doing strategy and work. Hamza-Orlinska's (2017) study of subsidiaries of a multinational firm in Poland shows that the universal diversity strategy does not travel well from headquarters to subsidiaries. When the global diversity strategy travelled to the Polish subsidiary, it was met with a mixed reception, as it was unfit for the context. To address the challenges that global strategy faces with its deeply held assumption of universalism, some organisations choose to adapt their practices to the diverse needs of the workforce and the diverse requirements of local sectoral and national structures, such as law and culture.

Localisation of diversity strategy means that the local setting dictates diversity practices. This particular approach would allow local laws, customs and cultures to be respected and complied with. Even the most globalised and universal strategic efforts need to be locally implemented. Thus, the local approach to diversity strategy overcomes the strategy and practice divide. However, the local approach may suffer as the local context may have certain blind spots, hegemonic discourses of diversity and taboos (Tatli et al., 2012). Through the localisation of diversity interventions, such biases and taboos could be internalised into the system and remain unquestioned and unresolved (Özbilgin et al., 2015). The localised approach could also be problematic in organisations which operate in multiple locations with distinctly different structures and cultures. In that case, the localised approach to diversity strategy could generate an uneven set of practices across the organisation. For example, suppose in one country, child labour or women's lowly pay is customary. In another country, these are outlawed or targeted by organisational policy. In that case, the organisation may suffer from inconsistencies in its diversity strategy, and this could bring considerable legal and reputational damage to the organisation if made public.

To overcome the problems that the universal-local application of diversity strategy faces, organisations often opt for a transversal strategy which considers both consistency and localisation needs (Özbilgin, 2019b). The transversal approach works with the identification of common terms, definitions and priorities across multiple local settings and the designing of a universal strategy which draws on shared understanding and priorities. Then the organisation allows for local practice subject to the idiosyncratic needs in each location. The transversal approach provides possibilities for the local networks to build on the experiences of each other. They could develop contexts of learning and cross-fertilisation of ideas. However, similar to the previous two approaches, the transversal approach may suffer from struggles of power and influence among localities of an organisation (Karabacakoglu and Özbilgin, 2010). Such symbolic and material struggles due to imbalances among localities (i.e. between the headquarters and branches with varying degrees of power and influence) may hinder progress.

Another approach to connecting diversity and strategy requires top-down, bottom-up and multilevel strategy-making practices which deliberately bring in diversity and inclusion to foster designs that transform organisations with diversity across levels and demographic backgrounds in mind. One such example of transformative strategy-making is described at the university sector included diverse stakeholders to shape strategy (Bakoğlu and Yildiz, 2016; Bakoğlu et al., 2016). Considering strategy and diversity together allows organisations to craft strategies that cater for the needs of diverse groups with inclusion, fairness and sustainability.

Organisations have the strategic choice to consider workforce diversity as a resource, which could be mobilised to reach organisational goals, such as improved shareholder value, better workplace relations and well-being at work and sustainable and positive contributions to the external stakeholders and the environment. Organisations use universalist, localised or transversal strategies to manage workforce diversity with varying degrees of success and limitations.

THE PROCESS APPROACH TO MANAGING DIVERSITY

Strategic models of diversity do not account for how diversity strategy is implemented. For this, there are alternative process models of diversity management (Nishii et al., 2018; Nishii and Özbilgin, 2007), which specify the antecedents, activities and outcomes of diversity management. The process model of diversity management explains the conditions which make diversity management possible, including leadership support, a supportive organisational culture and climate, a conducive socio-political context and the maturity and resourcefulness of the diversity management efforts in the organisation (Nishii and Özbilgin, 2007).

If the preconditions of diversity management are ready, typically, the organisation would have leadership and top management team support for diversity interventions, there would be a culture and climate of diversity and inclusion and a general level of preparedness for diversity management activities. Once the antecedents of diversity management are in place, diversity management activities could be developed. Diversity management activities are discussed in a subsequent section in this chapter. The process model outlines the range of diversity management interventions which are specific to the needs of the organisation. Nishii and Özbilgin (2007) propose that diversity management should understand what diversity means for that specific organisation. Defining diversity is a very political act (Özbilgin and Erbil, 2023a, 2023b). Defining diversity from the worker's perspective, from a collective and solidaristic stance, from employers' or a macro societal perspective signifies different political approaches to diversity. Therefore, the primary activity in the process approach to diversity management is to understand the politics of definitions and fix an agreed definition of diversity that captures the multiplicity of interests and stakeholders.

Inclusion and exclusion of certain categories of diversity and how each strand is afforded different resource allocations are underpinned by organisational priorities, contextual considerations (Özbilgin, 2019a) and contextual dynamics (Marfelt and Muhr, 2016). Once diversity is defined in an organisation, a diversity policy or approach could be crafted. Diversity policy could state the definitions, types of diversity and the kinds of activities which the organisation plans under the banner of diversity management. Diversity management activities could range from writing of policy and definitions to conducting surveys, collecting data to understand the particular needs of the organisation, giving training and education to staff to raise awareness and developing the organisation's systems and structures to accommodate diversity effectively and changing the culture and fundamental assumptions of the organisation to in line with the needs of the workforce diversity. Diversity management activities present a rich repertoire of actions based on organisational priorities and contextual considerations.

The third aspect of the process model is the consequences of diversity management. In Chapter 4, we outlined what research highlights as consequences of diversity. Effective management of diversity could alleviate negative consequences of workforce diversity, such as exclusionary and discriminatory practices and backlash and resistance to diversity. The literature on diversity management stipulates that once an organisation engages with diversity beyond training and education and considers diversity as a way to change, the organisation may accrue some benefits, such as improvements in performance, reduction in reactions to diversity programmes, improvements to innovative potential and employee engagement and commitment (Dobbin and Kalev, 2022).

The process approach of diversity management involves the exploration of antecedents, correlates and consequences of diversity. It could help organisations prepare their climate, culture and leadership support for workforce diversity interventions and also engages with the impact of these interventions. If successful, the process model could engender further support for diversity interventions. However, the process model generally lacks an appreciation of whose responsibility it is to prepare the organisational culture, climate and structure and whose responsibility it is to deliver and monitor diversity management activities and their impact. Particularly for organisations operating in divergent contexts or with devolved lines of authority and diverse product and service lines, organisations need to develop an approach sensitive to context beyond the process.

THE CONTEXTUAL APPROACH TO MANAGING DIVERSITY

As explained in the previous chapter, context gives meaning and purpose to diversity management interventions. Context has four dimensions. These are time, place, culture and symbols. Temporal context shapes the way that diversity interventions are path-dependent. There is a maturity timeline for diversity management interventions. Organisations starting their diversity works may choose to conduct employee surveys and issue diversity policy statements. When they become more mature in the process, they may offer training interventions and connect these interventions with organisational change initiatives that attempt to change cognition, affect, behaviours, as well as organisational structures and cultures. Diversity categories also change over time (Scott, 2018). New categories are legitimated, and new diversity management tools and measures emerge. So the temporal context indicates where the organisation is and where it can go in its historical journey of managing diversity. As we explained in the previous chapter, organisations may experience setbacks and backlash in their diversity management efforts.

Spatial context or geography also gives meaning to diversity management. What it means to manage diversity does not travel national, sectoral and regional borders. For example, in the UK, it is customary for organisations to collect gender, age, ethnicity, religion/belief, sexual orientation and disability diversity data for monitoring purposes. However, the same practice is unlawful in countries such as Germany, France and Italy due to variations in discrimination and equality laws (Klarsfeld et al., 2014). In some countries, such as France, even the term 'diversity management' is contested, as diversity is not viewed as a resource. Instead, the French institutions use the term 'management and diversity' to underline the need for management practices to become sensitive to diversity demands (Chanlat et al., 2013; Chanlat and Ozbilgin, 2019). Categories of diversity are often specific to location and spatial context. While class diversity is not protected by law in the UK, it is a silent/taboo form of diversity that continues to lead to uneven and disproportionate outcomes for individuals. The meaning of class is not the same in different countries. For example, in the Indian context, the caste system would present a similar diversity category as the class diversity in the UK (Mahalingam, 1998). Yet in India, there are legal arrangements to facilitate social mobility across castes. In African countries, tribal diversity could be divisive as class diversity in the UK (Zoogah, 2016). Although recent scholarship by Romani et al. (2021) it is possible to consider class diversity as part of diversity management repertoires, class diversity remains an unregulated and unsupported form of diversity internationally. While diversity policy and theory can be universalist in their discourse, diversity interventions are often adapted to the needs, priorities and hegemonic concerns of the local context (Ozbilgin and Chanlat, 2018). Therefore, Klarsfeld et al. (2019) argue that to contextualise diversity and equality, locally relevant and context-sensitive theoretical frameworks should be explored and developed.

The cultural context is a significant determinant of diversity management (Peretz and Knappert, 2021). Cultural context refers to the meaning-generating mechanisms of deeply held assumptions, norms, rules and artefacts of a social group. Cultural context manifests at multiple levels. There is a cosmopolitan cultural context that transcends national cultural contexts, building on cross-cultural interconnections as the riches of a multicultural community (Zapata-Barrero, 2019; Kucukaltan and Ozbilgin, 2019b). Cosmopolitanism, multicultural and intercultural approaches foster diversity interventions built around the coexistence of individuals from different cultural backgrounds. Cultural diversity discourses often accept nationality and national culture as proxies for culture (Syed and Kramar, 2010). However, industrial and organisational cultural contexts could be stronger than national cultures in shaping cultural assumptions and norms of behaviour, affect and cognition at work (Spender, 1989). Organisational, industrial, national and international cultural contexts and ethos inform diversity management and how it works in those cultural settings. What organisations in the pharmaceutical industry do in terms of diversity management would be very different to what organisations in the creative and cultural industry do. Forson's (2013) work on black businesswomen illustrates the interconnectedness of macro-, meso- and micro-level context on the work-life balance experiences of this group of participants. Industrial recipes (i.e. entrepreneurship and business) and inter- and intracultural encounters legitimate different kinds of diversity concerns (Kucukaltan, 2021). There are also differences in terms of the cultural context in small, medium and large organisations (Kucukaltan and Ozbilgin, 2019b) as well as among public, private and voluntary sectors in their cultural priorities of diversity management.

The symbolic context refers to the symbolic mechanisms that exist to establish the implicit value of any phenomenon. The symbolic context is imbued with explicit and implicit structures and relations of power in any given field. Diversity management would be located in a symbolic context, where diversity could be valorised or denigrated. Navigating the symbolic context could help diversity actors understand enablers and barriers to effective management of diversity and where power, rules and resources reside across and outside the organisation. Bourdieu and Wacquant (2013) refer to symbolic capital as the overall respectability and recognition that individuals accrue through mobilising their social, economic and cultural capitals. Symbolic violence occurs when an individual's different forms of capital are denigrated and devalued in a field of relations (Krais, 1993). The symbolic context determines the value of diversity management. Küskü et al. (2021 and 2022) show that in a context where there is systemic symbolic violence against diversity, diversity interventions could be ignored and devalued. While demands for equality, diversity and inclusion at work increase the symbolic value of diversity management, backlash and populist objections denigrate diversity management. Nentwich et al. (2015) explain that achieving social change towards gender equality requires discursive and material activism and recognising the historically entrenched symbiotic relationships. Aharoni Lir (2020) exemplifies this idea in relation to Wikipedia, showing that a public space being open to all does not ensure women's symbolic participation in the production of online knowledge and that interventive steps must be taken to ensure women's contributions to the website. Akanji et al. (2020) show that managers symbolically undervalue single individuals' work-life arrangement and their social commitments. Organisations attend to the symbolic context of diversity interventions by highlighting why and how diversity management is aligned with organisational priorities and processes.

The contextual approach to diversity management would help organisations craft a diversity management approach tailored to their specific location, present priorities in their diversity journey, normative expectations and power relations and structures that need negotiating. The context approach highlights what is practical and possible for organisations to manage diversity.

THE MULTILEVEL APPROACH TO MANAGING DIVERSITY

Diversity management attracted theorisation from micro, meso and macro levels of analysis. At the micro level, diversity management scholarship focuses on individual-level management practices, such as diversity management training, awareness raising and unconscious bias training, drawing on methods and approaches of organisational and industrial psychology (Otaye-Ebede, 2018). The macro-level focus of diversity management research has been on changes to structures and systems that govern workforce diversity and their effectiveness, drawing on sociologically oriented methods and theorisation (Kalev et al., 2006). At the meso-organisational level, diversity management scholarship draws on management and organisation studies literature, focusing on human resource and culture change processes that management interventions could achieve (Kossek and Lobel, 1996; Kossek et al., 2006). Single-level studies provide a sharper focus on aspects of diversity management. However, they suffer from some limitations. Individual-level framing of diversity management does not capture institutional mechanisms and social structures which impact diversity management in organisations. Meso-level management theorisation on diversity may miss out on how individuals receive these interventions and whether they are embedded in social and institutional structures and cultures. Macro-level studies of diversity management may fail to capture individual agency and meso-level organisational mechanisms.

Recent scholarship recognises the limitations of studies with single-level and mono-disciplinary focus, calling for and conducting multilevel investigations of diversity management (Hennekam et al., 2019; Jackson and Joshi, 2004). Multilevel approaches are particularly useful in exploring contexts underexplored in diversity scholarship (Shen et al., 2014; Syed, 2010; Syed and Özbilgin, 2009). Inclusion of macro, meso and micro levels provides an interdisciplinary reading of diversity management, connecting structural concerns with organisational processes and individual cognition, behaviour and affect. The nested approaches to context could locate micro-individual perceptions, behaviours and affect in the context of meso organisational dynamics and macro-level structures and cultures. Such nested multilevel approaches provide an understanding of diversity management in its specific context. For example, Ozkazanc-Pan and Muntean (2018) show how the multilevel influences at individual, organisational and societal level shape gender relations in technology entrepreneurship. The authors argue that unpacking gender inequalities in this field requires interventions addressing multilevel inequality structures.

Nishii et al. (2018, p. 76) explain that even when multilevel investigations are conducted, cross-level concerns remain underexplored:

> Once an organization adopts a diversity practice, a variety of factors influence the felt motivation among managers to implement the practice. Employees' perceptions of the enacted practice are, in turn, influenced by their assessment of the personal gain they might derive from the practice, as well as the perceived authenticity of the signals that the intended practice sends. Employees' practice-specific reactions shape their attitudinal reactions, which relate to behavioural responses. How these individual-level attitudes and behaviours translate to emergent, higher-level outcomes is still unclear, however.

The multilevel approach to diversity management transcends the limitations of single-level studies. However, the multilevel approach brings theoretical and methodological complexity, which could render diversity research harder to conduct and deliver. The theoretical challenge of exploring nested multilevel approaches and cross-level interactions is partly addressed by the relational approach.

THE RELATIONAL APPROACH TO MANAGING DIVERSITY

The relational approach to diversity management combines a multilevel approach with a relational understanding. Relationality is a process through which any social phenomenon gains meaning in its relationality to another phenomenon (Özbilgin, 2006; Tatli et al., 2014; Özbilgin and Vassilopoulou, 2018). Understanding the micro-individual level invariably requires an understanding of meso-organisational and macro-socioemotional contexts that give meaning to the micro level. When taken out of its nested context and its situatedness in any web of relations, the social phenomenon cannot be understood. For example, diversity management has a specific meaning at a given time, in a given organisational and industrial context and in its broad macro-social and national context.

Syed and Özbilgin (2009) argue in their exposition of the relational approach to diversity management that the micro, meso and macro level of analyses should be situated in their historical context. The relational approach is used widely to explore diversity management contexts that are emic, idiosyncratic or unusual. Forstenlechner et al. (2012) examined localisation quotas as part of diversity management in the United Arab Emirates, drawing on a relational approach. This study involved situating quotas in their relational context with references to UAE history and comparative perspectives in relation to other countries with quotas and local responses at organisational and individual levels. Hennekam et al. (2017) explored diversity management in the Middle East and North Africa through the relational framework. Dobusch (2021) used a relational perspective to locate the inclusion and exclusion of autistic individuals in the diversity management vernacular. Jamali (2009) explored enablers and barriers women entrepreneurs face in developing countries using the relational perspective.

Studies using the relational perspective of diversity management typically attend to the idiosyncratic historical, cultural, spatial and symbolic context in which their diversity phenomenon resides, showing its interplay and situatedness across multiple levels of analysis. Marfelt and Muhr (2016) critique a focus on the diversity context as external to individuals and organisations and propose a relational approach to diversity. Relational perspective adds to the riches of exploration of diversity that gains new meanings across different relational contexts. The relational perspective also explores diversity management beyond dominant West European and North American theorisations, allowing for insights into how diversity management operates in the Global South and less charted territories.

At the institutional level, the relational approach manifests at the point of individuals encountering institutions in their life course. Adopting a sociological notion of institutions, we can consider the family, healthcare, education, welfare state, employment, police and the law as institutions that individuals encounter in their lives. At the point of this encounter, there is a relational context which emerges as individual intersections meet with institutional intersections. For example, LGBTQ+ individuals are often born into families with cis-gender and heterosexual norms. Similarly, in a classroom or employment, students and staff come from diverse backgrounds and meet the rather limited intersections of the institutions, running often with colonial, heteronormative, classist and sexist assumptions. Most institutions have biased processes, routines and structures, which need to be attended to. The notion of institutional racism (Kamasak et al., 2021) in the case of policing and hidden curriculum (Baykut et al., 2022) in the case of education, and resultant demands for race duty and decolonisation, highlight the need for transforming institutions. The relational approach to managing diversity in all these cases is to change and transform the institutions rather than the individuals who encounter them. Changing institutional intersections may include making them more inclusive, free from bias and safe spaces (Rosemary, 2011) for individuals who are different to the norm to join as equal participants.

The relational approach is now widely adopted to explore diversity management in uncharted territories and to cover the interplay between diversity management with its macro context and the individual agency of the diversity actors. The relational approach also reveals the dynamics of power in diversity management. Other approaches could miss out on how power and resource implications of diversity and how relations of power inform the meaning, content and effectiveness of diversity management practices.

THE MATURITY APPROACH TO MANAGING DIVERSITY

The maturity approach to diversity management refers to the path dependence of diversity management interventions (Jonsen and Özbilgin, 2014). The maturity approach posits that the depth of diversity interventions is contingent upon several factors (Wieczorek-Szymańska, 2017), such as the support for diversity in the socio-political context, resourcing of diversity and the maturity of diversity management in the organisation. If diversity has limited support in the macro context, it is poorly resourced and is a new journey for the organisation, organisational efforts may focus on shallow-level activities, such as information giving and receiving, such as employee surveys, writing a diversity policy and offering training. Noon et al. (2013) caution about the limited and often ineffective nature of hyperformalised information gathering and giving processes in managing diversity. Suppose diversity has a supportive context, resources and maturity. In that case, more advanced level activities, such as human resource management interventions and organisational development activities, could be part of diversity management interventions. However, suppose there is strong support, high resourcing levels and much maturity in diversity management. In that case, organisations could take interventions which transform cultures, structures and institution-making practices in line with the demands of a diverse workforce.

In their study of diversity management in the USA, South Africa and Norway, Vassilopoulou et al. (2013) explore different levels of maturity that diversity management discourses and practices have in these countries, leading to a different emphasis on breadth and depth of diversity management interventions. Karam (2022) explores the treatment of diversity in the Lebanese context, showing how the path and context dependence leads to particular maturity and setbacks in some strands of diversity management. In exploring diversity biases in algorithms, Vassilopoulou et al. (2022) use the maturity approach to offer a path for algorithmic hygiene, which can ensure the effective elimination of bias in algorithmic processes.

The maturity approach to diversity offers the potential for organisations to understand the depth of their diversity interventions as contingent upon external and internal support and enablers. The maturity approach could help organisations craft practical and realistic agendas for diversity interventions in line with their unique external and internal resources and constraints.

DIVERSITY MANAGEMENT INTERVENTIONS AND ACTIVITIES

Diversity management interventions and activities have a wide repertoire. Depending on the approach to diversity management adopted, organisations and actors in the field of diversity management may choose interventions and activities that are fit for purpose. Earlier formulations of diversity management interventions focused on employee surveys, collection of diversity data, awareness raising about diversity, training on diversity issues, organisation development activities that support diversity management, work-life interface activities and flexible human resource management arrangements (Bartz, 1990). Even these earlier suggestions of diversity interventions focused on multiple levels: information receiving and giving (e.g. conducting employee opinion surveys, writing diversity statements and conducting training and awareness raising for diversity issues), organisational change interventions (e.g. human resource management interventions, flexible work arrangements, work-life interface policies and remote and working-from-home policies) and culture change interventions (e.g. organisational change for diversity and inclusion, organisational development for diversity and inclusion and strategic diversity management). Depending on the maturity of the diversity management programme, organisations can move from information-related activities to organisational development. If there is considerable support for diversity and the maturity of these activities, organisations could take on a strategic approach to managing diversity (Guler, 2022).

As we discussed in earlier chapters, different disciplines of social science have informed the development of diversity management and the kind of interventions that are offered at the organisational level. The humanities discipline has built connections between social movements, moral philosophy and diversity interventions. The discipline of law has helped organisations to develop formalised statements for diversity management, such as diversity statements, anti-discrimination, harassment and bullying statements and legal compliance training for diversity management. The discipline of psychology informs the dominant paradigm in diversity management interventions with an emphasis on changing cognition, affect and behaviour in organisations, informing mentoring, coaching, allyship, diversity training and unconscious bias training (Yavuz Sercekman, 2023). The discipline of economics and finance has provided means of assessing economic and financial aspects of diversity, informing policies which seek to combat diversity pay gaps, the single bottom-line arguments for diversity. Disciplines of sociology and anthropology (Chanlat, 2017) have informed the development of connections between diversity interventions and cultural change in organisations, including institutional duty for diversity, regulation of work, extracurricular and holiday arrangements in culturally and diversity sensitive ways, formation of employee resource groups and diversity networks for different categories of diversity, building partnerships with trade unions, community organisations and charities for diversity. The discipline of business and management has shaped the way diversity management interventions moved from operational considerations to strategic concerns of organisations, including strategic diversity management approaches, inclusive leadership development activities (Korkmaz et al., 2022), connecting diversity with the organisational, team and individual performance, building top-down and bottom-up lines of responsibility for diversity management in organisations. The discipline of education shapes how organisations tackle diversity management as part of their education and training programmes and consider communication effectiveness as part of diversity training. The discipline of design and engineering has considered access and adjustments to spatial regulation in organisations for diversity and inclusion.

Diversity management interventions in organisations that are novices to diversity start with building dialogue and conversations around diversity management. It is important to understand what diversity is within that specific organisational setting and identify the level of organisational preparedness regarding leadership support and diversity climate. Leaders are not naturally inclined to support diversity management interventions. There is a paradox of atypical leader emergence. While leadership support for diversity is essential for the effectiveness of diversity interventions, leadership diversity is sorely lacking (Bebbington and Özbilgin, 2013). Further, Aycan and Shelia (2019) explain that there are worries about leadership (WAL) (i.e. psycho-social conditions which prevent talented individuals from emerging as leaders). It is important that leadership development is considered an essential aspect of diversity management at this early stage. Without leadership support, diversity management interventions may be stillborn. Once a general understanding of diversity is garnered through dialogue with stakeholders, diversity definitions, statements and policies could be shaped. In this phase, it is important to note that these policies serve as bylaws, and organisations become responsible and accountable by issuing statements. Hoque and Noon (2004) caution about diversity statements becoming empty shells if the organisation does not effectively monitor and ensure compliance.

Developing a business case for diversity management interventions is important for overcoming the trust deficit that the leadership may suffer when approving diversity interventions. Such business case arguments bring together not only a single bottom line but also triple bottom-line rationales, including impact on individual welfare, financial viability and environmental sustainability. The business case arguments also consider how diversity interventions and their impact will be measured, monitored and reported and the lines of responsibility and accountability when compliance is not achieved. Diversity training could be offered across the organisation using blended and experiential learning techniques. Organisations can set up interventions to bias-proof their practices, policies and institutional arrangement and eliminate cognitive and unconscious biases at work. Diversity interventions need the development of allies and champions as well, particularly to tackle resistance and backlash. Mentoring and coaching activities could be offered to foster better awareness and to change patterns of recruitment, development and promotion at work. Lantz-Deaton et al. (2018) show that mentoring alone cannot eliminate gender barriers to leadership. However, mentorship could be used as part of a set of measures.

Diversity management interventions need to focus on what needs fixing at work to promote diversity and inclusion. Most interventions for diversity management focus on individuals to fix workers' cognition, behaviour and emotion, which can be biased (Yavuz Sercekman, 2023). At the team level, biases may emerge at the interpersonal level (Holmes IV et al., 2019). Diversity management interventions could also seek to fix interpersonal relations to secure interpersonal inclusion (Bourke, 2022). At the level of organisations, diversity management interventions could fix organisational routines, spatial and temporal arrangements, socialisation and work patterns to make them more accommodating of diversity.

Organisations have different starting points for diversity. What an organisation could do in terms of diversity management is path-dependent and contingent upon the maturity of its diversity programme. Suppose an organisation is starting its diversity programme. In that case, it needs to start with activities such as information collecting (monitoring of diversity) and information giving (education and training, writing of policy and proofing of organisational documents for bias). However, if the organisation has a mature diversity programme and if diversity is well legitimated internally and if there is a supportive culture and climate and a supportive political context organisation could engage in deeper-level diversity interventions, such as making the human resource management practices more flexible and accommodating of diversity and changing representation across the organisation, developing organisations systems and structures so that they are free from bias and that they cater better for the needs of a diverse workforce.

ILLUSTRATIVE CASE: DIVERSITY MANAGEMENT FAILURES

There is increased attention to the failure of diversity interventions, especially when diversity interventions are limited to training and individual development rather than organisational transformation (Noon, 2018; Dobbin and Kalev, 2018). The long lineup of scholars in the field of equality, diversity and inclusion (EDI) have suggested that EDI interventions should focus on institutional transformation, systemic change and organisational development (Cockburn, 1991; Acker, 2006; Syed and Ozbilgin, 2019). Despite evidence which shows that diversity interventions should target systemic change if they are to be successful (Singleton et al., 2021), this idea is largely ignored in favour of fixing individuals from diverse backgrounds (i.e. women [Wittenberg-Cox, 2013], black, Asian and minority ethnic, LGBT+ individuals) through training, mentoring schemes and practices that target individual changes. This illustrative case provides a political backdrop to how institutional and systemic aspects of equality and diversity are ignored.

Since the late 1980s, diversity management has become a significant domain of managerial practice that attempts to foster diversity to garner positive organisational outcomes. However, since the early 2000s, studies on the effectiveness of diversity interventions have started casting a shadow on the extent to which diversity interventions led to positive outcomes. Dobbin and Kalev (2022), in their book on failures of diversity management, draw on the US national data to show that some forms of diversity interventions have failed to generate desirable outcomes for diversity in organisations. Remarkably training programmes on unconscious bias, harassment and bullying and workforce diversity have not led to the desirable and positive outcomes they originally intended to generate. Scholars such as Noon (2018) in the UK have also shown that interventions that focus on tackling individual biases instead of institutional forms of discrimination are doomed to fail. Instead, UKRI research (2021) has shown that interventions that transform institutional systems, structures and temporal and spatial arrangements have generated positive outcomes. Chapman et al. (2022) study demonstrated that long-term commitment to diversity interventions generates more positive organisational outcomes.

Neoliberalism is a political and economic ideology with underlying assumptions and values. Stiglitz (2012) argues that neoliberalism, if untamed, could be detrimental to human rights and civil liberties in countries which lack social and legal regulatory measures to curb the corrosive power of the market and capitalist expansion. Neoliberalism comes with values of deregulation (i.e. belief in the self-regulation of the market for moral concerns, such as diversity and equality), individualism (Özbilgin and Slutskaya, 2017) (i.e. a belief that diversity is an individual rather than a collective issue) and financialisation (i.e. a belief that financialisation would support diversity) (Yavuz Sercekman and Ceviker, 2023). Unfortunately, these assumptions are hotly contested in recent years and found to fail when subjected to evidence and scrutiny. The deregulation of organisations and markets causes the shifting of responsibility for promoting diversity to the voluntary interventions of organisations. Voluntarism or self-regulation of organisations is remarkably ineffective (Jonsen et al., 2013), as the evidence suggests, in promoting gender and other forms of diversity at work. Most of the advances organisations make in diversity management focus on legally and socially endorsed categories. For example, the efforts to improve the number of women and minority ethnic leaders in the UK have been dampened by the voluntaristic nature of these interventions compared to advances that Scandinavian and North European countries have made with their coercive measures, such as gender quotas (Seierstad and Huse, 2017).

The individualist tendencies in the neoliberal context also serve to tarnish the effectiveness of diversity management. The neoliberal framing of diversity is often a set of qualities that an individual has in the workplace. However, this definition underplays the role of collectives which gives meaning to the diversity categories to which an individual belongs. This individualist definition severs the link between an individual and their community which supports them to have the rights and liberties they enjoy at work. Individualisation of diversity at work also diminishes the bargaining power of individuals who are expected to negotiate their diversity-based needs with the employers individually. Withdrawal of trade unions and social movements from the diversity management negotiations could weaken the individual regarding their negotiation power at work.

Finally, one of the outcomes of financialisation in the neoliberal system has been how diversity management is tied to single bottom-line arguments in its early days. The business case based on single bottom-line arguments proved too narrow for organisations to manage diversity effectively. Financialisation as an underpinning value of neoliberalism denigrates the value of human rights, civil liberties and social justice arguments which give diversity legitimacy. Financialisation is particularly detrimental to the public services and voluntary service sectors, which operate with different logic, bringing competition among workers, where the operating logic should be the provision of a service to all.

Diversity, when it is not managed effectively, could be a source of both positive and negative outcomes. Management in ways incongruent with the social, economic and political system and without attention to the responsibilisation of key actors leads to failures of workforce diversity interventions. Effective management of diversity could help organisations combat adversarial treatment of diversity and promote a way of approaching diversity as a resource that could be mobilised, cultivated and developed. This paradigmatic shift happened in enlightened organisations before the 2000s. However, the idea of managing diversity was not embraced with the same breadth and depth across different contexts, causing diversity management failures.

CONCLUSION

In this chapter, we explored the management of diversity, covering its key approaches and interventions, which account for the riches and limitations of diversity management. The chapter starts with diversity as a strategic concern. The second approach is managing diversity as a process with antecedents, correlates and consequences. The process model makes it possible for diversity managers to set the scene for diversity interventions and prepare the organisation in line with adequate cultural, material and moral preparation. Then several diversity management interventions could be crafted to fit the contextual requirements and garner expected outcomes. The contextual approach to diversity management involves crafting a diversity intervention with the geographic, historical, cultural and symbolic circumstances of the organisation. The multilevel approach recognises the interplay between macro social, political and economic context; meso organisational relations; and micro individual choices and chances in shaping diversity interventions. The relational approach situates diversity interventions in the multilevel relational context across history. The maturity approach combines contextual contingencies with the depth of diversity interventions, articulating three levels of information giving and receiving and structural and cultural changes as diversity interventions. The chapter also has a section on specific diversity interventions typically used in organisations to manage diversity. There is also an illustrative case of failure of diversity interventions.

CHAPTER 7

REGULATING DIVERSITY IN AND AROUND ORGANISATIONS

Beyond the management of diversity, which we explored earlier, diversity is regulated in and around the organisation. Regulation is defined as an assertion of rules to change behaviour. OECD (2022, p. 1) defines economic regulation as the 'imposition of rules by the government, backed by the use of penalties that are intended specifically to modify the economic behaviour of individuals and firms in the private sector'. Beyond economic regulation as defined by OECD, regulation is widely used in social, political and technological fields to shape behaviour and ensure compliance. Regulation may happen at multiple levels, and it is also not limited to the relationship between the government, organisations and individuals. To understand how diversity is regulated, it is important to understand what regulation is and how it manifests in different forms. Regulation takes place in a multilayered way ranging from self-regulation (i.e. individuals regulating their own choices and chances) to regulation in groups and social and legal regulation. Regulation may take voluntary or coercive forms, involve multiple parties, such as individuals, their reference groups, institutions, such as family, law, healthcare, education and employment, among others, organisations in the public, private and voluntary sectors and national- and international-level social and political agencies.

REGULATION OF DIVERSITY: A MULTILEVEL FRAMEWORK

There are micro, meso and macro levels of regulation. At the individual level, individuals may introduce ideas, values and concerns about forms of diversity. Individuals are capable of self-regulating, learning about diversity and changing their behaviours. Individual-level regulation is fundamental to the regulation of diversity in organisations, which devolved responsibility with diversity management to individual-level responsibilisation. Individuals are uniquely capable of self-regulating, particularly if they are enlightened by Levinasian ethics of alterity (Bruna and Bazin, 2018). Much post-feminist literature, such as Sandberg's (2013) famous book *Lean In*, focuses on the responsibilisation of individuals and their self-regulation to seek inclusion at work. Self-regulation discourse has been powerful in advancing our understanding of how individuals could self-lead and self-manage (Dharani et al., 2021). Critiques of the self-regulation paradigm highlight the limitations of self-regulation in light of collective concerns (Villesèche et al., 2022). One critique of self-responsibilisation is how organisations tend to tackle sexual harassment and bullying through unconscious bias training alone, which Taksa and Thornthwaite (2022) explain that individual awareness raising and responsibilisation have been ineffective as measures to eradicate sexist behaviours in the Australian Federal Parliament. At the meso level, teams and organisations regulate their and employees' behaviours and establish normative structures. Organisational-level regulation includes diversity management interventions, as well as other normative and coercive pressures within and outside the organisation shaping diversity-related behaviours. At the macro level, there are social movements, government agencies, equality regulators, industry-level recipes and international actors that regulate beliefs and practices of diversity (Özbilgin and Erbil, 2021b).

Although regulation happens at multiple levels, there is an intricate interplay between these levels of regulation that shapes beliefs and practices of diversity. In their work on individual

DOI: 10.4324/9780367824044-8

and collective status beliefs in relation to gender diversity, Hogg and Ridgeway (2003) define two paths, one from individual to collective and another from collective to individual regulation of status beliefs. Individual beliefs about diversity, if shared by a social group, may be taken up as collective concerns and shape demands for legitimacy, protection and promotion of a particular form of diversity and difference. Holck and Muhr (2017) suggest norm-criticial reflexivity to strengthen demands for diversity and difference. When such demands gain wider recognition through social movements, they could be more widely adopted and lead to normative changes in the social context. Social movements, if effectively represented, may affect regulatory changes at the macro national and international levels. There is also a macro-to-micro-level regulatory push. Once certain forms of diversity are legitimated at the macro level, they could give normative pressure to shape the policies and practices of organisations and the beliefs, thoughts, emotions and behaviours of individuals.

Adopting Reynaud's (2003) perspective, focusing on three ideal-typical forms of regulation within the organisation and social system (autonomous, coercive and joint) and overtaking this theoretical model to critically address the issues of our hyper-complexified, volatile and super-diversified postmodernity, Bruna (2016a, 2016b, 2020, 2022) pleads in favour of a 'pluralistic social regulation'. The latter could be able to recognise, balance and reconcile the heterogeneous and often competing calls, needs and interests from main internal diversity actors (Tatli, 2011; Bruna, 2014) and, more globally, from diversity stakeholders and contribute to drive and implement a regulated and, thus, aligned, efficient and effective diversity change process. Regulation in practice takes multiple forms across multiple levels. There is also an interplay between levels that shape beliefs and practices of diversity. Later, we explore different forms of regulation based on the level of enforcement, including voluntary, social and coercive regulation.

REGULATION OF DIVERSITY: A MULTIFACETED FRAMEWORK

Regulation of diversity takes three different forms: First, much of the diversity regulation in organisations takes voluntary form for categories of diversity which are not supported by laws or when diversity interventions go beyond the legal requirements. Second, diversity regulation could be coercive, resting on legal and other forms of enforcement. The third form of regulation is relational regulation, which rests on the relationship between actors of significance in diversity. Later, we explore these three forms of diversity regulation in greater detail.

Voluntary regulation of diversity

The liberal economic turn, spearheaded by national leaders since the 1970s, such as Ronald Regan in the USA, Margaret Thatcher in the UK and Turgut Ozal in Turkey and subsequent leaders of liberalised economies have pushed for several reforms. These reforms promoted the deregulation of international trade, the adoption of private sector logic for the operation of public and voluntary sector organisations, the weakening of social and solidaristic struggles for equality and the promotion of competitive and individualist agendas. In this neoliberal context, individuals, organisations and markets are responsible for their choices and chances. This liberal turn has transformed the character of public sector work and the social welfare system in particular by bringing financial and competitive logic into sectors and fields of work which operated with principles of upholding public service, compassion and the common good. Regulation of diversity in this market-driven political-economic system has been recrafted to fit with the logic of the times. In countries with advanced industrial and democratic traditions, this transition has meant that the responsibility for regulating diversity is pushed to the voluntarism of the market. In line with this ideological shift, new laws were also introduced to responsibilise the market, shifting the responsibility for equality, diversity and inclusion from the welfare state to the market. This period has seen the emergence of business case arguments to push the voluntary regulation of diversity and to convince corporate leaders of the viability of voluntary regulation. While anti-discriminatory and equality legislation were enforced, the market and organisations were allowed to regulate their diversity interventions voluntarily. Voluntarism remains the modus operandi for the regulation of diversity management practices internationally (2011). Critical social scientists criticise the limitations of the voluntary regulation of diversity in terms of its ineffectiveness in fostering equal outcomes and promoting inclusion at work (Demougin et al., 2021; Healy, 2016). Noon (2007) identified that the business case arguments of voluntary regulation have largely failed in promoting racial equality in the UK.

In countries where democratic and legal tradition remains weak, equality laws remain ceremonial and ineffective, yielding poor outcomes and toxic contexts for managing diversity (Küskü et al., 2021, 2022). Stiglitz argues that in countries where democracy is weak, liberalisation of the economy had human costs and harmed the already fragile human rights and civil liberties in those countries. Küskü et al. (2021) demonstrate that a liberal economic system and the lack of measures to protect diversity have led to a toxic context in Turkey, where diversity remained unregulated and weakened. However, in countries such as the UK, where there is a tradition of a welfare state, despite a weekend one after many decades of liberal economic assault, the legal regulation of diversity has shifted the responsibility to protect and look after diversity from the welfare state to the market and organisations. One particularly poignant example of this transition has been the disability discrimination laws, which originally stipulated a broad umbrella of welfare state subsidies for individuals with disabilities and an extremely small quota, which was discriminatory against disabled individuals in the UK (Morris, 2006). The revised disability discrimination act brought about a progressive stance on disability, suggesting that instead of a quota, organisations should provide reasonable adjustments to accommodate individuals with disabilities. This major shift in policy was welcome in terms of the responsibilisation of organisations. However, it concealed the shift of responsibility from the welfare state to the market regulation of disability. Many disability activists concurrently protested against the withdrawal of state subsidies and unemployment benefits for disability.

The expansion of neoliberalism has been informed by three interlinked values: a belief in individualism, a belief in voluntarism and competition (Özbilgin and Slutskaya, 2017). The values valorise voluntarism which moves the responsibility for regulating diversity from the state-sponsored welfare state to the market through the voluntary responsibilisation of organisations. Voluntary regulation of diversity means that organisations craft their diversity interventions. The voluntary regulation of diversity has been extensively criticised for its failure and ineffectiveness in promoting equality and inclusion (Özbilgin and Tatli, 2011; Noon, 2007).

Coercive regulation of diversity

The voluntary regulation provides limited normative pressure on organisations to tackle entrenched forms of inequality and discrimination. Coercive regulation is often described by rules that are produced and enforced as law by political structures as national laws and binding international agreements. Coercive regulation of diversity refers to the binding enforcement of diversity practices, with punitive measures for non-compliance. Coercive regulation takes many forms, including affirmative action programmes (Bacchi, 2000), diversity quotas (Mensi-Klarbach et al., 2021; Forstenlechner et al., 2012) and a range of reporting requirements, such as pay gap reporting (Healy and Ahamed, 2019; Milner, 2019).

Coercive regulation often receives backlash and resistance, as it seeks to alter historically entrenched forms of inequality with radical measures. For example, the affirmative action programmes in the USA, considered the single most divisive regulations in US history (Fobanjong, 2001), have received considerable backlash not only from the white population but also from minority ethnic groups for their radical nature. Gender quotas in Scandinavian countries are another example of coercive regulation, which received backlash at the point of their introduction (Seierstad and Huse, 2017). However, coercive measures can have unintended consequences, as they are often blunt measures for changing entrenched ways that diversity is treated. Huse (2016) offered the notion of golden skirts to explain the emergence of a class of women in multiple boardroom positions in response to the coercive regulation of gender quotas. While the gender quotas radically shifted female representation in the boardroom, this numerical shift needs to be queried further. Forstenlechner et al. (2012) study show that coercive regulation of localisation quotas in the United Arab Emirates originally worked against principles of merit and received backlash from organisations. However, changing cultural capital and investments in human development in the region need to be considered for the future effectiveness of such coercive measures.

Coercive regulation of diversity sets a strong tone for responsibility among diversity management actors. Özbilgin and Tatli (2011) explain that while trade unions, social movements and employee networks are generally in favour of coercive regulation, neoliberal market actors, such as employers and governments, tend to favour voluntarism. As neoliberalism takes root in democratic countries, the coercive regulation of diversity becomes infrequent. The coercive regulation puts the responsibility for governing diversity issues to the state and its regulators. In countries with strong coercive regulation, the provision of equality, diversity and inclusion could be considered the domain of social welfare and a state-level governance issue. While coercive regulation provides a strong impetus for organisations to engage with diversity issues, it often provides a blunt instrument for deeper-level transformation, overcoming institutional discrimination and combatting subtle forms of discrimination and bias in organisations.

Coercive regulation for diversity management is offered when voluntary measures do not shift persistent inequalities and discrimination and when there is an appetite for change. However, coercive measures are often radical and blunt instruments for change and receive backlash and resistance, as they often aim to disturb uneven power relations. The choice between mildly effective voluntary measures and relatively radical coercive measures depends on the relational regulation context that we explore later. The relational regulation context often dictates the taste for voluntary and coercive measures, with references to the power and influence of significant actors in the diversity industry.

Relational regulation of diversity

For organisations to regulate diversity management effectively, normative pressure is important (McHugh and Perrault, 2018). Voluntarism, as we explained later in the context of a moral and legal vacuum, may not be sufficient to push organisations to take diversity concerns seriously. Relational regulation refers to the normative pressures that impose diversity-related duties and expectations on organisations. Relational regulation includes social regulation (Klarsfeld et al., 2012; Hyman et al., 2012; Klarsfeld, 2009), employee networks-based regulation (Colgan and McKearney, 2012; Huber, 2013), employee collectives and trade unions-based regulation (Lucio and Perrett, 2009; Greene et al., 2005) and community- and customer-based (Park et al., 2022) regulation. What separates relational regulation from voluntary regulation is the regulatory power in relational regulation resides in the relational engagement of these pressure groups with diversity management discourses and practices. Each of these relational actors has varying degrees of power and influence in shaping diversity management practices across different socio-political systems and industrial contexts.

Relational actors' pressures provide the impetus for organisations to regulate diversity, informing the rationales by which diversity interventions are crafted. Relational regulation is how diversity concerns are translated into the design of diversity interventions. Social movements, trade unions and internal and external stakeholders, customers and communities provide a relational regulation context that shapes the current and future moral landscape and taste for workplace diversity. Similarly, there is industrial-level relational regulation. Industrial recipes suggest that each industry regulates workplace relations uniquely, which could not be explained only by national or organisational-level analyses. (Spender, 1989). Relational regulation provides an awareness that influences social mores that could subsequently lead to stronger forms of coercive regulation, the compliance to which could become difficult if the organisations do not prepare in advance. Thus, progressive organisations follow changes in the relational regulation context to understand and capture them in the design of their diversity management practices and policies.

As part of the relational regulation, customer and user groups could pressure organisations to consider human rights, social justice and equality (Seidman, 2007). When it becomes evident that an organisation is engaging in ethically objectionable practices, such as exploitation and discrimination, customer protests could cause considerable damage. Olcott and Storebeck (2022) report on how two companies compete over race relations and how an executive's behaviour in one leads to reputation damage and internal redress with conflicting outcomes. Therefore, many organisations today consider organisational brand and reputation in line with practices of diversity and inclusion at work. This woke turn in the corporate world has been a significant achievement of the social movements (Özbilgin and Erbil, 2021b). Oruh (2014) explains that the new media could enhance the relational regulation of employee voice through trade unions, which are significant actors in the relational regulation of work towards equality. Although relational regulation may be an important driver for diversity activities, it may not provide sufficient impetus for organisations to implement deep-level diversity activities or tackle issues which fall outside the gaze of customers and the public. We are invited to believe that relational pressure could provide sufficient impetus for organisations to manage diversity effectively. Such a relational approach to regulation is important yet insufficient for advancing diversity and inclusion in organisations. Vassilopoulou (2017) criticises the tendency in some organisations to take such relational pressures at face value and engage in diversity management practices only to improve their image and to window dress. In the next section, we focus on other forms of regulation with stronger formal and institutional structures.

Relational regulation operates well when there is a supportive diversity industry. The diversity industry refers to individual and institutional actors that are involved in or have stakes in the regulation of diversity. There is a diverse industry in countries with strong social movements and advanced democratic and welfare traditions. Relational regulation in a multi-factor context would generate normative pressure to regulate diversity. However, Tatli and Özbilgin (2012a) show that when the socio-political context supports voluntarism and powerful actors are pushing for voluntary regulation of diversity, which is the case in the UK, relational regulation may generate voluntaristic outcomes. Thus, relational regulation is progressive and supportive if the dominant forces which regulate diversity are supportive. This is not always the case, as we explained in the rise of backlash and setbacks against diversity. For example, Kornau et al. (2022) show in the case of Germany and Turkey that the institutional actors resist ideas of equality, diversity and inclusion, which result in an unsupportive regulatory context. To understand the constitution of relational regulation, we need to explore the key actors: at the micro level, there are allies, champions and change agents who are dedicated to progressing diversity and inclusion; at the meso-organisational level, there are diversity and inclusion professionals, academics in research institutions that conduct research offer courses and degree programmes in diversify management; and at the macro level, there are regulatory bodies and charters which push for equality and diversity. However, actors in the relational regulation context have divergent views regarding voluntarist versus coercive choices for progressing diversity agendas. The key success of the diversity industry has been the legitimacy that it has garnered for discourses and practices of diversity. Nevertheless, the diversity industry also suffers from blind spots in those countries where the industry is strong yet has a halo effect on progress. For example, despite over 50 years of equality legislation, there is little progress towards closing diversity pay gaps (Healy and Ahamed, 2019). When a social justice concern is raised, relevant authorities respond by saying they have the requisite measures. There is often resistance to change in diversity matters when actors in the field have sunk costs associated with previous interventions, even if they were ineffective. Thus, a strong diversity industry may entrench some systemic problems, which it tries to tackle through less effective regulatory approaches such as voluntarism.

Relational regulation offers normative pressures to organisations to craft their diversity management in line with the relational expectations of key actors in the diversity industry. However, relational regulation is entrenched in the interfield struggles of the diversity industry, which is often torn between voluntary regulation and radical coercive measures. Therefore, relational regulation remains sensitive to the needs and relative power and influence of key actors in the diversity industry.

THE NEW DEAL FOR REGULATING DIVERSITY: TOWARDS POSTHUMAN DIVERSITY

Workforce diversity is a mature field of research. Yet there are workforce diversity concerns which are neglected and left underexplored. Those silent aspects are likely to emerge and shape the future of workforce diversity. In this section, we discuss one of those silent aspects, the deal between human diversity, nature and technology. In the first and subsequent chapters, we discussed the failure of the old deal between humans, nature and technology. In this chapter, we contemplate a new deal between humans, nature and technology.

There are serious global challenges, such as climate change, migration, extinction of species, disruptive innovation, wars, health crises and an upsurge of totalitarian and populist movements. Regulation of diversity is central to all these challenges as the dispossessed, disenfranchised and disadvantaged are more susceptible and vulnerable to crises and challenges. For effective regulation of these global challenges, Verhulst et al. (2019) argue that data and data-driven policy would be pivotal. In this section, we move the focus from human diversity to posthuman diversity for a new deal between human diversity, the environment and technology. We first discuss why human diversity would be enriched by building intersectional solidarity with biodiversity and techno diversity arguments. Then we explore the biodiversity context and how the relationship with human diversity needs a new deal. We posit the incorporation of nature as a possible venue for regulatory progress. The final section focuses on techno diversity or cyborg diversity and the problematic nature of ownership structures and value chains in disruptive technological innovation. We propose changing ownership structures and bringing value chain arguments to promote an even relationship between humans and technology.

Human diversity: intersectional solidarity

Humanism, which inspired the discourses of equality, diversity and inclusion, is predicated on the dominion that humans have over other species of life and technology. However, this uneven relationship where humans dominate nature and technology is shaken by global challenges.

Human diversity is supported by social movements which are distinctly different to those which promote biodiversity and techno diversity. Diversity concerns are less likely to garner power and influence if they lack global reach and intersectional solidarity from other social movements. (Özbilgin and Erbil, 2021b). Global challenges divide interest across climate change, refugee crisis, health crises, disruptive innovation and inequalities, among others. There is a possibility of establishing intersectional solidarity between actors that support human diversity and those who struggle to protect the environment and better regulate technology. In this section, we will explore the necessity for considering intersectional solidarity between these three major strands of diversity.

Individuals can show solidarity with others sharing similar concerns (Meliou et al., 2021). However, most shared concerns remain narrow if we focus on single strands of diversity. Gender diversity alone would not address ethnic, class and sexual orientation diversity concerns. Intersectionality theory (Crenshaw, 1991) suggests possibilities for showing solidarity across fault lines to galvanise stronger support for diversity. Intersectional solidarity is how individuals can collaborate across categories of diversity to support progressive agendas for change. Let us consider the case of human diversity in light of biodiversity and techno diversity. Such intersectional forms of diversity are already emerging, with eco-feminism and techno-feminism and diversity movements gaining intersectional character to support each other's progressive agendas. Evidence of this intersectional turn is also evident with presentations on interspecies diversity, animal labour, rights and exploitation, technology and diversity, gig economy and diversity, algorithmic justice and cyborg diversity in established conferences in the field of equality, diversity and inclusion (Özbilgin and Erbil, 2023d).

Intersectional solidarity offers human diversity concerns to be taken up by wider groups of people as part of progressive agendas. Organisational efforts to regulate diversity across human diversity, biodiversity and techno diversity could also be bridged to see possibilities of more appropriate design that can accommodate these three strands of diversity to provide a level playing field between them.

Biodiversity: empowering environment as a legal entity

The relationship between humans and nature is not only skewed because of the uneven nature of this relationship. Human consumption and human carbon emissions and damage to nature have created climate change with drastic consequences for biodiversity as well as another significant impetus for climate migration (Bellard et al., 2012; McLeman, 2018). Climate change and global warming, which are caused by the historical carbon emissions of industrialised countries, now add to global inequalities by having a more devastating impact on developing and less developed countries, such as Pakistan, which suffered from floods (Devi, 2022), and Kenya, which suffers from chronic droughts (Haile et al., 2020). Climate change is radicalising life on earth. Climate migration and migration induced by wars, conflicts, poverty and poor governance will change social demography across all parts of the world. Climate change is also having a disproportionately negative impact on disadvantaged communities and less developed regions of the world. The COP summit in Egypt 2022 has highlighted the consequences of climate change on workforce diversity. Developed countries and countries of the Global North are invited to offset the impact they have on developing countries, where much of the manufacturing for consumption in the Global North is taking place (Harris et al., 2022). Climate change and the growth of human populations are putting biodiversity under strain, as we explained in the earlier chapters of this book.

Biodiversity is under threat, and the extinction of many life forms and species is a major global concern. Abrahamic and Judeo-Christian religions, in contrast to received wisdom from education and environmental science, are founded upon the dominion of humans over other life forms (Hayes and Marangudakis, 2001), and often, the relationship between humans and the environment is shaped by corporate interests (see Ayaz Arda and Bayraktar, 2018). However, as we explained in Chapter 1, many species of life are already extinct or facing extinction because of the way human life is prioritised over all other life forms.

Humans place themselves on the top of the pyramid of interspecies diversity. Interspecies diversity refers to the level of safety, importance, utility and rights afforded to different species of life by humans (Willett, 2014). Interspecies diversity is a concern which gets some recognition among equality scholars today (Coulter, 2016; Blattner et al., 2019; Knight and Sang, 2020). Humans impose a hierarchy on all species regarding their relative utility, desirability, aesthetics, rights and engagement for humans. For example, humans treat cockroaches with contempt and cats with compassion in their homes. Some species of life could be seen as pests, weeds or toxic, and some could be viewed as a source of energy, food, companion, transport and guide or guard for humans. This hierarchical organisation of interspecies diversity is predicated on the dominion of humans over nature. While humans have benefited from the exploits of this hierarchically superior position, the threat of extinction of species challenges the sustainability of this uneven relationship. There is a need to question the old deal between humans and other species of life and explore new ways of organising this relationship to end the extinction of species and provide possibilities for sustaining nature.

There is a hierarchy of life forms and species because of the human-centric organisation of life in the world. For example, humans tend to afford more empathy towards great apes and other sentient life when compared to cockroaches, for example. Eco-feminists and queer/trans scholars have seen the utility of solidarity across interconnections between interspecies and human diversity (Kirts, 2021; Gaard, 2011). Interesting to note that gender discrimination extends beyond the human species. Female animals are exploited extensively due to their reproductive and milk-producing qualities. Other species are used as pets to cater for human affection and emotional needs, as food to cater for hunger, as games for hunting and as labourers to carry objects, work under precarious conditions, retrieve materials, hunt and even as sex workers. Blount-Hill (2021) suggests that social identity can be used to navigate the uneven relationship between humans and nonhuman species because humans replicate the uneven relationships of dominations they have with each other in their encounters with other species. There has been little or no recognition of the rights of animals and other species in nature, except for a few where the rights are solely tied to human ownership and owners are given responsibilities and rights over other species to care for and make use of them.

Animal labour is a relatively well-studied subject (Blattner et al., 2019). Many animal species work for humans. Common and more visible examples are equids in farms and therapy, dogs in police services and as guides for individuals with disabilities and rats, rabbits and monkeys as laboratory test subjects. Exploitation, discrimination and disenfranchisement are not only human concerns (Erbil, 2021). Humans afford variable degrees of empathy and agency to some species, which leads to diverse choices and chances for each species of life. Humans impose an interspecies hierarchy based on the relative utility, disutility, aesthetics and social, economic and psychological engagement between any species and humans. Humans often present themselves at the top of this hierarchy, dominating all life and the environment.

There are calls for ethical and multi-actor approaches to take radical action to save the ecology (e.g. Chanlat, 2022). Reparation of the uneven deal between humans and nonhuman species will require action at multiple levels. At the macro level, the root causes of the extinction of some species need to be addressed through investment by developed countries to offset the devastation to nature in less developed regions. At the (inter)national level, it is possible to afford nature and nonhuman life forms legal status so that their rights to life and labour can be defended by coercive, voluntary and relational regulation. Incorporation of nature will mean giving nature legal recognition similar to the legal status that corporations have. This will allow nature to be protected against encroachment (Erbil and Özen-Aytemur, 2023). At the organisational level, nonhuman diversity and its value and right to life and work could be recognised and protected. At the individual level, Fraser and Taylor (2018) explain that there are many cases of interspecies solidarity, compassion and care between humans and nonhumans, drawing examples from companion animals. These macro-, meso- and micro-level possibilities of intersectional solidarity between humans and nature could be used to galvanise support for more sustainable and egalitarian futures for humans and nature.

Techno diversity: challenging ownership and value chains of technology

Technological changes have transformed the way we live. Particularly during the Covid19 pandemic, technology has been extensively used to facilitate various forms of temporal and spatial flexibility at work and life, including the emergence of blended learning technologies, technology-supported transportation and food delivery systems and AI-enabled services across all industries. We abbreviate these emergent and diverse technological innovations as techno diversity in this section. The interface between humans and disruptive technological innovations has brought about new complexities to techno diversity. The emergence of artificial intelligence, complex algorithmic systems, e-learning, e-health, e-government, e-commerce and AI-led gig economy and platform economy has brought techno diversity to every aspect of our individual and institutional lives (Engin et al., 2019). Vassilopoulou et al. (2022) highlight that these technological advances have not eliminated but entrenched many human biases in technology (see also Kelan, 2022). The authors explain that the scientific nature of technological innovation comes with the assumption that these algorithmic developments would be bias free. Scientism is the naive valorisation of scientific advances in technological innovation as innocuous, objective and bias-free. The authors explain that widespread scientism has caused biases in human resource management algorithms and AI systems to be left unattended. Diaz (2022) reports that arguments for free and liberal space are used to cover up sexism in Metaverse, the virtual environment in which women continue to get harassed and targeted. Adeyemo (2021) explain that technology is never neutral to ethnic and gender diversity and requires monitoring for democratic accountability.

Algorithms, algorithm-based artificial intelligence systems and other new technology have entered all industries and forms of work and formed the basis of the fast-growing, AI-led gig economy (Kamasak et al., 2023; Özbilgin et al., 2023b). Such technological advances and their industrial use have a considerable impact on workforce diversity. The old assumptions about human governance of algorithms are revised as algorithmic systems have become so sophisticated that effective governance of these systems is no longer possible. Disruptive technological innovations have been changing the relationship between humans with technology. Similar to the relationships that humans historically had with nature, humans also have a relationship of domination with technology, with the assumption that humans control and use technology to their advantage. With radical and disruptive advances in technology, many fields of technology are now beyond the control of individuals and teams.

Algorithmic governance is complicated by unexpected consequences, which leave moral and regulatory vacuums. Recent studies investigating the management of the well-being of employees through an online advice line evidenced some counterproductive results. While the advice line enabled employees to increase their knowledge about health at work, it also triggered some individualistic behaviours, such as employees with mental health–related problems attempting to solve their problems through the knowledge-based website without contacting their line managers for appropriate support. On some occasions, this process of self-management was not effective (Valsecchi et al., 2021; Balta et al., 2021). In this case and others, as the algorithmic system is not recognised as a legal entity, it is hard to identify who is responsible for the impact on humans and the environment.

Regulation of algorithms, AI systems, automation, robot use and the gig economy, in general, is too slow to capture the dynamism and speed of growth in these sectors. The meteoric growth of the gig economy has meant that regulation of EDI in the sector has lagged behind other sectors. The gig economy, such as AI-led retail and food delivery, transportation companies and e-commerce, has created opportunities for workers who are excluded or underemployed in the traditional labour markets. For example, in London, black cab drivers were over 90 per cent white British. Black, minority, ethnic and Asian migrant/refugee workers have always found it difficult to seek employment as black cab drivers. With the expansion of AI-led private car hire companies, jobs were created for migrant and refugee workers and other groups of discouraged workers in companies such as Uber in London. Phung et al. (2021) demonstrate that Uber has served to destigmatise migrant and refugee drivers in Canada.

Despite the positive impacts of the gig economy and its extensive flexible forms of work on discouraged and disenfranchised groups to access employment and economic activity, disruptive technological innovations and their economic systems have raised other concerns. For example, automation and technological innovation have caused considerable deskilling and job losses for individuals who worked in recently automated jobs. This includes phone operators for taxi companies, packing and some delivery services, and supply chain and logistic administrators have been broadly replaced by new algorithmic systems. While technological innovations appear to have fostered flexibility for individuals who are previously discouraged from joining the economic activity, they also caused job losses.

Beyond reports of the positive and negative impact of techno diversity on human diversity, ownership and value chain concerns have the most pressing impacts on human diversity. Most technological innovation is based on gathering information and using stakeholders to design new algorithms and AI systems. However, once an algorithmic system is launched, owners garner all the value created by stakeholders and the value chain in design. Investors and owners accrue the income generated through techno diversity, automation, robots and AI. Excessive earnings from the AI-led gig economy have created over 1 million USD millionaires (Özbilgin and Erbil, 2021a). The Oxfam report on global income inequality showed that the super-rich 1 per cent of the world took two-thirds of the new wealth created since the pandemic. The report calls for new forms of taxation to rebalance wealth distribution. Undoubtedly, the gig economy has a significant uneven impact on income distribution, as the gig economy companies can avoid taxation, pay relatively low wages to workers and cause deskilling (Özbilgin et al., 2023b). Although much is known about the impact of algorithms and the gig economy on workforce diversity, there has been little provocation on what could be done to restore the distributive justice that robot labour/AI-led gig economy has disrupted. A unique exception is Brabet et al.'s (2020) contestation of the oligopolistic nature of digital platform firms and their destructive competitive strategies. Authors argue for open and collaborative digital platforms and recognise the problems with the current oligopolistic model. Another problem with the digital platforms and AI-led gig economy has been that the income accrued from automation, algorithms, AI systems and robots has paid the owners of these disruptive technologies generously. However, the impact of these technological innovations has not been positive on other actors in the value chain (Özbilgin and Erbil, 2023c). This has led to the emergence of new super-rich among owners of e-commerce, platform and AI-led gig companies. Hao (2022) explains that the warped ownership structure of AI usurps all the value generated in the value chain, causing the emergence of new colonisation and a major divide between the haves and have-nots (see also Janssens and Zanoni, 2021). These are alarming signs of how AI ownership and value chains lead to poor governance of AI, generating toxic outcomes for many actors in the value chain.

It is time to move from identification of the problem to crafting solutions for problematic ownership and value chains of AI technologies. First, the ownership structure of the technology value chain could be transformed. In the current model, ownership is held by investors. Other actors are brought in for the co-design of technological products. Moving from diversity-led co-design to diversity-led ownership could transform the uneven nature of the ownership and income structures. Many technological products are developed using co-design, where stakeholders, including end users, innovators and community representatives from diverse backgrounds, are drawn together to co-innovate and co-design products. However, this democratic and diversity-led co-design practice is not translated into transformed co-ownership structures. Organisations instrumentalise a diverse range of actors for co-design but do not share the income generated from technological products in the same way. Thus, ownership presents a problematic structure that creates an uneven outcome for actors that help organisations design technological products. As a solution, organisations can move from co-design to co-ownership of products through which the economic and social spoils of technological innovation could be shared more fairly. For this to happen, there is a need for awareness of the negative consequences of the instrumentalisation of organisational actors in the co-design process and the detrimental effects of organisations abandoning co-design actors without sharing profits accrued through technological innovation. Co-ownership with other actors could transform this uneven relationship.

The second possibility is to recognise the key problem of algorithmic governance for equality, diversity and inclusion: the lack of responsibility and legal personhood afforded to AI systems. Techno diversity, that is, AI systems, algorithmic bundles and robots, could be recognised as legal entities (Özbilgin and Erbil, 2023c; Erbil, 2023). Similar to our suggestion to incorporate nature to give it legal representation and personhood, techno diversity could also be given legal status for better governance. Techno diversity gaining status as a legal entity would allow financial regulation of techno diversity, prevent all value and profits from being seized by investors and disruptive innovation from being taxed and allow its impact on human diversity to be better regulated. There is a role for digital humanities (Mahony, 2018) scholars to consider uneven power relations among a diverse range of actors in the expansion of e-commerce and the digital economy,

We proposed a shift to posthuman diversity by building intersectional solidarity among social movements that promote human diversity, biodiversity and techno diversity. However, social movements are not sufficient to regulate diversity in organisations. There were some calls for global and international organisations to provide consistency and equality in their practices in their local practices (Lauring, 2013) and, to a lesser extent, across their value chains. There are global initiatives, declarations and conventions, such as the Universal Declaration of Human Rights, CEDAW and Sustainable Development Goals (SDGs). These global, international and national drivers to regulate suggest that there will be a greater focus in the future on how global organisations practise diversity and whether they deliver a consistent and fair allocation of resources and generate fair outcomes across their value chains (Özbilgin et al., 2016). However, it is important to acknowledge the hierarchies of diversity each of these organisations and conventions involves. For example, the SDGs have a wedding cake hierarchy in which some SDGs, remarkably SDG 17, are considered the top tier, the cherry on the cake (SDG, 2022). To understand the deep hierarchies of diversity, it is possible to examine how much funding and budget are allocated to each diversity category. While some organisations may commit considerable resources to diversity, often, the allocation of budgets to each category of diversity demonstrates their uneven commitment to different categories of diversity.

Despite normative pressure from international interventions and conventions, most diversity literature and studies are heavily embedded in local rationales, concerned only with national-level diversity concerns or comparative exploration of diversity across different national contexts. Neither of these dominant traditions is sufficient to explore how multinational organisations can tailor their diversity interventions to fit local circumstances and how this creates uneven treatment of diversity. In this section, we explored how human diversity, biodiversity and techno diversity could be considered together to strengthen the governance of diversity to face the challenges of the future.

ILLUSTRATIVE CASE: RESPONSIBILISATION IN A NEOLIBERAL CONTEXT FOR POSTHUMAN DIVERSITY

One of the myths of the neoliberal economic system is that market forces could help regulate diversity voluntarily. Özbilgin and Slutskaya (2017) demonstrate that this neoliberal myth merely entrenches three detrimental values of neoliberalism: deregulation, individualisation and competition. These three values lead to the deterioration of work conditions, employment and labour market participation of individuals from historically disadvantaged groups. First, deregulation strips them from historically earned rights, as these are no longer protected. Across many categories of diversity, equality laws have been contested in recent years as impositions to the operation of the market and moral traditions of societies. For example, there has been an extensive deterioration of gender-equality laws, such as challenges to the reproductive rights of women in the USA, Poland and other countries and the withdrawal of Turkey from the Istanbul Convention, which seeks to protect women against violence.

Second, individualisation of the diversity debate means that workers are invited to consider their particular difference as a reference point for negotiating inclusion and equality. Such individualisation came when the solidarity among workers through trade unions was strained in developed countries. The weakening of the collective understanding of diversity led to the possibility of the individual framing of diversity, which reduced the individual workers' negotiation power with the employers. For example, research shows that the gender pay gap remained resistant to change across developed countries (OECD, 2021).

Third, there has been competitive logic and resultant financialisation in diversity discourses, which moved the debate around equality, diversity and inclusion from moral justifications (i.e. EDI as the right thing to do) to instrumental and performance measures in organisations (i.e. EDI as a profitable and performance-enhancing thing to do) (Özbilgin, 2017; Lorenzo and Reeves, 2018). Diversity is often presented as a competitive resource for organisations. This change generated a body of literature around the business case for diversity. However, many authors have cautioned that the relationship between diversity and organisational outcomes is not always unidirectional and positive. Diversity could lead to several negative outcomes, such as lowering workplace harmony, inducing communication problems and causing workplace disputes. Instead, Özbilgin et al. (2016) demonstrated that to accrue positive outcomes of diversity, organisations need to invest in diversity and transform their systems, processes and structures to accommodate diversity. Thus, the responsibility for generating benefits of diversity rests more with organisations than individuals from atypical socio-demographic backgrounds.

There is a misconception among some scholars and sections of the public that diversity when it is left to its own devices will self-regulate. Research shows that diversity, when not regulated and left unsupported in terms of institutions, resources and discourses, leads to toxic consequences. The toxic triangle of diversity is when diversity is left to self-regulate, it is not supported by legal and institutional regulation and policy discourses. Küskü et al. (2021) show that the toxic triangle of diversity leaves diversity vulnerable to labour market dynamics and further entrenches the disenfranchisement of underrepresented and marginalised groups. There has been a libertarian and neoliberal turn in the treatment of workforce diversity in line with many other aspects of work organising (Küskü et al., 2022; Özbilgin and Slutskaya, 2017; Aydin and Özeren, 2018). The responsibilisation of individuals marks the libertarian turn, which places the onus on individuals for their choices and chances in life. At the same time, the state and organisations could gradually shed their responsibility to provide safety nets for individuals (Greenhalgh et al., 2021). The decline of welfare systems and the emergence of individualised career norms and ideals, such as protean careers and self-made entrepreneurship, have created the image that individuals can manage their career and life projects without social and economic safety nets (e.g. Karatas-Ozkan, 2018). While the libertarian ideology worked fine for individuals who are resource-rich and who have access to symbolic power and respectability in their context, the libertarian turn has been largely harmful to those individuals coming from disadvantaged backgrounds, as their changes and choices of controlling their lives remained increasingly slim.

To challenge the focus on individual responsibility for workforce diversity in which each individual is responsible for their diverse identities, there is a need for institutional and national responsibilisation. This may take the forms of systemic treatment of diversity and exploration of institutional intersections.

CONCLUSION

Attacks on public demands for equality, diversity and inclusion are understandable. The woke-rati (i.e. public who demand social justice) are substantial enough internationally to impact political, economic and social life through their demands for change. We outlined the setbacks, backlash and attacks on diversity beliefs as knee-jerk reactions to the woke turn in international public opinion. Most social movements start with the moral entrepreneurship of a single individual or a critical event that captures the need for recognising, protecting and promoting a form of diversity. If there is an appetite in a group or society for such an awareness, that category of difference may be legitimated and promoted. Such collective decisions lead to wider social movements and may be taken up by nation-states and international organisations as significant concerns for regulation. Once adopted as a regulatory concern, diversity could be legitimated, protected and promoted.

The future of workforce diversity will be shaped by changes in the demographic, social, cultural and political context and shifts in the moral landscape. Diversity is regulated at multiple levels and facets. Individual-level demands for equality, freedom, justice and solidarity often find meaning in collectives which turn to social movements, which in turn shape back the very values and demands of individuals for the legitimation of equality for new forms of diversity and difference. Thus, there is an interplay between micro-individual and macro-international regulation of diversity as they constitute each other.

However, it would be wrong to assume that diversity is regulated only in constructive ways. Many forms of diversity, including gender, ethnicity and sexuality, are still denigrated through formal and social regulations across many contexts. In this chapter, we focused mainly on the supportive regulation of diversity. At the international macro level, social movements give recognition and legitimacy to forms of difference and diversity. Demands of social movements are translated to formal regulation at the macro-international level through organisations such as the UN and ILO and supranational organisations such as the OECD and European Union. International-level regulation of diversity encourages transposition to the national level and could impact individual values and social regulations across multiple levels.

Broadening of the categories of diversity has created a fragmented field of regulation in which there are hierarchies of resourcing and practice. Some categories of diversity are regulated with stronger emphasis, such as gender, ethnicity and disability. Other categories remain unattended in policy and practice circles. Overall, most discussions of diversity in social sciences focus on human diversity and the superiority of humans over other life forms and technology. In this chapter, we showed that these assumptions are challenged by global warming, the extinction of species and disruptive technological innovations that radicalised and polarised economic and social life. In response to these radical changes, this chapter addresses the uneven relationship between human diversity, biodiversity and techno diversity. Broadening diversity categories can level the playing field between humans, the environment and technology and provide a diversity-led solution to the global challenge of destroying the natural environment and widening inequalities due to poor technology governance, ownership and income flows.

The new deal between human diversity, biodiversity and techno diversity can build intersectional solidarity between social movements that support human diversity and biodiversity and locate techno diversity and its governance as a concern for humans and the environment. One radical agenda proposition is to recognise the natural environment and algorithmic systems as legal entities and to assess their ownership, rights, responsibility and accountability in line with their legal agency. Incorporating the natural environment will allow individuals and social movements to defend the rights of the natural environment in legal ways. Differently, legal identity for algorithmic systems and techno diversity can make it possible to address the warped structure of ownership and income generation in e-commerce and platform economies which are offshoots of innovation in techno diversity. The current model of ownership and income structure of algorithmic systems means that the owners of companies accrue all the income generated through algorithmic and robot labour. Other stakeholders, such as innovators, developers and controllers, are left with low pay and conditions. The impact of techno diversity to the natural environment is also poorly governed. Recognition as a legal entity would ensure that techno diversity, such as robots, algorithmic systems and their uses in social and economic life, will assume human-like responsibilities to human diversity and biodiversity. The legal status could also help improve ownership and income structure. We explain how the new deal between human diversity, biodiversity and techno diversity offers diversity-led and sustainable solutions to several global challenges.

REFERENCES

Acker, J. (2006). Inequality regimes: Gender, class, and race in organizations. *Gender & Society*, 20(4), 441–464.

Adam-Troian, J., Mahfud, Y., Urbanska, K., & Guimond, S. (2021). The role of social identity in the explanation of collective action: An intergroup perspective on the Yellow Vests movement. *Journal of Applied Social Psychology*, 51(6), 560–576.

Adeyemo, B. (2021). I'm a Black woman and the metaverse scares me – Here's how to make the next iteration of the internet inclusive. *The Conversation*. https://theconversation.com/im-a-black-woman-and-the-metaverse-scares-me-heres-how-to-make-the-next-iteration-of-the-internet-inclusive-173310?utm_source=twitter&utm_medium=bylinetwitterbuttonvia@ConversationUS

Adler, N. J., & Aycan, Z. (2018). Cross-cultural interaction: What we know and what we need to know. *Annual Review of Organizational Psychology and Organizational Behavior*, 5, 307–333.

Aharoni Lir, S. (2020). Strangers in a seemingly open-to-all website: The gender bias in wikipedia. *Equality, Diversity and Inclusion: An International Journal*, 40(7), 801–818.

Aharoni Lir, S., & Ayalon, L. (2022). The wounded lion -ageism and masculinity in the Israeli film industry. *Frontiers Psychology*, 13.

Aharoni Lir, S., & Ayalon, L. (2023). The celluloid hurdles: Israeli women film directors in the prism of gender and time. In N. Haring, R. Maierhofer, & B. Ratzenböck (eds.), *Gender and age in popular culture*. Bielefeld: Transcript Publishing.

Ahmed, S., & Swan, E. (2006). Doing diversity. *Policy Futures in Education*, 4(2), 96–100.

Ahonen, P., Tienari, J., Meriläinen, S., & Pullen, A. (2014). Hidden contexts and invisible power relations: A foucauldian reading of diversity research. *Human Relations*, 67(3), 263–286.

Akanji, B., Mordi, C., Simpson, R., Adisa, T. A., & Oruh, E. S. (2020). Time biases: Exploring the work – life balance of single Nigerian managers and professionals. *Journal of Managerial Psychology*, 35(2), 57–70. https://doi.org/10.1108/JMP-12-2018-0537

Akinci, I. (2020). Culture in the 'politics of identity': Conceptions of national identity and citizenship among second-generation non-Gulf Arab migrants in Dubai. *Journal of Ethnic and Migration Studies*, 46(11), 2309–2325.

Akron, S., Feinblit, O., Hareli, S., & Tzafrir, S. S. (2016). Employment arrangements diversity and work group performance. *Team Performance Management*, 22(5/6), 310–330. https://doi.org/10.1108/TPM-11-2015-0053

Aktürk, Ş. (2012). *Regimes of ethnicity and nationhood in Germany, Russia, and Turkey*. Cambridge: Cambridge University Press.

Al Ariss, A. (2010). Modes of engagement: Migration, self-initiated expatriation, and career development. *Career Development International*, 15(4), 338–358. https://doi.org/10.1108/13620431011066231

Al Ariss, A., & Ozbilgin, M. (2010). Lebanese skilled immigrants in France: Cultural and social capital. In *Politics, culture and the Lebanese diaspora* (pp. 22–38).

Al Ariss, A., Özbilgin, M., Tatli, A., & April, K. (2014). Tackling whiteness in organizations and management. *Journal of Managerial Psychology*, 29(4), 362–369.

Alba, R., Reitz, J. G., & Simon, P. (2012). National conceptions of assimilation, integration, and cohesion. In M. Crul, J. Schneider, & F. Lelie (eds.), *The changing face of world cities: Young adult children of immigrants in Europe and the United States* (pp. 44–64). New York: Russell Sage Foundation.

Alcázar, F. M., Fernández, P. M. R., & Gardey, G. S. (2013). Workforce diversity in strategic human resource management models: A critical review of the literature and implications for future research. *Cross Cultural Management: An International Journal*, 20(1), 39–49

Al Dahdah, M. (2021). Technodiversity and digital colonialism in pandemic times. *Revue d'Anthropologie des Connaissances*, 15(2).

American Psychological Association. (2021). *Apology to people of color for APA's role in promoting, perpetuating, and failing to challenge racism, racial discrimination, and human hierarchy in US*. www.apa.org/about/policy/racism-apology

Anthias, F. 2005. Social stratification and social inequality: Models of intersectionality and identity. In F. Devine, M. Savage, J. Scott, & R. Compton (eds.), *Rethinking class: Cultures, identities and lifestyles*. London: Bloomsbury.

Antonini, F. (2019). Pessimism of the intellect, optimism of the will: Gramsci's political thought in the last miscellaneous notebooks. *Rethinking Marxism*, 31(1), 42–57. https://doi.org/10.1080/0 8935696.2019.1577616

Apfelbaum, E. P., Norton, M. I., & Sommers, S. R. (2012). Racial color blindness: Emergence, practice, and implications. *Current Directions in Psychological Science*, 21(3), 205–209.

April, K. (2021a). The narratives of racism in South Africa. In P. Daya & K. April (eds.), *12 lenses into diversity in South Africa* (pp. 11–31). Randburg: KR Publishing.

April, K. (2021b). The new diversity, equity and inclusion (DEI) realities and challenges. In P. Norman (ed.), *HR: The new agenda* (pp. 119–132). Randburg, SA: KR Publishing.

April, K., & Blass, E. (2010). Measuring diversity practice and developing inclusion. *Dimensions*, 1(1), 59–66.

April, K., & Dharani, B. (2021). Diversity and entrepreneurship in South Africa: Intersections and purposive collaboration. In K. April & B. Zolfaghari (eds.), *Values-driven entrepreneurship and societal impact: Setting the agenda for entrepreneuring across (Southern) Africa* (pp. 241–254). Randburg, SA: KR Publishing.

April, K., Dharani, B., & April, A. (2023). *Lived experiences of exclusion in the workplace: Psychological and behavioural effects.* Bingley, UK: Emerald Publishing.

April, K., Ephraim, N., & Peters, B. K. G. (2012). Diversity management in South Africa: Inclusion, identity, intention, power and expectations. *African Journal of Business Management*, 6(4), 1749–1759. https://doi.org/10.5897/AJBM11.1184

April, K., & Peters, B. K. G. (2011). Communal versus individual modalities of work: A South African investigation. In R. F. Littrell & P. S. Nel (eds.), *Leadership & management studies in sub-Sahara Africa volumes II and III* (pp. 51–99). San Diego, CA: University Readers.

Aras, N. E. G., Kabadayi, S., Ozeren, E., & Aydin, E. (2021). Right to health and access to healthcare services for refugees in Turkey. *Journal of Services Marketing*, 35(7), 962–976.

Archer, M. S. (2003). *Structure, agency and the internal conversation.* Cambridge, UK: Cambridge University Press.

Arda, O. A., Bayraktar, E., & Tatoglu, E. (2019). How do integrated quality and environmental management practices affect firm performance? Mediating roles of quality performance and environmental proactivity. *Business Strategy and the Environment*, 28(1), 64–78.

Areheart, B. A. (2008). When disability isn't just right: The entrenchment of the medical model of disability and the goldilocks dilemma. *Indiana Law Journal*, 83, 181.

Armitage, L. (2020). Explaining backlash to trans and non-binary genders in the context of UK gender recognition act reform. *INSEP – Journal of the International Network for Sexual Ethics and Politics*, 8(SI), 5–6.

Armitage, R., & Nellums, L. B. (2020). The COVID-19 response must be disability inclusive. *The Lancet Public Health*, 5(5), e257.

Ashley, L., & Empson, L. (2012). Differentiation and discrimination: Understanding social class and social exclusion in leading law firms. *Human Relations*, 65(2), 139–161. https://doi.org/10.1177/0018726712455833

Atatüre, M., Englund, D., Vamivakas, N., Lee, S. Y., & Wrachtrup, J. (2018). Material platforms for spin-based photonic quantum technologies. *Nature Reviews Materials*, 3(5), 38–51.

Avery, D. R., Volpone, S. D., & Holmes IV, O. (2018). Racial discrimination in organizations. In J. Colella & E. B. King (eds.), *The Oxford handbook of workplace discrimination* (pp. 89–109). New York: Oxford University Press.

Ayaz Arda, O., & Bayraktar, E. (2018, July). Environmental management and organizational performance: Environmental performance as a mediator. In *Academy of management proceedings* (Vol. 2018, No. 1, p. 13375). Briarcliff Manor, NY: Academy of Management.

Aycan, Z., Kanungo, R. N., & Mendonca, M. (2014). *Management and organizations in cross-cultural context.* London: Sage Inc.

Aycan, Z., & Shelia, S. (2019). 'Leadership? No, thanks!' a new construct: Worries about leadership. *European Management Review*, 16(1), 21–35.

Aycan, Z., Shyncs, B., Sun, J., Felfe, J., & Saher, N. (2013). Convergence and divergence of paternalistic leadership: A cross-cultural investigation of prototypes. *Journal of International Business Studies*, 44(9), 962–969.

Aydin, E., & Ozbilgin, M. F. (2019). *Exploring the interplay between the aims and the context of LGBTI+ organising: The case of LGBTI+ organisations in Turkey and the UK.* LGBT+ Studies Turkey, Transnational Press, London, 9–32.

Aydin, E., & Özeren, E. (2018). Rethinking workforce diversity research through critical perspectives: Emerging patterns and research agenda. *Business & Management Studies: An International Journal*, 6(3), 650–670.

Aydin, E., & Özeren, E. (2020). Inclusion and exclusion of sexual minorities at organisations: Evidence from LGBT NGOs in Turkey and the UK. *Journal of Organizational Change Management*, 33(3), 567–578.

Babacan, S. (2019). *Grup fay hatları, grup içi çatışma ve grup performansı ilişkilerinde grup sargınlığı ve hedef karşılıklı bağlılığın etkisi üzerine bir araştırma* (Doctoral dissertation, Muğla Sıtkı Koçman University, Muğla).

Bacchi, C. (2000). The seesaw effect: Down goes affirmative action, up comes workplace diversity. *Journal of Interdisciplinary Gender Studies*, 5(2), 64–83.

Bach, D. R., & Dayan, P. (2017). Algorithms for survival: A comparative perspective on emotions. *Nature Reviews Neuroscience*, 18(5), 311–319.

Bağlama, S. H. (2020). Intersectionality in Zadie Smith's fiction: Race, gender and class. In M. Sarıoğlan & S. H. Bağlama (eds.), *Critical studies in social sciences and humanities* (pp. 21–38). Livre de Lyon.

Bakoğlu, R. (2010). *Çağdaş Stratejik Yönetim* (Contemporary Strategic Management). İstanbul: Beta Yayınları.

Bakoğlu, R. (2014). New business model: The contemporary way of strategy creation. *10th international strategic management conference*, Rome, 19–21 July 2014.

Bakoğlu, R., Öncer, A. Z., Yıldız, M. L., & Güllüoğlu, A. N. (2016). Strategy development process in higher education: The case of marmara university. *12th international strategic management conference*, 28–30 October 2016, Antalya, Procedia- Social and Behavioral Sciences, 234 (2016), 36–45.

Bakoğlu, R., & Yıldız, M. L. (2016). *Üniversitelerde Strateji Geliştirme Sürecinde Uygulamalı Durum Analizleri* (Situation Analysis with Practice on Strategy Development Process at Universities) (pp. 1–26). İstanbul: Beta Publication. ISBN: 978-605-333-802-4.

Baldwin, A. (2017). Climate change, migration, and the crisis of humanism. *WIREs Climate Change*, 8, e460. https://doi.org/10.1002/wcc.460

Ball, P. (2020). *The Gene Delusion*, 10 June 2020. www.newstatesman.com/class-race-genetics-science-human-diversity-charles-murray-review, accessed 11 April 2021.

Balta, M., Valsecchi, R., Papadopoulos, T., & Bourne, D. J. (2021). Digitalization and co-creation of healthcare value: A case study in occupational health. *Technological Forecasting and Social Change*, 168, 120785.

Bandura, A., Barbaranelli, C., Caprara, G. V., & Pastorelli, C. (1996). Mechanisms of moral disengagement in the exercise of moral agency. *Journal of Personality and Social Psychology*, 71(2), 364–374.

Bartels-Ellis, F., Özbilgin, M. F., & Gibbs, P. (2019). Introduction to the challenges of international diversity management. In *Global diversity management* (pp. 1–8). Cham: Springer.

Bartlett, R. L. (1996). Discovering diversity in introductory economics. *Journal of Economic Perspectives*, 10(2), 141–153.

Bartz, D. E., Hillman, L. W., Lehrer, S., & Mayhugh, G. M. (1990). A model for managing workforce diversity. *Management Education and Development*, 21(4), 321–326.

Baykut, S., Erbil, C., Ozbilgin, M., Kamasak, R., & Bağlama, S. H. (2022). The impact of the hidden curriculum on international students in the context of a country with a toxic triangle of diversity. *The Curriculum Journal*, 33(2), 156–177.

BBC (2018). *Pride in London sorry after anti-trans protest*. www.bbc.co.uk/news/uk-england-london-44757403

BBC (2021). *'Greed' and 'capitalism' helped UK's vaccines success, says PM*, original 24 March 2021. www.bbc.co.uk/news/uk-politics-56504546, accessed 25 March 2021.

Beattie, J. C. (1990). Prohibiting marital status discrimination: A proposal for the protection of unmarried couples. *Hastings Law Journal*, 42, 1415.

Beauregard, A. T., Arevshatian, L., Booth, J. E., & Whittle, S. (2018). Listen carefully: Transgender voices in the workplace. *The International Journal of Human Resource Management*, 29(5), 857–884.

Bebbington, D., & Özbilgin, M. (2013). The paradox of diversity in leadership and leadership for diversity. *Management International/International Management/Gestiòn Internacional*, 17, 14–24.

Becker, G. S. (2009). *Human capital: A theoretical and empirical analysis, with special reference to education*. Chicago: University of Chicago Press.

Bell, K., & Bevan, G. (2021). Beyond inclusion? Perceptions of the extent to which Extinction Rebellion speaks to, and for, Black, Asian and Minority Ethnic (BAME) and working-class communities. *Local Environment*, 26(10), 1205–1220.

Bell, M. (2018). Adapting work to the worker: The evolving EU legal framework on accommodating worker diversity. *International Journal of Discrimination and the Law*, 18(2–3), 124–143.

Bell, M., Özbilgin, M. F., Beauregard, T. A., & Sürgevil, O. (2011). Voice, silence, and diversity in 21st century organizations: Strategies for inclusion of gay, lesbian, bisexual, and transgender employees. *Human Resource Management*, 50(1), 131–146.

Bellard, C., Bertelsmeier, C., Leadley, P., Thuiller, W., & Courchamp, F. (2012). Impacts of climate change on the future of biodiversity. *Ecology Letters*, 15(4), 365–377.

Benschop, Y. (2001). Pride, prejudice and performance: Relations between HRM, diversity and performance. *The International Journal of Human Resource Management*, 12(7), 1166–1181. https://doi.org/10.1080/09585190110068377

Berros, M. V. (2021). Challenges for the implementation of the rights of nature: Ecuador and bolivia as the first instances of an expanding movement. *Latin American Perspectives*, 48(3), 192–205.

Beveridge, W. (1942). *Social insurance and allied services* (Vol. 942). London: HMSO.

Biden, J. (2022). *The biden plan to advance LGBTQ+ Equality in America and around the world.* https://joebiden.com/lgbtq-policy/#

Bird, S. R. (1996). Welcome to the men's club: Homosociality and the maintenance of hegemonic masculinity. *Gender & Society*, 10(2), 120–132.

Birhane, A., & van Dijk, J. (2020, February). Robot rights? Let's talk about human welfare instead. *Proceedings of the AAAI/ACM conference on AI, ethics, and society* (pp. 207–213). https://doi.org/10.1145/3375627.3375843

Bjögvinsson, E., Ehn, P., & Hillgren, P. A. (2012). Design things and design thinking: Contemporary participatory design challenges. *Design Issues*, 28(3), 101–116.

Blaine, B. E., & Brenchley, K. J. M. (2020). *Understanding the psychology of diversity.* Thousand Oaks, CA: SAGE Publications.

Blattner, C. E., Coulter, K., & Kymlicka, W. (eds.). (2019). *Animal labour: A new frontier of interspecies justice.* Oxford: Oxford University Press.

Blau, F. D. (1996). Where are we in the economics of gender?: The gender pay gap. *National Bureau of Economic Research.* https://www.nber.org/system/files/working_papers/w5664/w5664.pdf

Blau, F. D., & Kahn, L. M. (2003). Understanding international differences in the gender pay gap. *Journal of Labor Economics*, 21(1), 106–144.

Blau, F. D., & Kahn, L. M. (2007). The gender pay gap: Have women gone as far as they can?. *Academy of Management Perspectives*, 21(1), 7–23.

Blazer, D. G., & Hernandez, L. M. (eds.). (2006). *Genes, behavior, and the social environment: Moving beyond the nature/nurture debate.* Washington, DC: Academies Press.

Bleijenbergh, I., Peters, P., & Poutsma, R. (2010). Diversity management beyond the business case. *Equality, Diversity and Inclusion*, 29(5), 413–421.

Blount-Hill, K. L. (2021). Proposing a social identity theory of interspecies dominance. *Biological Conservation*, 254, 108969.

Boehm, S. A., Baumgaertner, M. K., Dwertmann, D. J., & Kunze, F. (2011). Age diversity and its performance implications – Analysing a major future workforce trend. In *From grey to silver* (pp. 121–141). Berlin & Heidelberg: Springer.

Booth, A. L., Francesconi, M., & Frank, J. (2003). A sticky floors model of promotion, pay, and gender. *European Economic Review*, 47(2), 295–322.

Bourdieu, P. (1984). *Distinction: A social critique of the judgement of taste.* Cambridge, MA: Harvard University Press.

Bourdieu, P. (1987). What makes a social class? On the theoretical and practical existence of groups. *Berkeley Journal of Sociology*, 32, 1–17.

Bourdieu, P. (2020). Outline of a theory of practice. In S. Seidman & J. Alexander (eds.), *The new social theory reader* (pp. 80–86). New York, NY: Routledge.

Bourdieu, P. and Wacquant, L. J. D. (1992). *An invitation to reflexive sociology.* Chicago, IL: University of ChicagoPress.

Bourdieu, P., & Wacquant, L. J. D. (2013). Symbolic capital and social classes. *Journal of Classical Sociology*, 13(2), 292–302.

Bourke, J. (2022). *It's the little things: A qualitative study of the nature and role of interpersonal inclusion in fostering individual performance in project teams* (Doctoral dissertation, Brunel University London).

Bourke, J., & Espedido, A. (2019). Why inclusive leaders are good for organizations, and how to become one. *Harvard Business Review*, 29.

Bourke, J., & Espedido, A. (2020). The key to inclusive leadership. *Harvard Business Review*, 6.

Box, R. C., Marshall, G. S., Reed, B. J., & Reed, C. M. (2001). New public management and substantive democracy. *Public Administration Review*, 61(5), 608–619.

Brabet, J. A. (2010). Le champ contesté de la responsabilité sociale des entreprises. *Revue Internationale de Psychosociologie*, 16(38), 31–41.

Brabet, J. A., & Beierlein, L. (2017, June). Taking global value chains seriously. Studying GVCs: Why and how? In *European academy of management 2017 conference, "making knowledge work" (EURAM 2017)*.

Brabet, J. A., Bruna, M.-G., Chanlat, J.-F., & Labulle, F. (2019). The French model and the discriminations towards visible minorities at work. In *Race discrimination and management of ethnic diversity and migration at work* (International Perspectives on Equality, Diversity and Inclusion, Vol. 6) (pp. 35–57). Bingley: Emerald Publishing Limited. https://doi.org/10.1108/S2051-233320190000006003

Brabet, J. A., Taksa, L., & Vercher-Chaptal, C. (2020, December). From oligopolistiic digital platforms to open/cooperative ones? In *European academy of management-EURAM*, EURAM, Dublin, Ireland. ⟨hal-03228385⟩

Bradley, H., Healy, G., & Mukherjee, N. (2005). Multiple burdens: Problems of work-life balance for ethnic minority trade union activist women. In *Work-life balance in the 21st century* (pp. 211–229). London: Palgrave Macmillan.

Brennan, J. (2022). Diversity for justice vs. diversity for performance: Philosophical and empirical tensions. *Journal of Business Ethics*, 1–15.

Brown, S., & Kelan, E. (2020). *Gender and Corporate Boards: The route to a seat at the table*. Abington: Routledge.

Brubaker, R. (2017). Why populism? *Theory and Society*, 46(5), 357–385.

Bruna, M. G. (2014). L'heptagone de la diversité: Dynamiques stratégiques et jeux d'acteurs dans la conduite d'une politique de diversité. *Management & Sciences Sociales*, 17, 69–86.

Bruna, M. G. (2016a). Des acteurs, des règles et des savoirs: Régulation sociale et apprentissage collectif dans une politique diversité. *Management Avenir*, 86(4), 163–192.

Bruna, M. G. (2016b). Dynamique de changement, exercice de la réflexivité et apprentissage managérial dans la conduite d'une démarche transformationnelle de diversité. *La Revue des Sciences de gestion*, 5–6(281–282), 121–136.

Bruna, M. G. (2020). Du diagnostic stratégique à l'alignement: Explorer les conditions d'efficience d'une démarche RSE. *Gestion 2000*, 37(6), 67–85.

Bruna, M. G. (2021). Du besoin de régulation à l'heure de la Covid-19. *Question(s) de Management*, 34, 118–119.

Bruna, M. G. (2022). Des dynamiques d'alignement, des cercles d'apprentissage et des boucles régulatoires. *Proposition d'une méthode de conduite du changement en matière de diversité en entreprise, manuscrit d'Habilitation à Diriger les Recherches en Sciences de Gestion, sous la coordination du Prof. J.-F. Chanlat*, Université Paris-Dauphine-PSL, Paris.

Bruna, M. G., & Bazin, Y. (2018). Answering Levinas' call in organization studies. *European Management Review*, 15(4), 577–588.

Bruna, M. G., Chanlat, J. F., & Chauvet, M. (2017). Conducting a diversity policy as a management change agent: A key issue to an organisation's performance. In *Management and diversity* (Vol. 4, pp. 37–57). London: Emerald Publishing Limited.

Bruna, M. G., Chanlat, J. F., & Özbilgin, M. (2021). Mot des rédacteurs invités: Les promesses et les défis de la confiance/Word from the Guest Editors: The Promise and Challenges of Trust/Palabras de los redactores invitados: Las promesas y los desafios de la confianza. *Management International/International Management/Gestiòn Internacional*, 25(6), 10–21.

Bruna, M. G., & Ducray, L. F. (2018). *Repenser la diversité au travail à l'ère postmoderne. Les diversités en milieux de travail. Discrimination, égalité des chances et inclusion.* Canada Québec: Presses de l'Université Laval.

Brundtland, G. H. (1987). Our common future – Call for action. *Environmental Conservation*, 14(4), 291–294.

Buche, A., Jungbauer-Gans, M., Niebuhr, A., & Peters, C. (2013). Diversität und erfolg von organisationen/Diversity and organizational performance. *Zeitschrift für Soziologie*, 42(6), 483–501.

Bunderson, J. S., & Sutcliffe, K. M. (2002). Comparing alternative conceptualizations of functional diversity in management teams: Process and performance effects. *Academy of Management Journal*, 45(5), 875–893.

Cahusac, E., & Kanji, S. (2014). Giving up: How gendered organizational cultures push mothers out. *Gender, Work & Organization*, 21(1), 57–70.

Calvard, T. (2020). *Critical perspectives on diversity in organizations*. London: Routledge.

Cantle, T. (2012). Interculturalism: For the era of globalisation, cohesion and diversity. *Political Insight*, 3(3), 38–41.

Cardinale, B. J., Duffy, J. E., Gonzalez, A., Hooper, D. U., Perrings, C., Venail, P., . . . & Naeem, S. (2012). Biodiversity loss and its impact on humanity. *Nature*, 486(7401), 59–67.

Carmichael, F., Darko, C., Kanji, S., & Vasilakos, N. (2022). The contribution of girls' longer hours in unpaid work to gender gaps in early adult employment: Evidence from Ethiopia, India, Peru and Vietnam. *Feminist Economics*, 1–37. ISSN: 1354–5701.

Carroll, A. B. (1991). The pyramid of corporate social responsibility: Toward the moral management of organizational stakeholders. *Business Horizons*, 34(4), 39–48.

Casini, A. (2016). Glass ceiling and glass elevator. *The Wiley Blackwell Encyclopedia of Gender and Sexuality Studies*, 1–2.

Castles, S. (1995). How nation-states respond to immigration and ethnic diversity. *Journal of Ethnic and Migration Studies*, 21(3), 293–308.

Cava, P. (2016). Cisgender and cissexual. *The Wiley Blackwell Encyclopedia of Gender and Sexuality Studies*, 1–4.

Ceci, S. J., & Williams, W. M. (eds.). (1999). *The nature – nurture debate: The essential readings*. Oxford: Blackwell Publishing.

Census (2021). *Coronavirus (COVID-19) related deaths by ethnic group*. England and Wales, 2 March 2020 to 15 May 2020. www.ons.gov.uk/peoplepopulationandcommunity/birthsdeathsandmarriages/deaths/articles/coronaviruscovid19relateddeathsbyethnicgroupenglandandwales/2march-2020to15may2020

Chamberlain, K. (2000). Methodolatry and qualitative health research. *Journal of Health Psychology*, 5(3), 285–296.

Chanlat, J. F. (2014). Language and thinking in organization studies: The visibility of French OS production in the Anglo-Saxon OS field. *International Journal of Organizational Analysis*, 22(1), 70–88.

Chanlat, J. F. (2017). Management, diversity, equal opportunity, and social cohesion in France: The republic resistant to differences☆. In *Management and diversity* (Vol. 3, pp. 63–89). London: Emerald Publishing Limited.

Chanlat, J. F. (2020). La catastrophe sanitaire actuelle: un fait social total. *Le Libellio d'AEGIS*, 16(7), 3–30.

Chanlat, J. F. (2022). Rethinking organizations and society from an ethical perspective. *Organizações & Sociedade*, 29, 123–150.

Chanlat, J. F., Dameron, S., Dupuis, J. P., de Freitas, M., & Ozbilgin, M. (2013). Management et Diversité: lignes de tension et perspectives. *Management International/International Management/Gestiòn Internacional*, 17, 5–13.

Chanlat, J. F., & Ozbilgin, M. (2019). *Management et diversité. Approches thématiques et défis sociopolitiques* (Tome 2). Quebec, Canada: Presses de l'Université Laval.

Chanlat, J.-F. & Ozbilgin, M. (2023). Context. In S. Nkomo & A. Klarsfeld (eds.), *Edward Elgar encyclopedia of diversity and management*. Cheltenham, UK: Edward Elgar Publisher.

Chapman, G., Nasirov, S., & Özbilgin, M. (2022). Workforce diversity, diversity charters and collective turnover: Long-term commitment pays. *British Journal of Management*, 33(1), 33–50.

Charles, M. (2003). Deciphering sex segregation: Vertical and horizontal inequalities in ten national labor markets. *Acta Sociologica*, 46(4), 267–287.

Chatterjee, I. (2021). *Alt-right movement: Dissecting racism, patriarchy and anti-immigrant Xenophobia*. New Delhi, India: SAGE Publishing.

Chicha, M. T. (2006). *A comparative analysis of promoting pay equity: Models and impacts*. Geneva: ILO.

Chicha, M. T. (2012). Discrimination systémique et intersectionnalité: la déqualification des immigrantes à Montréal. *Canadian Journal of Women and the Law*, 24(1), 82–113.

China ABC (2021). *Ethnic groups in China*. http://english.www.gov.cn/archive/china_abc/2014/08/27/content_281474983873388.htm, accessed 31 March 2021.

Cho, S., Kim, A., & Mor Barak, M. E. (2017). Does diversity matter? Exploring workforce diversity, diversity management, and organizational performance in social enterprises. *Asian Social Work and Policy Review*, 11(3), 193–204.

Choroszewicz, M., & Kay, F. (2020). The use of mobile technologies for work-to-family boundary permeability: The case of Finnish and Canadian male lawyers. *Human Relations*, 73(10), 1388–1414. https://doi.org/10.1177/0018726719865762

Chou, R. S., & Feagin, J. R. (2015). *Myth of the model minority: Asian Americans facing racism.* Abingdon, UK: Routledge.

Choudaha, R., & Van Rest, E. (2018). Envisioning pathways to 2030: Megatrends shaping the future of global higher education and international student mobility. *Journal of International Student Mobility,* 6(1), 1–12.

Christensen, J. F., Mahler, R., & Teilmann-Lock, S. (2021). GenderLAB: Norm-critical design thinking for gender equality and diversity. *Organization,* 28(6), 1036–1048.

Chui, M., Manyika, J., & Miremadi, M. (2016). Where machines could replace humans – and where they can't (yet). *McKinsey Quarterly,* July 1.

Cin, F. M. (2017). Understanding context: Political history, gender politics and education provision in Turkey. In *Gender justice, education and equality* (pp. 47–74). Cham: Palgrave Macmillan.

CIPD (2021). *CIPD responds to commission on race and ethnic disparities report.* www.cipd.co.uk/about/media/press/310321commission-race-ethnic-disparities#gref

Clynes, M. E., & Kline, N. (1960). *Cyborgs and space,* Astronautics, September, 26–27 and 74–75. Reprinted in Gray, Mentor, and Figueroa-Sarriera. 1995. IN: The cyborg handbook.

Cochrane, A. (2016). Labour rights for animals. In R. Garner & S. O'Sullivan (eds.), *The political turn in animal ethics* (pp. 15–32). London, UK: Rowman & Littlefield International.

Cockburn, C. (1991). *In the way of women: Men's resistance to sex equality in organizations.* Ithaca: ILR Press.

Cockburn, C. (2010). Gender relations as causal in militarization and war: A feminist standpoint. *International Feminist Journal of Politics,* 12(2), 139–157.

Coleman, H. L., Casali, S. B., & Wampold, B. E. (2001). Adolescent strategies for coping with cultural diversity. *Journal of Counseling & Development,* 79(3), 356–364.

Colgan, F., & McKearney, A. (2012). Visibility and voice in organisations: Lesbian, gay, bisexual and transgendered employee networks. *Equality, Diversity and Inclusion: An International Journal,* 31(8), 750–764.

Collier, P. (2001). Implications of ethnic diversity. *Economic Policy,* 16(32), 128–166.

Conley, H., & Page, M. (2017). Revisiting Jewson and Mason: The politics of gender equality in UK local government in a cold climate. *Gender, Work & Organization,* 24(1), 7–19.

Cook, K. S., & Hegtvedt, K. A. (1983). Distributive justice, equity, and equality. *Annual Review of Sociology,* 217–241.

Corritore, M., Goldberg, A., & Srivastava, S. B. (2020). Duality in diversity: How intrapersonal and interpersonal cultural heterogeneity relate to firm performance. *Administrative Science Quarterly,* 65(2), 359–394.

Cotofan, M., De Neve, J. E., Golin, M., Kaats, M., & Ward, G. (2021). *Work and well-being during COVID-19: Impact, inequalities, resilience, and the future of work.* World Happiness Report, 153–190.

Coulter, K. (2016). *Animals, work, and the promise of interspecies solidarity.* New York: Palgrave Macmillan US.

CRED Report (2021). *Independent report: The report of the commission on race and ethnic disparities, The Commission's report into racial and ethnic disparities in the UK.* www.gov.uk/government/publications/the-report-of-the-commission-on-race-and-ethnic-disparities

Crenshaw, K. (1989). *Demarginalizing the intersection of race and sex: A black feminist critique of antidiscrimination doctrine, feminist theory and antiracist politics* (pp. 139–167). Chicago: University of Chicago Legal Forum.

Crenshaw, K. (1991). Mapping the margins: Intersectionality, identity politics, and violence against women of color. *Stanford Law Review,* 43, 1241–1299.

CRPD (2008). *UN convention on the rights of persons with disabilities.* https://treaties.un.org/Pages/ViewDetails.aspx?src=TREATY&mtdsg_no=IV-15&chapter=4

Cumming-Bruce, N. (2021, April 19) U.N. panel is scathing in its criticism of a British report on race. *The New York Times.* www.nytimes.com/2021/04/19/world/europe/britain-race-united-nations-boris-johnson.html

D'Almada-Remedios, R., Groutsis, D., Kaabel, A., & O'Leary, J. (2021). *Counting culture: Towards a standardised approach to measuring and reporting on workforce cultural diversity in Australia.* Sydney: Diversity Council Australia.

Dea, S. (2016). *Beyond the binary: Thinking about sex and gender.* Peterborough, ON, Canada: Broadview Press.

Degener, T. (2016). Disability in a human rights context. *Laws,* 5(3), 35.

Demougin, P., Gooberman, L., Hauptmeier, M., & Heery, E. (2021). Revisiting voluntarism: Private voluntary regulation by Employer Forums in the United Kingdom. *Journal of Industrial Relations,* 63(5), 684–705. https://doi.org/10.1177/00221856211038308

Deshpande, A. (2015). Caste and diversity in India. In *The Elgar companion to social economics* (2nd ed.). Cheltenham, UK: Edward Elgar Publishing.

Devi, S. (2022). Pakistan floods: Impact on food security and health systems. *The Lancet*, 400(10355), 799–800.

Dharani, B., & April, K. (2021). Locus of control and the happy entrepreneur. In K. April & B. Zolfaghari (eds.), *Values-driven entrepreneurship and societal impact: Setting the agenda for entrepreneuring across (Southern) Africa* (pp. 199–205). Randburg, SA: KR Publishing.

Dharani, B., April, K., & Harvey, K. (2021). *The poetic journey of self-leadership: Leadership development along stages of psychological growth*. Midrand, South Africa: Knowledge Resources.

Diaz, A. (2022). Disturbing reports of sexual assaults in the metaverse: 'It's a free show'. *New York Post*. https://nypost.com/2022/05/27/women-are-being-sexually-assaulted-in-the-metaverse/?utm_source=twitter_sitebuttons&utm_medium=site%20buttons&utm_campaign=site%20buttons via @nypost

DiTomaso, N., Post, C., & Parks-Yancy, R. (2007). Workforce diversity and inequality: Power, status, and numbers. *Annual Review of Sociology*, 33, 473–501.

Djabi, M., & Shimada, S. (2017). Generational diversity in organisation: A meta-analysis. In *Management and diversity*. London, UK: Emerald Publishing Limited.

D'Netto, B., & Sohal, A. S. (1999). Human resource practices and workforce diversity: An empirical assessment. *International Journal of Manpower*.

Dobbin, F., & Kalev, A. (2016). Why diversity programs fail and what works better. *Harvard Business Review*, 94(7–8), 52.

Dobbin, F., & Kalev, A. (2018). Why doesn't diversity training work? The challenge for industry and academia. *Anthropology Now*, 10(2), 48–55.

Dobbin, F., & Kalev, A. (2022). *Getting to diversity: What works and what doesn't*. Cambridge, MA: Harvard University Press.

Dobusch, L. (2021). The inclusivity of inclusion approaches: A relational perspective on inclusion and exclusion in organizations. *Gender, Work & Organization*, 28(1), 379–396.

Doci, E., Knappert, L., Nijs, S., & Hofmans, J. (2023). Unpacking psychological inequalities in organisations: Psychological capital reconsidered. *Applied Psychology*, 72(1), 44–63.

Donaldson S., Kymlicka W. (2019). Animal labour in a post-work society. In Blattner C., Coultner K., Kymlicka W. (Eds.), *Animal labour: A new frontier of interspecies justice?* (pp. 207–228). Oxford University Press: Oxford.

Durham, W. H. (1991). *Coevolution: Genes, culture, and human diversity*. Stanford, CA: Stanford University Press.

Dwyer, S., Richard, O. C., & Chadwick, K. (2003). Gender diversity in management and firm performance: The influence of growth orientation and organizational culture. *Journal of Business Research*, 56(12), 1009–1019.

Eatwell, R., & Goodwin, M. (2018). *National populism: The revolt against liberal democracy*. London: Penguin UK.

Ebers, M., Hoch, V. R., Rosenkranz, F., Ruschemeier, H., & Steinrötter, B. (2021). The European commission's proposal for an artificial intelligence act – A critical assessment by members of the robotics and AI law society (RAILS). *J*, 4(4), 589–603.

EHRC (2021). *Equality and human rights commission, your rights under the equality act 2010*. www.equalityhumanrights.com/en/advice-and-guidance/your-rights-under-equality-act-2010, accessed 31 March 2021.

Einhorn, C., & Andreoni, M. (2023, January 14). Ecuador tried to curb drilling and protect the Amazon. The opposite happened. *The New York Times*. www.nytimes.com/2023/01/14/climate/ecuador-drilling-oil-amazon.html?smid=tw-share

Eisenberg, L. (1995). The social construction of the human brain. *American Journal of Psychiatry*, 152(11), 1563–1575.

Elfira, M., Wibawarta, B., Esther, R., & Febriand, F. (2021). Working from home: Women between public and domestic spheres after the outbreak of COVID-19. *International Review of Humanities Studies*, 6(1).

Ellingsæter, A. L., & Leira, A. (eds.). (2006). *Politicising parenthood in Scandinavia: Gender relations in welfare states*. Bristol, UK: Policy Press.

Ellis, K. M., & Keys, P. Y. (2015). Workforce diversity and shareholder value: A multi-level perspective. *Review of Quantitative Finance and Accounting*, 44(2), 191–212.

Ely, R. J., & Thomas, D. A. (2001). Cultural diversity at work: The effects of diversity perspectives on work group processes and outcomes. *Administrative Science Quarterly*, 46(2), 229–273.

Engin, Z., & Treleaven, P. (2019). Algorithmic government: Automating public services and supporting civil servants in using data science technologies. *The Computer Journal*, 62(3), 448–460.

Englehart, N. A., & Miller, M. K. (2014). The CEDAW effect: International law's impact on women's rights. *Journal of Human Rights*, 13(1), 22–47.

Erbil, C. (2021). Hümanist Yönetim Yaklaşımı İnsanı Niçin Ehlileştiremez? Yapay Hiyerarşileri Hayvan Emeğinde Ekofeminizm ile Sorgulama Girişimi. In H. Kapu (ed.), *29. National management and organization congress procedia*. Kars, Turkey: Kars Kafkas University Press.

Erbil, C. (2023). Eleştirel Yönetim Çalışmaları Perspektifinden Dijitalleşme. In A. Yılmaz (ed.), *İş'te Dijitalleşme*. Ankara: Nobel Akademi Yayıncılık.

Erbil, C., & Özbilgin, M. (2023). Worker silence in a turbulent neoliberal context: The case of mass privatisation of sugar factories in Turkey. *Human Resource Management Journal* (pp. 1–21). https://doi.org/10.1111/1748-8583.12506

Erbil, C., Özbilgin, M., & Bağlama, S. H. (2023). Duality of language as a tool for integration versus mobility at work: Utility of a polyphonic perspective. In P. Lecomte, M. Vigier, C. Gaibrois, & B. Beeler (eds.), *Understanding the dynamics of language and multilingualism in professional contexts: Advances in language-sensitive management research* (pp. 155–168). Cheltenham, UK: Edward Elgar Publishing.

Erbil, C., & Özen-Aytemur, J. (2023). Emek ve Ekoloji: Yönetsel Yaklaşımlar ve Öneriler. In A. A. Cengiz & B. Uçkan Hekimler (eds.), *Emeğin Hallerine Dair*. Ankara, Turkey: Yeniinsan Yayınevi.

Faludi, S. (2009). *Backlash: The undeclared war against American women*. New York City: Crown.

Feagin, J. (2013). *Systemic racism: A theory of oppression*. London, UK: Routledge.

Fenech, A. E., Kanji, S., & Vargha, Z. (2021). Gender-based exclusionary practices in performance appraisal. *Gender, Work and Organization*, 27(2), 427–442.

Fine, Marlene G. (1996/1973). Cultural diversity in the workplace: The state of the field. *The Journal of Business Communication*, 33(4), 485–502.

Fink, M. (2021). *The EU artificial intelligence act and access to justice*. Brussels, Belgium: EU Law Live.

Fitzsimmons, S., Ozbilgin, M., Nkomo, S. M., & Thomas, D. C. (2022). Equality, diversity and inclusion in international business: A review and research agenda. In *Academy of management proceedings* (Vol. 2022, No. 1, p. 15655). Briarcliff Manor, NY: Academy of Management.

Fletcher, O. (2022). UK financial services firms suffer from record skills shortage. *Insurance Journal*. www.insurancejournal.com/news/international/2022/08/10/679477.htm

Fobanjong, J. (2001). *Understanding the backlash against affirmative action*. Hauppauge, New York: Nova Publishers.

Fogel, R. W. (1994). *Without consent or contract: The rise and fall of American slavery*. New York City: WW Norton & Company.

Fogel, R. W. (2003). *The slavery debates, 1952–1990: A retrospective*. Baton Rouge, LA: LSU Press.

Foley, R. A., & Lahr, M. M. (2011). The evolution of the diversity of cultures. *Philosophical Transactions of the Royal Society of London. Series B, Biological Sciences*, 366(1567), 1080–1089. https://doi.org/10.1098/rstb.2010.0370

Forson, C. (2013). Contextualising migrant black business women's work-life balance experiences. *International Journal of Entrepreneurial Behavior & Research*, 19(5), 460–477. https://doi.org/10.1108/IJEBR-09-2011-0126

Forstenlechner, I., Lettice, F., & Özbilgin, M. F. (2012). Questioning quotas: Applying a relational framework for diversity management practices in the United Arab Emirates. *Human Resource Management Journal*, 22(3), 299–315.

Foss, N., & Klein, P. (2022). Why do companies go woke? *Academy of Management Perspectives*, 36(1), 1–16.

Foster, D. (2018). The health and well-being at work agenda: Good news for (disabled) workers or just a capital idea? *Work, Employment and Society*, 32(1), 186–197.

Fox, K. (2014). *Watching the English: The hidden rules of English behavior revised and updated*. London, UK: Nicholas Brealey.

Fox, S., & Stallworth, L. E. (2005). Racial/ethnic bullying: Exploring links between bullying and racism in the US workplace. *Journal of Vocational Behavior*, 66(3), 438–456.

Frank, R. (2008). *Richistan: A journey through the American wealth boom and the lives of the new rich*. New York City: Currency.

Frank, R. (2011). *The high-beta rich: How the manic wealthy will take us to the next boom, bubble, and bust*. York City: Crown Pub.

Fraser, H., & Taylor, N. (2018). *Women, anxiety, and companion animals: Toward a feminist animal studies of interspecies care and solidarity* (p. 155). Animaladies: Gender, Animals, and Madness.

Friedman, S., & Laurison, D. (2020). *The class ceiling: Why it pays to be privileged.* Policy Press.

Friedrich, C. J. (2013). 3. The unique character of totalitarian society. In *Totalitarianism* (pp. 47–60). Cambridge, MA: Harvard University Press.

Gaard, G. (2011). Ecofeminism revisited: Rejecting essentialism and re-placing species in a material feminist environmentalism. *Feminist Formations*, 23(2), 26–53.

Galbreath, J. (2018). Is board gender diversity linked to financial performance? The mediating mechanism of CSR. *Business & Society*, 57(5), 863–889.

Galizzi, G., Meliou, E., & Steccolini, I. (2021). Experiences and challenges with gender budgeting and accounting. Moving towards gender-responsive form of accountability? *Public Money and Management*, 41(7), 499–501.

Galletta, S., Mazzù, S., Naciti, V., & Vermiglio, C. (2022). Gender diversity and sustainability performance in the banking industry. *Corporate Social Responsibility and Environmental Management*, 29(1), 161–174.

Gardenswartz, L., Rowe, A., Digh, P., & Bennett, M. (2003). *The global diversity desk reference: Managing an international workforce.* San Francisco: Pfeiffer.

Garland, F., & Travis, M. (2018). Legislating intersex equality: Building the resilience of intersex people through law. *Legal Studies*, 38(4), 587–606.

Gash, V. (2009). Sacrificing their careers for their families? An analysis of the penalty to motherhood in Europe. *Social Indicators Research*, 93(3), 569–586.

Georgiadou, A., Metcalfe, B., Dickerson von Lockette, N., & Groutsis, D. (eds.). (2021). Special issue, Gender, bodies and identities in organization: Postcolonial critiques. *Gender, Work and Organization*, 28(5), 1719–1725.

Gezici Yalçın, M., & Tanriverdi, V. (2018). "Kavanozu Açan" Erkeklerle "Kafasını Kullanabilen" Kadınlar: Erkek Üniversite Öğrencilerinin Erkeklik Müzakereleri. *Masculinities: A Journal of Identity and Culture*, 9–10, 129–167.

Gezici Yalçın, M., & Tanriverdi, V. (2020). Cinsiyet farklarının inşasında ve bu farkların ortadan kaldırılmasında cinsiyet ifadesinin rolü. *Vira Verita E-Journal: Interdisciplinary Encounters*, 11, 82–114.

Gibbon, P., Bair, J., & Ponte, S. (2008). Governing global value chains: An introduction. *Economy and Society*, 37(3), 315–338.

Gibbs, P. (2018). The marketingization of higher education. In M. Peters (ed.), *Encyclopedia of educational philosophy and theory.* Singapore: Springer.

Gill, R., Kelan, E. K., & Scharff, C. M. (2017). A postfeminist sensibility at work. *Gender, Work & Organization*, 24(3), 226–244.

Gillborn, D., Bhopal, K., Crawford, C. E., Demack, S., Gholami, R., Kitching, K., Kiwan, D., & Warmington, P. (2021). *Evidence for the commission on race and ethnic disparities.* Working Paper. Birmingham, UK: University of Birmingham.

Goc, K., & Kusku, F. (2020). Sustainable human resources management from the language of reports. *Research Journal of Business and Management (RJBM)*, 7(2), 95–115.

Gong, Y., Chow, I. H. S., & Ahlstrom, D. (2011). Cultural diversity in China: Dialect, job embeddedness, and turnover. *Asia Pacific Journal of Management*, 28(2), 221–238.

Gonzalez, J. A., & DeNisi, A. S. (2009). Cross-level effects of demography and diversity climate on organizational attachment and firm effectiveness. *Journal of Organizational Behavior: The International Journal of Industrial, Occupational and Organizational Psychology and Behavior*, 30(1), 21–40.

Goodman, S., Sirriyeh, A., & McMahon, S. (2017). The evolving (re) categorisations of refugees throughout the "refugee/migrant crisis". *Journal of Community & Applied Social Psychology*, 27(2), 105–114.

Gowder, P. (2013). The rule of law and equality. *Law and Philosophy*, 32(5), 565–618.

Graff, A., Kapur, R., & Walters, S. D. (2019). Introduction: Gender and the rise of the global right. *Signs: Journal of Women in Culture and Society*, 44(3), 541–560.

Greene, A. M., Kirton, G., & Wrench, J. (2005). Trade union perspectives on diversity management: A comparison of the UK and Denmark. *European Journal of Industrial Relations*, 11(2), 179–196.

Greenhalgh, T. (1999). Narrative based medicine in an evidence based world. *BMJ*, 318(7179), 323–325.

Greenhalgh, T., Ozbilgin, M. F., & Contandriopoulos, D. (2021). Orthodoxy, illusio, and playing the scientific game: A Bourdieusian analysis of infection control science in the COVID-19 pandemic. *Wellcome Open Research*, 6.

Greenhalgh, T., Ozbilgin, M. F., Prainsack, B., & Shaw, S. (2019). Moral entrepreneurship, the power-knowledge nexus, and the Cochrane "crisis". *Journal of Evaluation in Clinical Practice*, 25(5), 717–725.

Greenhalgh, T., Ozbilgin, M. F., & Tomlinson, D. (2022). How COVID-19 spreads: Narratives, counter narratives, and social dramas. *BMJ*, 378.

Greenhalgh, T., & Russell, J. (2009). Evidence-based policymaking: A critique. *Perspectives in Biology and Medicine*, 52(2), 304–318.

Griffiths, M., & Yeo, C. (2021). The UK's hostile environment: Deputising immigration control. *Critical Social Policy*, 41(4), 521–544.

Gross, N., Jacobs, C. E., Marar, R., & Lewis, A. (2022). 'This school is too diverse': Fragile feelings among white boys at elite independent schools. *Whiteness and Education*, 1–19.

Groutsis, D., Cooper, R., & Whitwell, G. (2018b). *Beyond the pale: Cultural diversity and non-executive directors of the ASX100*. University of Sydney, the Australian Human Rights Commission and Australian Institute of Company Directors, Australia.

Groutsis, D., Kaabel, A., & Wright, C. (2023). Temporary migrants as dehumanised 'Other' in the time of COVID-19: We're all in this together? *Work, Employment and Society*. https://doi.org/10.1177/09500170221142723

Groutsis, D., Martin, L., Lattouf, A., Soutphommasane, T., Lumby, C., Young, N., Crawford, J., & Robertson, A. (2022). *Who gets to tell Australian stories 2.0*. Sydney: Multicultural Development Association.

Groutsis, D., O'Leary, J., & Russell, G. (2018a). Capitalizing on the cultural and linguistic diversity of mobile talent: Lessons from an Australian study. *International Journal of Human Resource Management*, 29(11), 1821–1845.

Groutsis, D., van den Broek, D., & Harvey, W. (2015). Transformations in network governance: The case of migration intermediaries. *Journal of Ethnic and Migration Studies*, 41(10), 1558–1576.

Groutsis, D., Vassilopoulou, J., Kyriakidou, O., & Özbilgin, M. F. (2020). The "new" migration for work phenomenon: The pursuit of emancipation and recognition in the context of work. *Work, Employment and Society*, 34(5), 864–882.

Guerrero, M. (2022). Does workforce diversity matter on corporate venturing? *Economics of Innovation and New Technology*, 31(1–2), 35–53.

Guler, S. (2022). *Strategic management of equality, diversity, and inclusion in organisations and its impact on team performance* (PhD thesis, Brunel Business School, Brunel University London).

Gulson, K., Benn, C., Kitto, K., Knight, S., & Swift, T. (2021). Algorithms can decide your marks, your work prospects and your financial security. How do you know they're fair? *The Conversation*. https://theconversation.com/algorithms-can-decide-your-marks-your-work-prospects-and-your-financial-security-how-do-you-know-theyre-fair-171590

Gwiazda, A. (2021). Right-wing populism and feminist politics: The case of Law and Justice in Poland. *International Political Science Review*, 42(5), 580–595.

Haile, G. G., Tang, Q., Hosseini-Moghari, S. M., Liu, X., Gebremicael, T. G., Leng, G., . . . & Yun, X. (2020). Projected impacts of climate change on drought patterns over East Africa. *Earth's Future*, 8(7), e2020EF001502.

Halkitis, P. N., & Krause, K. D. (2021). COVID-19 in LGBTQ populations. *Annals of LGBTQ Public and Population Health*, 1(4), 249–253.

Hammack, P. L., Frost, D. M., & Hughes, S. D. (2019). Queer intimacies: A new paradigm for the study of relationship diversity. *The Journal of Sex Research*, 56(4–5), 556–592.

Hamza-Orlinska, A. (2017). Corporate commitment to diversity in the local perspective of the Polish subsidiary of a multinational corporation: A qualitative exploratory study. *Journal of Corporate Responsibility and Leadership*, 4(4), 19–33.

Handlovsky, I., Bungay, V., Oliffe, J., & Johnson, J. (2018). Developing resilience: Gay men's response to systemic discrimination. *American Journal of Men's Health*, 12(5), 1473–1485.

Hansen, K., & Seierstad, C. (2017). Introduction: CSR and diversity management. In *Corporate social responsibility and diversity management* (pp. 1–40). Cham: Springer.

Hao, K. (2022). Artificial intelligence is creating a new colonial world order. *MIT Technology Review*. www.technologyreview.com/2022/04/19/1049592/artificial-intelligence-colonialism/

Haraway, D. (2006). A cyborg manifesto: Science, technology, and socialist-feminism in the late 20th century. In *The international handbook of virtual learning environments* (pp. 117–158). Dordrecht: Springer.

Hardin, G. (1968). The tragedy of the commons: The population problem has no technical solution; it requires a fundamental extension in morality. *Science*, 162(3859), 1243–1248.

Harris, J., Jain, S., & Codur, A. M. (2022). *Climate conference COP27: Focus on agriculture and forests*. https://sites.tufts.edu/gdae/files/2022/11/ClimatePolicyBrief-16_2022.pdf

Harrison, D. A., & Klein, K. J. (2007). What's the difference? Diversity constructs as separation, variety, or disparity in organizations. *Academy of Management Review*, 32(4), 1199–1228.

Harrison, D. A., Price, K. H., & Bell, M. P. (1998). Beyond relational demography: Time and the effects of surface-and deep-level diversity on work group cohesion. *Academy of Management Journal*, 41(1), 96–107.

Haslam, N. (2006). Dehumanization: An integrative review. *Personality and Social Psychology Review*, 10(3), 252–264.

Haslam, N. (2011). Genetic essentialism, neuroessentialism, and stigma: Commentary on Dar-Nimrod and Heine (2011). *Psychological Bulletin*, 137(5), 819–824. https://doi.org/10.1037/a0022386

Hayes, B. G., & Marangudakis, M. (2001). Religion and attitudes towards nature in Britain. *The British Journal of Sociology*, 52(1), 139–155.

Healy, G. (2016). Diversity management. In *Encyclopedia of human resource management*. Cheltenham, UK: Edward Elgar Publishing Limited.

Healy, G., & Ahamed, M. M. (2019). Gender pay gap, voluntary interventions and recession: The case of the British financial services sector. *British Journal of Industrial Relations*, 57(2), 302–327.

Healy, G., Bradley, H., & Forson, C. (2011). Intersectional sensibilities in analysing inequality regimes in public sector organizations. *Gender, Work & Organization*, 18(5), 467–487.

Healy, G., Özbilgin, M., & Aliefendioğlu, H. (2005). Academic employment and gender: A Turkish challenge to vertical sex segregation. *European Journal of Industrial Relations*, 11(2), 247–264.

Hecan, M., & Farhaoui, F. (2021). The coercive power and democratic transition in the post-uprising Middle East and North Africa. *Democratization*, 1–20. https://doi.org/10.1080/13510347.2021.1897788

Hennekam, S., Bacouel-Jentjens, S., & Yang, I. (2019). Ethnic diversity management in France: A multilevel perspective. *International Journal of Manpower*, 40(3), 365–378. https://doi.org/10.1108/IJM-07-2018-0236

Hennekam, S., Peterson, J., Tahssain-Gay, L., & Dumazert, J.-P. (2018). Managing religious diversity in secular organizations in France. *Employee Relations*, 40(5), 746–761. https://doi.org/10.1108/ER-06-2017-0142

Hennekam, S., Richard, S., & Özbilgin, M. (2023). How social structures influence the labour market participation of individuals with mental illness: A Bourdieusian perspective. *Journal of Management Studies*, 60(1), 174–203.

Hennekam, S., Tahssain-Gay, L., & Syed, J. (2017). Contextualising diversity management in the Middle East and North Africa: A relational perspective. *Human Resource Management Journal*, 27(3), 459–476.

Hennessy, R., & Ingraham, C. (1997). *Materialist feminism: A reader in class, difference, and women's lives*. London, UK: Psychology Press.

Herring, C. (2009). Does diversity pay?: Race, gender, and the business case for diversity. *American Sociological Review*, 74(2), 208–224.

Hicks, D. A. (2002). Spiritual and religious diversity in the workplace: Implications for leadership. *The Leadership Quarterly*, 13(4), 379–396.

Hicks, S. (2003). The Christian right and homophobic discourse: A response to 'evidence' that lesbian and gay parenting damages children. *Sociological Research Online*, 8(4), 1–7.

Hill, R. J. (2009). Incorporating queers: Blowback, backlash, and other forms of resistance to workplace diversity initiatives that support sexual minorities. *Advances in Developing Human Resources*, 11(1), 37–53. https://doi.org/10.1177/1523422308328128

Hird, M. J. (2000). Gender's nature: Intersexuality, transsexualism and the "sex"/"gender" binary. *Feminist Theory*, 1(3), 347–364.

Hoffman, S. D. (1977). *Discrimination over the life-cycle: A longitudinal analysis of black-white experience-earnings profiles*. Ann Arbor, Michigan: University of Michigan.

Hogg, M. A., & Ridgeway, C. L. (2003). Social identity: Sociological and social psychological perspectives. *Social Psychology Quarterly*, 97–100.

Holck, L., & Muhr, S. L. (2017). Unequal solidarity? Towards a norm-critical approach to welfare logics. *Scandinavian Journal of Management*, 33(1), 1–11.

Holmes IV, O. (2019). The antecedents and outcomes of heteronormativity in organizations. In *Oxford encyclopedia of business and management*. Oxford: Oxford University Press.

Holmes IV, O. (2020a). Police brutality and four other ways racism kills Black people. *Equality, Diversity and Inclusion: An International Journal*, 39(4), 402–415. https://doi.org/10.1108/EDI-06-2020-0153

Holmes IV, O. (2020b). Sexuality blindness: A new frontier of diversity resistance. In K. M. Thomas (ed.), *Diversity resistance in organizations* (2nd ed., pp. 34–57). New York: Lawrence Erlbaum Associates.

Holmes IV, O., Jiang, K., Avery, D. R., McKay, P. F., Oh, I. S., & Tillman, C. J. (2021). A meta-analysis integrating 25 years of diversity climate research. *Journal of Management*, 47(6), 1357–1382.

Holmes IV, O., Lopiano, G., & Hall, E. V. (2019). A review of compensatory strategies to mitigate bias. *Personnel Assessment and Decisions*, 5(2), 23–34 (Special Issue: Reducing Discrimination in the Workplace).

Holmes IV, O., Whitman, M. V., Campbell, K., & Johnson, D. E. (2016). Exploring the social identity threat response framework. *Equality, Diversity and Inclusion: An International Journal*, 35(3), 205–220.

Home Office (2022). *Official statistics of hate crime, England and Wales, 2021 to 2022, Published 6 October 2022*. www.gov.uk/government/statistics/hate-crime-england-and-wales-2021-to-2022/hate-crime-england-and-wales-2021-to-2022

Hoque, K., & Noon, M. (2004). Equal opportunities policy and practice in Britain: Evaluating the "empty shell" hypothesis. *Work, Employment and Society*, 18(3), 481–506. https://doi.org/10.1177/0950017004045547

Huber, D. F. (2013). *Corporate diversity programs and employee networks: A study of congruence between organizational perspectives* (Doctoral dissertation, Capella University).

Hundschell, A. S., Backmann, J., Tian, A. W., & Hoegl, M. (2019, July). Inclusive work environments and multinational team performance: The role of team resilience. In *Academy of management proceedings* (Vol. 2019, No. 1, p. 13571). Briarcliff Manor, NY: Academy of Management.

Husain, L., Greenhalgh, T., Hughes, G., Finlay, T., & Wherton, J. (2022). Desperately seeking intersectionality in digital health disparity research: Narrative review to inform a richer theorization of multiple disadvantage. *Journal of Medical Internet Research*, 24(12), e42358. https://doi.org/10.2196/42358

Huse, M. (2016). The 'golden skirts': Lessons from Norway about women on corporate boards of directors. In *Diversity quotas, diverse perspectives* (pp. 29–42). London, UK: Routledge.

Hyman, R., Klarsfeld, A., Ng, E., & Haq, R. (2012). Introduction: Social regulation of diversity and equality. *European Journal of Industrial Relations*, 18(4), 279–292.

ILGA (2021). https://ilga.org/sites/default/files/downloads/ENG_ILGA_World_map_sexual_orientation_laws_dec2020.png

ILO (International Labour Organisation) (2021). *The need for social justice*. www.ilo.org/global/standards/introduction-to-international-labour-standards/need-for-social-justice/lang-en/index.htm%2013, accessed 31 March 2021.

Jackson, S. E., & Alvarez, E. B. (1992). Working through diversity as a strategic imperative. In S. E. Jackson (ed.), *The professional practice series. Diversity in the workplace: Human resources initiatives* (pp. 13–29). New York: Guilford Press.

Jackson, S. E., & Joshi, A. (2004). Diversity in social context: A multi-attribute, multilevel analysis of team diversity and sales performance. *Journal of Organizational Behavior: The International Journal of Industrial, Occupational and Organizational Psychology and Behavior*, 25(6), 675–702.

Jahoda, G. (2015). *Images of savages: Ancient roots of modern prejudice in Western culture*. London, UK: Routledge.

Jamali, D. (2009). Constraints and opportunities facing women entrepreneurs in developing countries: A relational perspective. *Gender in Management: An International Journal*, 24(4), 232–251.

Jammaers, E., Zanoni, P., & Williams, J. (2021). Not all fish are equal: A Bourdieuan analysis of ableism in a financial services company. *International Journal of Human Resource Management*, 32(11), 2519–2544.

Janssens, M., & Zanoni, P. (2021). Making diversity research matter for social change: New conversations beyond the firm. *Organization Theory*, 2, 1–21. http://doi.org/10.1177/26317877211004603

Jarzombek, M. (2016). *Digital Stockholm syndrome in the post-ontological age*. Minneapolis, MN: University of Minnesota Press.

Jennifer Ho, L. C., & Taylor, M. E. (2007). An empirical analysis of triple bottom-line reporting and its determinants: Evidence from the United States and Japan. *Journal of International Financial Management & Accounting*, 18(2), 123–150.

Jones, J. M., Dovidio, J. F., & Vietze, D. L. (2013). *The psychology of diversity: Beyond prejudice and racism*. Hoboken, NJ: John Wiley & Sons.

Jonsen, K., & Özbilgin, M. (2014). Models of global diversity management. In *Diversity at work: The practice of inclusion* (pp. 364–390). San Francisco: John Wiley & Sons, Inc.

Jonsen, K., Tatli, A., Özbilgin, M. F., & Bell, M. P. (2013). The tragedy of the uncommons: Reframing workforce diversity. *Human Relations*, 66(2), 271–294.

Joo, M. K., Kong, D., & Atwater, L. (2018, July). Workforce gender diversity, human resource practices, and organizational outcomes. In *Academy of management proceedings* (Vol. 2018, No. 1, p. 17603). Briarcliff Manor, NY: Academy of Management.

Joo, M. K., Lee, J.-Y., Kong, D. T., & Jolly, P. M. (2022). Gender diversity advantage at middle management: Implications for high performance work system improvement and organizational performance. *Human Resource Management*, 1–21. https://doi.org/10.1002/hrm.22159

Jung, C. G. (2010). *Synchronicity: An acausal connecting principle* (From Vol. 8. of the collected works of CG Jung) (New in paper). Princeton, NJ: Princeton University Press.

Jussupow, E., Benbasat, I., & Heinzl, A. (2020). Why are we averse towards algorithms? A comprehensive literature review on algorithm aversion. *Journal of Information Technology*, 35(1), 1–28.

Kakabadse, N. K., Figueira, C., Nicolopoulou, K., Hong Yang, J., Kakabadse, A. P., & Özbilgin, M. F. (2015). Gender diversity and board performance: Women's experiences and perspectives. *Human Resource Management*, 54(2), 265–281.

Kalev, A., Dobbin, F., & Kelly, E. (2006). Best practices or best guesses? Assessing the efficacy of corporate affirmative action and diversity policies. *American Sociological Review*, 71(4), 589–617.

Kamasak, R., & Ozbilgin, M. F. (2021). English medium instruction (EMI): Is it a vehicle to achieve linguistic and content knowledge or a marketing tool in higher education? In B. Christiansen & J. Branch (eds.), *The marketisation of higher education: Practices and policies* (pp. 321–341). London: Palgrave Macmillan.

Kamasak, R., Ozbilgin, M. F., Baykut, S., & Yavuz, M. (2020a). Moving from intersectional hostility to intersectional solidarity: Insights from LGBTQ individuals in Turkey. *Journal of Organizational Change Management*, 33(3), 456–476. https://doi.org/10.1108/JOCM-11-2018-0328

Kamasak, R., Ozbilgin, M. F., Kucukaltan, B., & Yavuz, M. (2020b). Regendering of dynamic managerial capabilities in the context of binary perspectives on gender diversity. *Gender in Management: An International Journal*, 35(1), 19–36.

Kamasak, R., Ozbilgin, M. F., & Yavuz, M. (2020c). Understanding intersectional analyses. In E. King, Q. Roberson, & M. Hebl (eds.), *Research on social issues in management on pushing understanding of diversity in organizations* (pp. 93–115). Charlotte: Information Age Publishing.

Kamasak, R., Özbilgin, M. F., Yavuz, M., & Akalin, C. (2019). Race discrimination at work in the United Kingdom. In *Race discrimination and management of ethnic diversity and migration at work*. London, UK: Emerald Publishing Limited.

Kamasak, R., Özbilgin, M. F., Yavuz, M., April, K., & Vassilopoulou, J. (2023). 'We can't go back to normal': Diversity management in global organisations: Introducing the global value chain (GVC) approach. In C. Maheshkar & V. Sharma (eds.), *Handbook of research on cross-cultural business and management*. Wilmington, DE: Vernon Press.

Kamasak, R., & Palalar Alkan, D. (2023). Parenthood in academia. In M. Ozbilgin (ed.), *International perspectives on equality, diversity and inclusion series*. Bingley: Emerald Publishing.

Kamasak, R., Palalar Alkan, D., & Yalcinkaya, B. (2023). Emerging trends of Industry 4.0 in equality, diversity and implementations. In B. Kucukaltan (ed.), *Contemporary approaches in equality, diversity and inclusion: Strategic and technological perspectives*. Bingley: Emerald Publishing.

Kanai, A., & Gill, R. (2020). Woke? Affect, neoliberalism, marginalised identities and consumer culture. *New Formations*, 102(102), 10–27.

Kanji, S., & Cahusac, E. (2015). Who am I? Mothers' shifting identities, loss and sensemaking after workplace exit. *Human Relations*, 68(9), 1415–1436.

Kanter, R. M. (1977). Some effects of proportions on group life. In *The gender gap in psychotherapy* (pp. 53–78). Boston, MA: Springer.

Karabacakoglu, F., & Özbilgin, M. (2010). Global diversity management at Ericsson: The business case. In *Cases in strategic management* (pp. 79–91). London: Mcgraw-Hill.

Karakas, F., Sarigollu, E., & Uygur, S. (2017). Exploring the diversity of virtues through the lens of moral imagination: A qualitative inquiry into organizational virtues in the Turkish context. *Journal of Business Ethics*, 141(4), 731–744.

Karakas, S., & Özbilgin, M. F. (2019). Reflections on definitions, methods, challenges of and ways forward for ethnic counting in Europe. In *Race discrimination and management of ethnic diversity and migration at work*. London, UK: Emerald Publishing Limited.

Karam, C. M. (2022). Understanding diversity in the Lebanese workplace: Legal protections in the context of protracted crises and occupation. In *Research handbook on new frontiers of equality and diversity at work* (pp. 132–159). Chetenham, UK: Edward Elgar Publishing.

Karatas-Ozkan, M. (2018). Diversity dimensions of entrepreneurship. In J.-F. Chanlat & M. Ozbilgin (eds.), *Management and diversity: Perspectives from different national contexts* (pp. 209–229) (International Perspectives on Equality, Diversity and Inclusion; Vol. 4). Bingley, UK: Emerald Group Publishing Limited. https://doi.org/10.1108/S2051-233320160000004011

Karatas-Ozkan, M., & Chell, E. (2015). Gender inequalities in academic innovation and enterprise: A bourdieuian analysis. *British Journal of Management*, 26(1), 109–125.

Karatas-Ozkan, M., Grinevich, V., Baines, L., & Baruch, Y. (2022). *Women leaders South West programme (WLSW): Experiences of people with disadvantaged backgrounds with leadership and (social) entrepreneurship in arts: Implications for entrepreneurial and policy ecosystems; Report*, November 2022. Southampton, UK: University of Southampton.

Karatas-Ozkan, M., Inal, G., & Ozbilgin, M. (2010). Turkish women entrepreneurs: Opportunities and challenges. In S. Fielden (ed.), *International research handbook on successful women entrepreneurs*. London, UK: SAGE Publications.

Kaytaz, E. S. (2015). At the border of 'Fortress Europe': Immigration detention in Turkey. In *Immigration detention* (pp. 73–82). London, UK: Routledge.

Kelan, E. K. (2009). Gender fatigue: The ideological dilemma of gender neutrality and discrimination in organizations. *Canadian Journal of Administrative Sciences/Revue Canadienne des Sciences de l'Administration*, 26(3), 197–210.

Kelan, E. K. (2014). From biological clocks to unspeakable inequalities: The intersectional positioning of young professionals. *British Journal of Management*, 25(4), 790–804.

Kelan, E. K. (2022). Automation anxiety and augmentation aspiration – Subtexts of the future of work. *British Journal of Management*. https://doi.org/10.1111/1467-8551.12679.

Kelly, M. P., Heath, I., Howick, J., & Greenhalgh, T. (2015). The importance of values in evidence-based medicine. *BMC Medical Ethics*, 16(1), 1–8.

Khasawneh, O. Y. (2018). Technophobia: Examining its hidden factors and defining it. *Technology in Society*, 54(1), 93–100.

Kidder, D. L., Lankau, M. J., Chrobot-Mason, D., Mollica, K. A., & Friedman, R. A. (2004). Backlash toward diversity initiatives: Examining the impact of diversity program justification, personal and group outcomes. *International Journal of Conflict Management*, 15(1), 77–102.

King, J. E., & Holmes IV, O. (2012). Spirituality, recruiting and total wellness: Overcoming challenges to organizational attraction. *Journal of Management, Spirituality, and Religion*, 9, 237–253.

Kipfer, S. (2019). What colour is your vest? Reflections on the yellow vest movement in France. *Studies in Political Economy*, 100(3), 209–231.

Kirby, A., & Gibbon, H. (2018). Dyslexia and employment. *Perspectives on Language and Literacy*, 44(1), 27–31.

Kirby, A., & Smith, T. (2021). *Neurodiversity at work: Drive innovation, performance and productivity with a neurodiverse workforce*. London, UK: Kogan Page Publishers.

Kircal Şahin, A. (2022). Migration experiences of the highly skilled and stay-at-home Turkish mothers in the UK. *Migration Letters*, 19(3).

Kırcal Şahin, A. (2023). *Yüksek Eğitimli Ev Hanımı Annelerin Uluslararası Göçü*. Istanbul, Turkey: Cinius Yayınları.

Kirton, G., & Greene, A. M. (2021). *The dynamics of managing diversity and inclusion: A critical approach*. London, UK: Routledge.

Kirts, L. (2021). Upsetting boundaries: Trans queer interspecies ecofeminisms. In G. Gaard & C. Willett (eds.), *Ecofeminism: Feminist intersections with other animals and the earth* (pp. 373–386). London, UK: Bloomsbury Academic.

Kiwan, N. (2011). Response to Annette: New friends and old foes? Diversity politics and national identity in Sarkozy's France. *Ethnicities*, 11(3), 403–407.

Klaesson, J., & Öner, Ö. (2021). Ethnic enclaves and segregation – Self-employment and employment patterns among forced migrants. *Small Business Economics*, 56, 985–1006.

Klaesson, J., Öner, Ö., & Pennerstorfer, D. (2021). Getting the first job: Size and quality of ethnic enclaves and refugee labor market entry. *Journal of Regional Science*, 61(1), 112–139.

Klarsfeld, A. (2009). Managing diversity: The virtue of coercion. In A. Konrad, P. Prasad, & J. K. Pringle (eds.), *Equality, diversity and inclusion at work: A research companion* (pp. 321–335). London, UK: SAGE Publications.

Klarsfeld, A., Booysen, L. A., Ng, E., Tatli, A., & Roper, I. (2014). *International handbook on diversity management at work: Country perspectives on diversity and equal treatment.* Cheltenham, UK: Edward Elgar Publishing.

Klarsfeld, A., Knappert, L., Kornau, A., Ngunjiri, F. W., & Sieben, B. (2019). Diversity in under-researched countries: New empirical fields challenging old theories? *Equality, Diversity and Inclusion,* 38(7), 694–704. https://doi.org/10.1108/EDI-03-2019-0110

Klarsfeld, A., Ng, E., & Tatli, A. (2012). Social regulation and diversity management: A comparative study of France, Canada and the UK. *European Journal of Industrial Relations,* 18(4), 309–327.

Knappert, L., Kornau, A., & Figengül, M. (2018). Refugees' exclusion at work and the intersection with gender: Insights from the Turkish-Syrian border. *Journal of Vocational Behavior,* 105, 62–82.

Knappert, L., van Dijk, H., & Ross, V. (2020). Refugees' inclusion at work: A qualitative cross-level analysis. *Career Development International,* 25(1), 32–48. https://doi.org/10.1108/CDI-01-2018-0021

Knappert, L., van Dijk, H., Yuan, S., Engel, Y., van Prooijen, J. W., & Krouwel, A. (2021). Personal contact with refugees is key to welcoming them: An analysis of politicians' and citizens' attitudes towards refugee integration. *Political Psychology,* 42(3), 423–442.

Knight, C., & Sang, K. (2020). 'At home, he's a pet, at work he's a colleague and my right arm': Police dogs and the emerging posthumanist agenda. *Culture and Organization,* 26(5–6), 355–371.

Koall, I. (2001). *Managing gender & diversity. Von der Homogenität zur Heterogenität in der Organisation der Unternehmung.* Münster: LIT-Verlag.

Kochan, T., Bezrukova, K., Ely, R., Jackson, S., Joshi, A., Jehn, K., . . . & Thomas, D. (2003). The effects of diversity on business performance: Report of the diversity research network. *Human Resource Management: Published in Cooperation with the School of Business Administration, The University of Michigan and in alliance with the Society of Human Resources Management,* 42(1), 3–21.

Köllen, T. (ed.). (2016). *Sexual orientation and transgender issues in organizations: Global perspectives on LGBT workforce diversity.* Berlin, Germany: Springer.

Köllen, T., Kakkuri-Knuuttila, M. L., & Bendl, R. (2018). An indisputable "holy trinity"? On the moral value of equality, diversity, and inclusion. *Equality, Diversity and Inclusion: An International Journal,* 37(5), 438–449.

Konrad, A. M., Prasad, P., & Pringle, J. K. (2005). *Workplace diversity.* London, UK: SAGE.

Korkmaz, A. V., van Engen, M. L., Knappert, L., & Schalk, R. (2022). About and beyond leading uniqueness and belongingness: A systematic review of inclusive leadership research. *Human Resource Management Review,* 100894, ISO 690.

Kornau, A., Knappert, L., Tatli, A., & Sieben, B. (2022). Contested fields of equality, diversity and inclusion at work: An institutional work lens on power relations and actors' strategies in Germany and Turkey. *The International Journal of Human Resource Management,* 1–35.

Kossek, E. E., & Lobel, S. A. (1996). *Managing diversity.* Cambridge, MA: Blackwell Publishers.

Kossek, E. E., Lobel, S. A., & Brown, J. (2006). Human resource strategies to manage workforce diversity. In A. M. Konrad, P. Prasad, & J. K. Pringle (eds.), *Handbook of workplace diversity* (pp. 53–74). Oxford: Oxford University Press.

Köybaşı, S. (2018). Yeni Bir Anayasal Hak Öznesi Olarak Hayvan – I. *Anayasa Hukuku Dergisi,* 7(13), 103–156.

Krais, B. (1993). *Gender and symbolic violence: Female oppression in the light of Pierre Bourdieu's theory of social* (p. 156). Bourdieu: Critical Perspectives.

Krause, E. L. (2001). "Empty cradles" and the quiet revolution: Demographic discourse and cultural struggles of gender, race, and class in Italy. *Cultural Anthropology,* 16(4), 576–611.

Krieger, L. H. (ed.). (2010). *Backlash against the ADA: Reinterpreting disability rights.* Michigan, Ann Arbor: University of Michigan Press.

Küçükaltan, B. (2018). Örgütsel Başarı-Performans Açısından Yönetim. In A. Akdemir (ed.), *Örgütlerin Yönetimi: Kavramsal-Kuramsal, Tematik ve Kurumsal Açılardan Yönetim* (pp. 356–371). Istanbul, Turkey: Beta Yayınları. ISBN: 978-605-242-233-5.

Kucukaltan, B. (2021). A cross-country study on women entrepreneurship through the CAGE analysis: Evidences from China and Turkey. *Optimum Ekonomi ve Yönetim Bilimleri Dergisi,* 8(1), 19–42. https://doi.org/10.17541/optimum.748424

Kucukaltan, B., & Ozbilgin, M. F. (2019a). Managing diverse talent in the global context. In: D. G. Collings, H. Scullion, & P. M. Caligiuri (eds.), *Global talent management* (2nd ed., pp. 200–209). London, UK: Routledge. ISBN: 978-1-138-71245-4.

Kucukaltan, B., & Ozbilgin, M. F. (2019b). Cosmopolitanism and entrepreneurship in Istanbul and London: A symbiotic relationship in context (Chapter 5). In N. Mouraviev & N. Kakabadse (eds.), *Entrepreneurship and global cities: Diversity, opportunity and cosmopolitanism*. London, UK: Routledge. ISBN: 978-0-367-14056-4.

Kurz, K., & Muller, W. (1987). Class mobility in the industrial world. *Annual Review of Sociology*, 13(1), 417–442.

Küskü, F., Aracı, Ö., & Özbilgin, M. F. (2021). What happens to diversity at work in the context of a toxic triangle? Accounting for the gap between discourses and practices of diversity management. *Human Resource Management Journal*, 31(2), 553–574.

Küskü, F., Araci, O., Tanriverdi, V., & Ozbilgin, M. F. (2022). Beyond the three monkeys of workforce diversity: Who hears, sees, and speaks up? *Frontiers in Psychology*, 13, 879862.

Küskü, F., Özbilgin, M., & Özkale, L. (2007, March). Against the tide: Gendered prejudice and disadvantage in engineering study from a comparative perspective. *Gender, Work and Organization*, 14(2), 109–129 (SSCI). ISSN: 0968–6673. https://doi.org/10.1111/J.1468-0432.2007.00335.X

Kusters, A. (2017). Autogestion and competing hierarchies: Deaf and other perspectives on diversity and the right to occupy space in the Mumbai suburban trains. *Social & Cultural Geography*, 18(2), 201–223.

Kyriakidou, O., Kyriacou, O., Özbilgin, M., & Dedoulis, E. (2016). Equality, diversity and inclusion in accounting. *Critical Perspectives on Accounting*, 35, 1–12.

Kyriakidou, O., & Ozbilgin, M. F. (eds.). (2006). *Relational perspectives in organizational studies: A research companion*. Cheltenham, UK: Edward Elgar Publishing. ISBN: 9781845421250.

Lambert, W. E., & Taylor, D. M. (1990). *Coping with cultural and racial diversity in urban America*. New York: Praeger Publishers.

Lang, R. (2009). The United Nations convention on the right and dignities for persons with disability: A panacea for ending disability discrimination? *Alter*, 3(3), 266–285.

Lantz-Deaton, C., Tabassum, N., & McIntosh, B. (2018). Through the glass ceiling: Is mentoring the way forward. *International Journal of Human Resources Development and Management*, 18(3/4), 167–197.

Laumann, E. O., Gagnon, J. H., Michael, R. T., & Michaels, S. (1994). *The socialorganization of sexuality: Sexual practices in the United States*. Chicago: University of Chicago Press.

Lauring, J. (2013). International diversity management: Global ideals and local responses. *British Journal of Management*, 24(2), 211–224.

Laville, S., & Watts, J. (2019, September 21). Across the globe, millions join the biggest climate protest ever. *The Guardian*. www.theguardian.com/environment/2019/sep/21/across-the-globe-millions-join-biggest-climate-protest-ever, accessed 25 March 2021.

Ledwith, S., & Colgan, F. (2003). Tackling gender, diversity and trade union democracy: A worldwide project? In *Gender, diversity and trade unions* (pp. 17–39). London, UK: Routledge.

Lepkowsky, C. M. (2017). Technological diversity: A cost-caving, person-centered alternative to systemic techno centric and technological provider bias. *Psychology and Behavioral Medicine Open Access Journal*, 1–7.

Lesińska, M. (2014). The European backlash against immigration and multiculturalism. *Journal of Sociology*, 50(1), 37–50. https://doi.org/10.1177/1440783314522189

Leslie, L. M., & Gelfand, M. J. (2008). The who and when of internal gender discrimination claims: An interactional model. *Organizational Behavior and Human Decision Processes*, 107(2), 123–140.

Leung, R., & Williams, R. (2019). #MeToo and intersectionality: An examination of the #MeToo movement through the R. Kelly scandal. *Journal of Communication Inquiry*, 43(4), 349–371. https://doi.org/10.1177/0196859919874138

Liedtka, J. (2015). Perspective: Linking design thinking with innovation outcomes through cognitive bias reduction. *Journal of Product Innovation Management*, 32(6), 925–938.

Linnehan, F., Chrobot-Mason, D., & Konrad, A. M. (2006). Diversity attitudes and norms: The role of ethnic identity and relational demography. *Journal of Organizational Behavior: The International Journal of Industrial, Occupational and Organizational Psychology and Behavior*, 27(4), 419–442.

Lopez Areu, M. (2018). Narendra Modi's Hindu populism: Reimagining the Indian nation. *Revista Cidob D Afers Internationals*, 119, 113–134.

Lorenzo, R., & Reeves, M. (2018). How and where diversity drives financial performance. *Harvard Business Review*, 1–5.

Lowndes, J. (2017). Populism in the United States. In *The Oxford handbook of populism* (pp. 232–247). Oxford, UK: Oxford University Press.

Lubensky, M. E., Holland, S. L., Wiethoff, C., & Crosby, F. J. (2004). Diversity and sexual orientation: Including and valuing sexual minorities in the workplace. In M. S. Stockdale & F. J. Crosby (Eds.), *The psychology and management of workplace diversity* (pp. 206–223). Oxford, UK: Blackwell Publishing.

Lucio, M. M., & Perrett, R. (2009). The diversity and politics of trade unions' responses to minority ethnic and migrant workers: The context of the UK. *Economic and Industrial Democracy*, 30(3), 324–347.

Ma, Q., & Tang, N. (2022). Too much of a good thing: The curvilinear relation between inclusive leadership and team innovative behaviors. *Asia Pacific Journal of Management*. https://doi.org/10.1007/s10490-022-09862-5

Macklin, R. (1999). *Against relativism: Cultural diversity and the search for ethical universals in medicine*. Oxford: Oxford University Press.

Mahalingam, R. (1998). *Essentialism, power and representation of caste: A developmental study* (Doctoral dissertation, University of Pittsburgh).

Mahony, S. (2018). Cultural diversity and the digital humanities. *Fudan Journal of the Humanities and Social Sciences*, 11(3), 371–388.

Maj, J. (2018). Embedding diversity in sustainability reporting. *Sustainability*, 10(7), 2487.

Maré, D. C., Fabling, R., & Stillman, S. (2014). Innovation and the local workforce. *Papers in Regional Science*, 93(1), 183–201.

Marfelt, M. M., & Muhr, S. L. (2016). Managing protean diversity: An empirical analysis of how organizational contextual dynamics derailed and dissolved global workforce diversity. *International Journal of Cross Cultural Management*, 16(2), 231–251.

Marquez, D. A. (2021). An attempt at democratizing resource allocation for social movements using decentralized autonomous organizations (Doctoral dissertation, Massachusetts Institute of Technology).

Mashiah, I. (2021). "Come and join us": How tech brands use source, message, and target audience strategies to attract employees. *The Journal of High Technology Management Research*, 32(2), 100418.

Massey, D. S., & Riosmena, F. (2010). Undocumented migration from Latin America in an era of rising US enforcement. *The Annals of the American Academy of Political and Social Science*, 630(1), 294–321.

Mayes, B. T., & Allen, R. W. (1977). Toward a definition of organizational politics. *Academy of Management Review*, 2(4), 672–678.

McCall, L. (2005). The complexity of intersectionality. *Signs: Journal of Women in Culture and Society*, 30(3), 1771–1800.

McDonald, D. M. (2003). Strategic human resource management approaches to workforce diversity in Japan – Harnessing corporate culture for organizational competitiveness1. *Global Business Review*, 4(1), 99–114.

McDonald, D. M. (2010). *The evolution of 'diversity management' in the USA: Social contexts, managerial motives and theoretical approaches* (pp. 1–17). Tokyo, Japan: Institute of Business Research, Daito Bunka University.

McGee, M. (2012). Neurodiversity. *Contexts*, 11(3), 12–13.

McHugh, P. J., & Perrault, E. (2018). Accelerating time: The effect of social pressures and regulation on board gender diversity post-IPO. *Journal of General Management*, 43(3), 95–105.

McIntosh, B., McQuaid, R., Munro, A., & Dabir-Alai, P. (2012). Motherhood and its impact on career progression. *Gender in Management*, 27(5), 346–364. https://doi.org/10.1108/17542411211252651

McKay, P. F., Avery, D. R., Tonidandel, S., Morris, M. A., Hernandez, M., & Hebl, M. R. (2007). Racial differences in employee retention: Are diversity climate perceptions the key? *Personnel Psychology*, 60(1), 35–62.

McLeman, R. (2018). Thresholds in climate migration. *Population and Environment*, 39(4), 319–338.

McPherson, M., Smith-Lovin, L., & Cook, J. M. (2001). Birds of a feather: Homophily in social networks. *Annual Review of Sociology*, 415–444.

McPherson Report (1999). *The Stephen Lawrence inquiry, report of an inquiry by Sir William Macpherson*. www.gov.uk/government/publications/the-stephen-lawrence-inquiry

Meliou, E. (2020). Family as a eudaimonic bubble: Women entrepreneurs mobilizing resources of care during persistent financial crisis and austerity. *Gender, Work and Organization*, 27(2), 218–235.

Meliou, E., & Edwards, T. (2018). Relational practices and reflexivity: Exploring the responses of women entrepreneurs to changing household dynamics. *International Small Business Journal*, 36(2), 149–168.

Meliou, E., & Mallett, O. (2022). Negotiating gendered ageing: Intersectional reflexivity and experiences of incongruity of self-employed older women. *Work Employment and Society*, 36(1), 101–118.

Meliou, E., Mallett, O., & Rosenberg., S (2019). Being a self-employed older woman: From discrimination to activism. *Work, Employment and Society*, 33(3), 529–538.

Meliou, E., Ozbilgin, M., & Edwards, T. (2021). How does responsible leadership emerge? An emergentist perspective. *European Management Review*, 18(4), 521–534.

Mensi-Klarbach, H., Leixnering, S., & Schiffinger, M. (2021). The carrot or the stick: Self-regulation for gender-diverse boards via codes of good governance. *Journal of Business Ethics*, 170(3), 577–593.

Mergen, A., & Ozbilgin, M. F. (2021a). Toxic Illusio in the global value chain the case of Amazon. In *Destructive leadership and management hypocrisy*. London, UK: Emerald Publishing Limited.

Mergen, A., & Ozbilgin, M. F. (2021b). Understanding the followers of toxic leaders: Toxic illusio and personal uncertainty. *International Journal of Management Reviews*, 23(1), 45–63.

Mershon, C., & Walsh, D. (2016). Diversity in political science: Why it matters and how to get it. *Politics, Groups, and Identities*, 4(3), 462–466.

Meyer, C. (2020). The commons: A model for understanding collective action and entrepreneurship in communities. *Journal of Business Venturing*, 35(5), 106034.

Milner, S. (2019). Gender pay gap reporting regulations: Advancing gender equality policy in tough economic times. *British Politics*, 14(2), 121–140.

Minbaeva, D. B., & Muratbekova-Touron, M. (2013). Clanism. *Management International Review*, 53(1), 109–139.

Minkowitz, T. (2017). CRPD and transformative equality. *International Journal of Law in Context*, 13(1), 77–86.

Mirzaei, A., Wilkie, D. C., & Siuki, H. (2022). Woke brand activism authenticity or the lack of it. *Journal of Business Research*, 139, 1–12. https://doi.org/10.1016/j.jbusres.2021.09.044

Mobley, M., & Payne, T. (1992). Backlash! The challenge to diversity training. *Training & Development*, 46(12), 45–52.

Modood, T. (2013). *Multiculturalism*. Hoboken, New Jersey: John Wiley & Sons.

Modood, T., Berthoud, R., Lakey, J., Nazroo, J., Smith, P., Virdee, S., & Beishon, S. (1997). *Ethnic minorities in Britain: Diversity and disadvantage. Series: PSI report (843)*. London: Policy Studies Institute. ISBN: 9780853746706.

Mohammadi, A., Broström, A., & Franzoni, C. (2017). Workforce composition and innovation: How diversity in employees' ethnic and educational backgrounds facilitates firm-level innovativeness. *Journal of Product Innovation Management*, 34(4), 406–426.

Monro, S., Carpenter, M., Crocetti, D., Davis, G., Garland, F., Griffiths, D., . . . & Aggleton, P. (2021). Intersex: Cultural and social perspectives. *Culture, Health & Sexuality*, 23(4), 431–440.

Moon, K.-K., & Christensen, R. K. (2020). Realizing the performance benefits of workforce diversity in the U.S. federal government: The moderating role of diversity climate. *Public Personnel Management*, 49(1), 141–165. https://doi.org/10.1177/0091026019848458

Mor Barak, M. E. (2016). *Managing diversity: Toward a globally inclusive workplace*. Thousand Oaks, CA: Sage Publications.

Mor Barak, M. E., Lizano, E. L., Kim, A., Rhee, M., Hsiao, H., & Brimhall, K. (2016). The promise of diversity management for climate of inclusion: A state of the art review and meta- analysis. *Journal of Human Service Organizations: Management, Leadership and Governance*, 40, 305–333.

Morelock, J. (2018). *Critical theory and authoritarian populism* (p. 298). London, UK: University of Westminster Press.

Morgan, G., & Pulignano, V. (2020). Solidarity at work: Concepts, levels and challenges. *Work, Employment and Society*, 34(1), 18–34.

Morris, J. (2006). Independent living: The role of the disability movement in the development of government policy. In *Cash and care: Policy challenges in the welfare state* (pp. 235–248). Bristol, UK: Policy Press.

Mushaben, J. M. (2017). Misrepresenting America's women: Trump's three-pronged attack on gender equality. *FEMINA*, 2, 147.

Muyia Nafukho, F., Roessler, R. T., & Kacirek, K. (2010). Disability as a diversity factor: Implications for human resource practices. *Advances in Developing Human Resources*, 12(4), 395–406. https://doi.org/10.1177/1523422310379209

Myeza, A., & April, K. (2021). Atypical Black leader emergence: South African self-perceptions. *Frontiers in Psychology*, 12.

Nanda, S. (2014). *Gender diversity: Crosscultural variations*. Long Grove, IL: Waveland Press, Inc.

Nentwich, J. C., & Kelan, E. K. (2014). Towards a topology of 'doing gender': An analysis of empirical research and its challenges. *Gender, Work & Organization*, 21(2), 121–134.

Nentwich, J. C., Ozbilgin, M. F., & Tatli, A. (2015). Change agency as performance and embeddedness: Exploring the possibilities and limits of Butler and Bourdieu. *Culture and Organization*, 21(3), 235–250.

Ng, E. S., & Sears, G. J. (2018). Walking the talk on diversity: CEO beliefs, moral values, and the implementation of workplace diversity practices. *Journal of Business Ethics*, 1–14.

Ng, E. S., Sears, G. J., & Bakkaloglu, M. (2021). White and minority employee reactions to perceived discrimination at work: Evidence of White fragility? *International Journal of Manpower*, 42(4), 661–682. https://doi.org/10.1108/IJM-12-2019-0535

Nicholls, A., & Teasdale, S. (2017). Neoliberalism by stealth? Exploring continuity and change within the UK social enterprise policy paradigm. *Policy & Politics*, 45(3), 323–341.

Nishii, L. H. (2013). The benefits of climate for inclusion for gender diverse groups. *Academy of Management Journal*, 56, 1754–1774.

Nishii, L. H., Khattab, J., Shemla, M., & Paluch, R. M. (2018). A multi-level process model for understanding diversity practice effectiveness. *Academy of Management Annals*, 12(1), 37–82.

Nishii, L. H., & Özbilgin, M. F. (2007). Global diversity management: Towards a conceptual framework. *The International Journal of Human Resource Management*, 18(11), 1883–1894.

Nkomo, S. M. (2019). The emperor has no clothes: Rewriting "race in organizations". In C. Cassell, A. Cunliffe, & G. Grandy (eds.), *Postmodern management theory* (pp. 463–489). London, UK: Routledge.

Nkomo, S. M., Bell, M. P., Roberts, L. M., Joshi, A., & Thatcher, S. M. (2019). Diversity at a critical juncture: New theories for a complex phenomenon. *Academy of Management Review*, 44(3), 498–517.

Noon, M. (2007). The fatal flaws of diversity and the business case for ethnic minorities. *Work, Employment and Society*, 21(4), 773–784.

Noon, M. (2018). Pointless diversity training: Unconscious bias, new racism and agency. *Work, Employment and Society*, 32(1), 198–209.

Noon, M., Healy, G., Forson, C., & Oikelome, F. (2013). The equality effects of the 'hyper-formalization' of selection. *British Journal of Management*, 24(3), 333–346.

Oberai, H., & Anand, I. M. (2018). *Unconscious bias: Thinking without thinking*. Human Resource Management International Digest.

OECD (2020). *All hands in? Making diversity work for all*. Paris: OECD Publishing. https://doi.org/10.1787/efb14583-en.

OECD (2021). *Gender wage gap (indicator)*. https://doi.org/10.1787/7cee77aa-en, accessed 13 December 2021.

OECD (2022). *Glossary of statistical terms*. https://stats.oecd.org/glossary/detail.asp?ID=3295

Oerlemans, W. G. M., Peeters, M. C. W., & Schaufeli, W. B. (2008). Ethnic diversity at work: An overview of theories and research. In K. Näswall, J. Hellgren, & M. Sverke (eds.), *The individual in the changing working life* (pp. 211–232). Cambridge: Cambridge University Press. https://doi.org/10.1017/CBO9780511490064.011

Offor, I. (2022). Global animal law and the problem of "globabble": Toward decoloniality and diversity in global animal law studies. *Asian Journal of International Law*, 1–30.

Olafsdottir, K. (2018). Iceland is the best, but still not equal: Søkelys på Norden. *Søkelys på arbeidslivet*, 35(1–02), 111–126.

Olcott, E., & Storebeck, O. (2022). Top Adidas executive rebuked in 'final warning' over comments on diversity. *Financial Times*. www.ft.com/content/7b852f73-e463-4458-809a-c1ba80607295

Oliver, M. (2013). The social model of disability: Thirty years on. *Disability & Society*, 28(7), 1024–1026.

Oliver, T. (2020). Is racism and bigotry in our DNA? *The Conversation*, 2 April 2020. https://theconversation.com/is-racism-and-bigotry-in-our-dna-135096

Omhand, K., Yamak, S., & Ogunseyin, M. (2023). The race to the top: The experiences and strategies of women of colour in UK academia. In *Symposium on the social inclusion of disadvantaged early career researchers, European academy conference*, 14–16 June, Dublin.

Opie, T., & Livingston, B. A. (2022). *Shared sisterhood: How to take collective action for racial and gender equity at work*. Cambridge, MA: Harvard Business Press.

Opstrup, N., & Villadsen, A. R. (2015). The right mix? Gender diversity in top management teams and financial performance. *Public Administration Review*, 75(2), 291–301.

Oruh, E. S. (2014). Giving voice to the people: Exploring the effects of new media on stakeholder engagement in the Nigerian trade union movement. *Management Research and Practice*, 6(3), 41–52.

Otaye-Ebede, L. (2018). Employees' perception of diversity management practices: Scale development and validation. *European Journal of Work and Organizational Psychology*, 27(4), 462–476.

Oxfam (2022). *Inequality Kills: The unparalleled action needed to combat unprecedented inequality in the wake of COVID-19 (summary)*. https://oxfamilibrary.openrepository.com/bitstream/handle/10546/621341/bp-inequality-kills-170122-summ-en.pdf

Özbilgin, M. (2006). 13 Relational methods in organization studies: A review of the field. *Relational Perspectives in Organizational Studies*, 244.

Özbilgin, M. (2017). Cinsellik ve Emek: Butler ve Bourdieu ile kazanımların kırılganlığını ve direnişi sorgulamak (in Turkish for Sexuality and Labour: Questioning the frailty of progress with Butler and Bourdieu). *KAOSQ+*, 5, 97–106.

Ozbilgin, M. (2018). *What the racial equality movement can learn from the global fight for women's rights*. https://theconversation.com/what-the-racial-equality-movement-can-learn-from-the-global-fight-for-womens-rights-105616

Özbilgin, M. (2019a). Farklilik, esitlik ve guc. In H. Yildiz & T. Okan (eds.), *Orgutlerde Guc ve Politika* (pp. 289–303). Istanbul: Beta Press.

Özbilgin, M. (2019b). Global diversity management. In *Global diversity management* (pp. 25–39). Cham: Springer.

Özbilgin, M., Beauregard, T. A., Tatli, A., & Bell, M. P. (2011). Work – life, diversity and intersectionality: A critical review and research agenda. *International Journal of Management Reviews*, 13(2), 177–198.

Özbilgin, M., & Bell, M. P. (2008). The rise of Cartesian dualism and marketization in academia. In *The Sage handbook of new approaches in management and organization* (pp. 268–269).

Ozbilgin, M., & Chanlat, J. F. (eds.). (2017). *Management and diversity: Perspectives from different national contexts*. Emerald Group Publishing.

Ozbilgin, M., & Chanlat, J. F. (2018). *Management et diversité, comparaisons internationales 01*. Presses de l'Université Laval.

Özbilgin, M., & Erbil, C. (2019). Yönetim Çalışmaları Alanındaki Kısır Yöntem İkilemlerini Dışaçekimsel ve Geçmişsel Yaklaşım ve Eleştirel Gerçekçilikle Yöntem Yelpazesine Dönüştürmek (Transforming the barren dichotomies of method in the field of management studies into a spectrum with abductive and retroductive approaches and critical realism). *Yönetim ve Çalışma Dergisi*, 3(1), 1–24.

Özbilgin, M., & Erbil, C. (2021a). Post-hümanist İnovasyon: Gig Ekonomi Özelinde Moto Kuryeli Teslimat Sektörü Örneklemi. *Sosyal Mucit Academic Review*, 2(1), 22–41. https://dergipark.org.tr/en/pub/smar/issue/62309/923729

Özbilgin, M. & Erbil, C. (2021b). Social Movements and Wellbeing in Organizations from Multi-level and Intersectional Perspectives: The case of the #blacklivesmatter Movement In Wall, T., Cooper, S. C. and Brough, P. (eds) *The SAGE Handbook of Organisational Wellbeing*, Sage: London.

Özbilgin, M., & Erbil, C. (2023a). Insights into equality, diversity, and inclusion. In B. Kucukaltan (ed.), *Contemporary approaches in equality, diversity and inclusion: Strategic and technological perspectives*. Bingley: Emerald Publishing.

Özbilgin, M., & Erbil, C. (2023b). Çeşitlilik: Disiplinlerarası Bir Bakış. In V. Tanrıverdi & S. Ercan (eds.), *Sosyal Psikolojide Çeşitlilik*. Nobel Akademik Yayıncılık.

Özbilgin, M., & Erbil, C. (2023c). Robot Emeği ve İnsan-Doğa-Teknoloji İlişkisinde Robot Emeğine Yeni Bir Yaklaşım. In A. A. Cengiz & B. Uçkan Hekimler (eds.), *Emeğin Hallerine Dair*. Yeni İnsan Yayınevi.

Özbilgin, M., & Erbil, C. (2023d). International diversity. In S. Nkoma, A. Klarsfeld, L. Taksa, & A. F. Bender (eds.), *Encyclopedia of diversity and management*. Edward Elgar Publishing.

Özbilgin, M., & Erbil, C. (2023e). LGBT+ in the Boardroom: A rainbow agenda for change. In M. Huse & S. Nielsen (eds.), *The research handbook on diversity and corporate governance*. Edward Elgar Publishing.

Özbilgin, M., Erbil, C., Baykut, S., & Kamasak, R. (2022a). Normalised, defensive, strategic and instrumental passing at work: A Goffmanian exploration of LGBTQ+ individuals passing at work in Turkey. *Gender, Work & Organization*, 30(3), 862–880. https://doi.org/10.1111/gwao.12928

Özbilgin, M., Erbil, C., Demirbağ, K. Ş., Demirbağ, O., & Tanriverdi, V. (2023c). Afet Yönetiminde Sorumluluğun Yeniden İnşası: Deprem, Sosyal Dramalar, Sosyal Politikalar. *Sosyal Mucit Academic Review*, 4(1), 71–112.

Özbilgin, M., Erbil, C., & Dipalma, A. (2022c). Migrant diversity: Introducing the migrant diversity category to diversity management. In G. Meardi (ed.), *Research handbook on migration and employment*. Edward Elgar Publishing.

Özbilgin, M., Erbil, C., & Odabasi, E. (2022b). Leaders with disabilities: A boardroom challenge. In J. Beatty, S. Hennekam, & M. Kulkarni (eds.), *De Gruyter handbook of disability and management*. De Gruyter.

Özbilgin, M., Gundogdu, N., & Akalin, C. (2023b). Artificial intelligence, Gig economy and precarity. In E. Meliou, J. Vassilopoulou, & M. Ozbilgin (eds.), *Diversity and precarious work during socio-economic upheaval*. Cambridge: Cambridge University Press.

Özbilgin, M., Kucukaltan, B., & Açar, A. (2019). Sycophancy as a factor that corrodes merit in academic life. *Business & Management Studies: An International Journal*, 7(5), 2828–2850. https://doi.org/10.15295/bmij.v7i5.1361

Özbilgin, M., Mulholland, G., Tatli, A., & Worman, D. (2008). *Managing diversity and the business case* (p. 4). London: Chartered Institute of Personnel and Development.

Özbilgin, M., Samdanis, M., & Arsezen, P. (2023a). Appearance as carnal capital and symbolic violence: An intersectional approach. In A. Broadbridge (ed.), *Handbook on appearance in the workplace: Impact on career development*. Cheltenham: Edward Elgar Publishing.

Özbilgin, M., & Slutskaya, N. (2017). Consequences of neo-liberal politics on equality and diversity at work in Britain: Is resistance futile? In *Management and diversity: Thematic approaches* (Vol. 4, pp. 319–334). Emerald Publishing Limited.

Özbilgin, M., & Syed, J. (2019). Future of diversity management. In *Managing diversity and inclusion: An international perspective* (p. 406).

Özbilgin, M., & Tatli, A. (2011). Mapping out the field of equality and diversity: Rise of individualism and voluntarism. *Human Relations*, 64(9), 1229–1253.

Özbilgin, M., Tatli, A., Ipek, G., & Sameer, M. (2016). Four approaches to accounting for diversity in global organisations. *Critical Perspectives on Accounting*, 35, 88–99.

Özbilgin, M., Tatli, A., & Jonsen, K. (2015). *Global diversity management: An evidence-based approach*. New York: Palgrave Macmillan.

Özbilgin, M., Tatli, A., & Jonsen, K. (2017). *Global diversity management: An evidence-based approach*. London: Bloomsbury Publishing.

Özbilgin, M., & Vassilopoulou, J. (2018). Relational methods in organization studies: A critical overview. In *Qualitative methodologies in organization studies* (pp. 151–177).

Özbilgin, M., & Woodward, D. (2004a). *Banking and gender: Sex equality in the financial services in Britain and Turkey*. London, UK: Macmillan Publisher.

Özbilgin, M., & Woodward, D. (2004b). 'Belonging' and 'otherness': Sex equality in banking in Turkey and Britain. *Gender, Work & Organization*, 11(6), 668–688.

Özbilgin, M., & Yalkin, C. (2019). Hegemonic dividend and workforce diversity: The case of 'biat' and meritocracy in nation branding in Turkey. *Journal of Management & Organization*, 25(4), 543–553. https://doi.org/10.1017/jmo.2019.39

Özcan, M. (2021). The bottleneck metaphor of leadership culture: How shared understandings about leadership develop in groups and impede diversity and effectiveness of leaders. *Frontiers in Psychology*, 12. https://doi.org/10.3389/fpsyg.2021.635751

Ozeren, E., & Aydin, E. (2016). What does being LGBT mean in the workplace? A comparison of LGBT equality in Turkey and the UK. In *Research handbook of international and comparative perspectives on diversity management*. Edward Elgar Publishing.

Ozgen, C., Nijkamp, P., & Poot, J. (2017). The elusive effects of workplace diversity on innovation. *Papers in Regional Science*, 96, S29–S49.

Ozkazanc-Pan, B. (2019). On agency and empowerment in a# MeToo world. *Gender, Work & Organization*, 26(8), 1212–1220.

Ozkazanc-Pan, B. (2021). Diversity and future of work: Inequality abound or opportunities for all? *Management Decision*, 59(11), 2645–2659. https://doi.org/10.1108/MD-02-2019-0244

Ozkazanc-Pan, B., & Clark Muntean, S. (2018). Networking towards (in)equality: Women entrepreneurs in technology. *Gender Work Organ*, 25, 379–400. https://doi.org/10.1111/gwao.12225

Özsoy, Z., Şenyücel, M., & Oba, B. (2022). *Gender diversity and inclusion at work: Divergent views from Turkey*. Taylor & Francis.

Ozturk, M. B. (2017). When freedoms collide: Competing claims for religious rights and sexual orientation equality at work and beyond. In *Management and diversity*. Emerald Publishing Limited.

Öztürk, M. B., & Özbilgin, M. (2014). From cradle to grave: The lifecycle of compulsory heterosexuality in Turkey. In *Sexual orientation at work* (pp. 166–179). Routledge.

Palalar Alkan, D., Kamasak, R., Yesildal, E., & Vassilopoulou, J. (2023). Ethnicity and precarity relationship: The refugee case in Turkey. In M. Meliou, J. Vassilopoulou, & M. Ozbilgin (eds.), *Diversity and precarious work during socio-economic upheaval: The missing link*. Cambridge: Cambridge University Press.

Palalar Alkan, D., Ozbilgin, M., & Kamasak, R. (2022). Social innovation in managing diversity: COVID-19 as a catalyst for change. *Equality, Diversity and Inclusion*, 41(5), 709–725. https://doi.org/10.1108/EDI-07-2021-0171

Palpacuer, F., Pérez, R., Tozanli, S., & Brabet, J. (2006). Financiarisation et globalisation des stratégies d'entreprise: le cas des multinationales agroalimentaires en Europe. *Finance contrôle stratégie*, 9(3), 165–189.

Papoutsi, C., Hargreaves, D., Hagell, A., Hounsome, N., Skirrow, H., Muralidhara, K., . . . & Finer, S. (2022). Group clinics for young adults living with diabetes in an ethnically diverse, socioeconomically deprived population: Mixed-methods evaluation. *National institute for health and care research*, Southampton (UK). PMID: 36063481.

Park, E. (2014). Ethical issues in cyborg technology: Diversity and inclusion. *NanoEthics*, 8(3), 303–306.

Park, Y. W., Voss, G. B., & Voss, Z. G. (2022). Advancing customer diversity, equity, and inclusion: Measurement, stakeholder influence, and the role of marketing. *Journal of the Academy of Marketing Science*, 1–24.

Parker, K., Horowitz, J., & Anderson, M. (2020). Amid protests, majorities across racial and ethnic groups express support for the Black lives matter movement. *Pew Research Center's Social & Demographic Trends Project*. https://policycommons.net/artifacts/616390/amid-protests-majorities-across-racial-and-ethnic-groups-express-support-for-the-black-lives-matter-movement/1597028/, accessed 28 December 2022. CID: 20.500.12592/tqmb46.

Patel, P., Hiam, L., Sowemimo, A., Devakumar, D., & McKee, M. (2020). Ethnicity and COVID-19. *BMJ*, 369.

Pearce, R. G., Wald, E., & Ballakrishnen, S. S. (2014). Difference blindness vs. bias awareness: Why Law firms with the best of intentions have failed to create diverse partnerships. *Fordham Law Review*, 83, 2407.

Pepper, A. (2022). Is animal labour a viable route to interspecies justice? *Politics and Animals*, 8, 12–17.

Pepper, S. C. (1926). Emergence. *The Journal of Philosophy*, 23(9), 241–245.

Peretz, H., & Knappert, L. (2021). The cultural lens. In *The Oxford handbook of contextual approaches to human resource management*, Chris Brewster, Emma Parry, Michael J. Morley (eds), Oxford Uni Press: Oxford pp. 25–52.

Peterson, R. S., & Gardner, H. K. (2023). Is your board inclusive – or just diverse? *Harvard Business Review*, in press. ISSN: 0017-8012.

Phinney, J. S. (1996). Understanding ethnic diversity: The role of ethnic identity. *American Behavioral Scientist*, 40(2), 143–152.

Phung, K., Buchanan, S., Toubiana, M., Ruebottom, T., & Turchick-Hakak, L. (2021). When Stigma doesn't transfer: Stigma deflection and occupational stratification in the sharing economy. *Journal of Management Studies*, 58, 1107–1139. https://doi.org/10.1111/joms.12574

Pichler, S., Ruggs, E., & Trau, R. (2017). Worker outcomes of LGBT-supportive policies: A cross-level model. *Equality, Diversity and Inclusion: An International Journal*.

Pichler, S., Varma, A., & Bruce, T. (2010). Heterosexism in employment decisions: The role of job misfit. *Journal of Applied Social Psychology*, 40(10), 2527–2555.

Piketty, T. (2013). *Capital in the 21st century*. Cambridge, MA: President and Fellows, Harvard College.

Pio, E., & Waddock, S. (2021). Invoking indigenous wisdom for management learning. *Management Learning*, 52(3), 328–346.

Pisano, G. P. (2017). Neurodiversity as a competitive advantage. *Harvard Business Review*, 1–9.

Pitts, D. W., & Recascino Wise, L. (2010). Workforce diversity in the new millennium: Prospects for research. *Review of Public Personnel Administration*, 30(1), 44–69.

Plaut, V. C. (2010). Diversity science: Why and how difference makes a difference. *Psychological Inquiry*, 21(2), 77–99.

Poggio, B. (2010). Vertical segregation and gender practices. Perspectives of analysis and action. *Gender in Management: An International Journal*.

Polanyi, K. (1944). *The great transformation: Economic and political origins of our time*. New York: Rinehart.

Polzer, J. T., Milton, L. P., & Swarm Jr, W. B. (2002). Capitalizing on diversity: Interpersonal congruence in small work groups. *Administrative Science Quarterly*, 47(2), 296–324.

Portier-Le Cocq, F. (2019). Theorising motherhood. In *Motherhood in contemporary international perspective* (pp. 1–17). Routledge.

Powell, G. N. (1999). Reflections on the glass ceiling: Recent trends and future prospects. In G. N. Powell (ed.), *Handbook of gender and work* (pp. 325–345). Sage Publications, Inc. https://doi.org/10.4135/9781452231365.n17

Prati, F., Crisp, R. J., & Rubini, M. (2021). 40 years of multiple social categorization: A tool for social inclusivity. *European Review of Social Psychology*, 32(1), 47–87. https://doi.org/10.1080/10463283.2020.1830612

Pringle, J. K. (2009). Positioning workplace diversity: Critical aspects for theory. In *Equality, diversity and inclusion at work: A research companion* (pp. 75–87).

Raco, M. (2018). Living with diversity: Local social imaginaries and the politics of intersectionality in a super-diverse city. *Political Geography*, 62, 149–159.

Reay, D. (2022). Still the elephant in the room. In *Routledge handbook of the sociology of higher education*.

Reddy, S., & Jadhav, A. M. (2019). Gender diversity in boardrooms – A literature review. *Cogent Economics & Finance*, 7(1), 1644703.

Regan, T. (2013). The case for animal rights. In *Ethics, humans and other animals* (pp. 179–188). Routledge.

Reilly, P., & Williams, T. (2016). *Global HR: Challenges facing the function*. Routledge.

Reskin, B. F., & Roos, P. A. (1990). *Job queues, gender queues: Explaining women's inroads into male occupations* (Vol. 105). Temple University Press.

Resnik, J. (2007). The democratisation of the education system in France after the second world war: A neo-Weberian glocal approach to education reforms. *British Journal of Educational Studies*, 55(2), 155–181.

Reynaud, J. D. (2003). Une théorie de la régulation sociale pour quoi faire. In Terssac G. De (ed.), *La Théorie de la régulation sociale de Jean-Daniel Reynaud. Débats et prolongements* (pp. 399–446). Paris: la Découverte.

Rhodes, C. (2021). *Woke capitalism: How corporate morality is sabotaging democracy*. Policy Press.

Richard, O. C., Barnett, T., Dwyer, S., & Chadwick, K. (2004). Cultural diversity in management, firm performance, and the moderating role of entrepreneurial orientation dimensions. *Academy of Management Journal*, 47(2), 255–266.

Ridgeway, C. L. (2001). Gender, status, and leadership. *Journal of Social Issues*, 57(4), 637–655.

Ripstein, A. (2001). *Equality, responsibility, and the law*. Cambridge: Cambridge University Press.

Roberson, Q. M. (ed.). (2013). *The Oxford handbook of diversity and work*. Oxford: Oxford University Press.

Roberson, Q. M. (2018). Diversity and Inclusion in the Workplace: A review, synthesis, and future research agenda. *Annual Review of Organizational Psychology and Organizational Behavior*.

Roberson, Q. M., Holmes IV, O., & Perry, J. L. (2017b). Transforming research on diversity and firm performance: A dynamic capabilities perspective. *Academy of Management Annals*, 11(1), 189–216.

Roberson, Q. M., King, E., & Hebl, M. (2020). Designing more effective practices for reducing workplace inequality. *Behavioral Science & Policy*, 6(1), 39–49.

Roberson, Q. M., Ryan, A. M., & Ragins, B. R. (2017a). The evolution and future of diversity at work. *Journal of Applied Psychology*, 102(3), 483.

Robinson, B. A. (2016). Heteronormativity and homonormativity. In *The Wiley Blackwell encyclopedia of gender and sexuality studies* (pp. 1–3).

Robinson, G., & Dechant, K. (1997). Building a business case for diversity. *Academy of Management Perspectives*, 11(3), 21–31.

Roehling, M. V., Roehling, P. V., & Pichler, S. (2007). The relationship between body weight and perceived weight-related employment discrimination: The role of sex and race. *Journal of Vocational Behavior*, 71(2), 300–318.

Romani, L., Holck, L., Holgersson, C., & Muhr, S. L. (2017). Diversity management and the scandinavian model: Illustrations from Denmark and Sweden☆. In *Management and diversity: Perspectives from different national contexts* (pp. 261–280). Emerald Publishing Limited.

Romani, L., Holck, L., & Risberg, A. (2019). Benevolent discrimination: Explaining how human resources professionals can be blind to the harm of diversity initiatives. *Organization*, 26(3), 371–390.

Romani, L., Zanoni, P., & Holck, L. (2021). Radicalizing diversity (research): Time to resume talking about class. *Gender Work Organisation*, 28, 8–23. https://doi.org/10.1111/gwao.12593

Romero, A. J., Edwards, L. M., Fryberg, S. A., & Orduña, M. (2014). Resilience to discrimination stress across ethnic identity stages of development. *Journal of Applied Social Psychology*, 44(1), 1–11.

Rose, D., & Harrison, E. (2007). The European socio-economic classification: A new social class schema for comparative European research. *European Societies*, 9(3), 459–490.

Rosemary, J. (2011). Witnessing embodiment: Trauma narrative and theory at the limit in field research and in the classroom. *Australian Feminist Studies*, 26(69), 297–317.

Rouine, I., Ammari, A., & Bruna, M. G. (2022). Nonlinear impacts of CSR performance on firm risk: New evidence using a panel smooth threshold regression. *Finance Research Letters*, 102721.

Roy, S., & Hossain, M. A. (2015). Women's empowerment through higher education: Case study of Begum Rokeya University, Rangpur, Bangladesh. *Human Rights International Research Journal*. ISSN: 2320–6942.

Rubin, J. D., Atwood, S., & Olson, K. R. (2020). Studying gender diversity. *Trends in Cognitive Sciences*, 24(3), 163–165.

Rushton, M. (2008). A note on the use and misuse of the racial diversity index. *Policy Studies Journal*, 36(3), 445–459.

Russell, A. E., Cambardella, C. A., Ewel, J. J., & Parkin, T. B. (2004). Species, rotation, and life-form diversity effects on soil carbon in experimental tropical ecosystems. *Ecological Applications*, 14(1), 47–60.

Ryan, M. K., Haslam, S. A., Morgenroth, T., Rink, F., Stoker, J., & Peters, K. (2016). Getting on top of the glass cliff: Reviewing a decade of evidence, explanations, and impact. *The Leadership Quarterly*, 27(3), 446–455.

Saba, T., Ozbilgin, M., Ng, E., & Cachat-Rosset, G. (2021). Guest editorial: Ineffectiveness of diversity management: Lack of knowledge, lack of interest or resistance? *Equality, Diversity and Inclusion: An International Journal*.

Saba, T., Vassilopoulou, J., Ng, E., & Ozbilgin, M. (2022). Guest editorial: Crossing boundaries and strengthening social connections through improved professional integration of immigrants. *Equality, Diversity and Inclusion: An International Journal*, 41(7), 953–958.

Sabir, M., Ali, Y., Khan, I., & Salman, A. (2022). Plants species selection for afforestation: A case study of the Billion Tree Tsunami Project of Pakistan. *Journal of Sustainable Forestry*, 41(6), 537–549.

Saglam, E. (2019). Commutes, coffeehouses, and imaginations: An exploration of everyday makings of heteronormative masculinities in public. In S. Sehlikoglu & F. Karioris (eds.), *The everyday makings of heteronormativity cross-cultural explorations of sex, gender, and sexuality* (pp. 45–64). Lexington.

Sakellari, M. (2021). Climate change and migration in the UK news media: How the story is told. *International Communication Gazette*, 83(1), 63–80. https://doi.org/10.1177/1748048519883518

Samdanis, M., & Özbilgin, M. (2020). The duality of an atypical leader in diversity management: The legitimization and delegitimization of diversity beliefs in organizations. *International Journal of Management Reviews*, 22(2), 101–119.

Sandberg, S. (2013). *Lean in-women, work and the will to lead*. Random House.

Savage, M. (2015). *Social class in the 21st century*. Penguin UK.

Sayce, S., & Özbilgin, M. F. (2014). Pension trusteeship and diversity in the UK: A new boardroom recipe for change or continuity? *Economic and Industrial Democracy*, 35(1), 49–69.

Scott, C. L. (2018). Historical perspectives for studying diversity in the workforce. In *Diversity in the workforce* (pp. 3–27). Routledge.

SDG (2022). *The SDGs wedding cake*. www.stockholmresilience.org/research/research-news/2016-06-14-the-sdgs-wedding-cake.html

Sear, R. (2021). Demography and the rise, apparent fall, and resurgence of eugenics. *Population Studies*, 75(sup1), 201–220. ISSN: 0032–4728. https://doi.org/10.1080/00324728.2021.2009013

Seidman, G. W. (2007). *Beyond the boycott: Labor rights, human rights, and transnational activism*. Russell Sage Foundation.

Seierstad, C. (2016). Beyond the business case: The need for both utility and justice rationales for increasing the share of women on boards. *Corporate Governance: An International Review*, 24(4), 390–405.

Seierstad, C., & Huse, M. (2017). Gender quotas on corporate boards in Norway: Ten years later and lessons learned. In *Gender diversity in the boardroom* (pp. 11–45).

Sennett, R. (1998). *The corrosion of character: The personal consequences of work in the new capitalism.* WW Norton & Company.

Sewell, T., Aderin-Pocock, M., Chughtai, A., Fraser, K., Khalid, N., Moyo, D., . . . & Cluff, B. (2021). *Commission on race and ethnic disparities: The report.* London: Commission on Race and Ethnic Disparities.

Shachaf, P. (2008). Cultural diversity and information and communication technology impacts on global virtual teams: An exploratory study. *Information & Management,* 45(2), 131–142.

Shahabuddin, M. (2016). *Ethnicity and international law: Histories, politics and practices.* Cambridge: Cambridge University Press.

Shakespeare, T. (2006). The social model of disability. *The Disability Studies Reader,* 2, 197–204.

Sheber, K. (2020). Legal rights for nature: How the idea of recognizing nature as a legal entity can spread and make a difference globally. *Hastings Env't'l LJ,* 26, 147.

Shen, J., Tang, N., & D'Netto, B. (2014). A multilevel analysis of the effects of HR diversity management on employee knowledge sharing: The case of Chinese employees. *The International Journal of Human Resource Management,* 25(12), 1720–1738.

Shih, M., Young, M. J., & Bucher, A. (2013). Working to reduce the effects of discrimination: Identity management strategies in organizations. *American Psychologist,* 68(3), 145.

Shiva, V., & Mies, M. (2014). *Ecofeminism.* Bloomsbury Publishing.

Shore, L. M., Randel, A. E., Chung, B. G., Dean, M. A., Holcombe Ehrhart, K., & Singh, G. (2011). Inclusion and diversity in work groups: A review and model for future research. *Journal of Management,* 37, 1262–1289. https://doi.org/10.1177/0149206310385943

Siebers, T. (2008). *Disability theory.* University of Michigan Press.

Silva, E. O. (2019). Donald Trump's discursive field: A juncture of stigma contests over race, gender, religion, and democracy. *Sociology Compass,* 13(12), e12757.

Simon, P. (2013). Collecting ethnic statistics in Europe: A review. *Accounting for Ethnic and Racial Diversity,* 22–47.

Simpson, R., & Morgan, R. (2020). 'Gendering' contamination: Physical, social and moral tain in the context of COVID-19. *Gender in Management: An International Journal,* 35(7/8), 685–691.

Simpson, R., Morgan, R., Lewis, P., & Rumens, N. (2021). Living and working on the edge: 'Place precarity' and the experiences of male manual workers in a UK seaside town. *Population, Space and Place,* 27(8), e2447.

Simpson, R., Morgan, R., Lewis, P., & Rumens, N. (2022). Landscape and work: 'Placing' the experiences of male manual workers in a UK seaside town. *Sociology,* 56(5), 839–858.

Sinclair-Chapman, V. (2015). Leveraging diversity in political science for institutional and disciplinary change. *PS: Political Science & Politics,* 48(3), 454–458.

Singleton, K. S., Murray, D. S. R., Dukes, A. J., & Richardson, L. N. (2021). A year in review: Are diversity, equity, and inclusion initiatives fixing systemic barriers? *Neuron,* 109(21), 3365–3367.

Sippola, A., & Smale, A. (2007). The global integration of diversity management: A longitudinal case study. *The International Journal of Human Resource Management,* 18(11), 1895–1916.

Smith, E. B., & Nkomo, S. M. (2021). *Our separate ways, with a new preface and epilogue: Black and White women and the struggle for professional identity.* Harvard Business Press.

Soliev, I., Janssen, M. A., Theesfeld, I., Pritchard, C., Pirscher, F., & Lee, A. (2021). Channeling environmentalism into climate policy: An experimental study of Fridays for Future participants from Germany. *Environmental Research Letters,* 16(11), 114035.

Soroka, S. N., Johnston, R., & Banting, K. G. (2006). *Ties that bind?: Social cohesion and diversity in Canada.* Montreal: Institute for Research on Public Policy.

Spender, J. C. (1989). *Industry recipes.* Oxford: Basil Blackwell.

Squires, J. (2007). *The new politics of gender equality.* Bloomsbury Publishing.

Stahl, G. K., Maznevski, M. L., Voigt, A., & Jonsen, K. (2010). Unraveling the effects of cultural diversity in teams: A meta-analysis of research on multicultural work groups. *Journal of International Business Studies,* 41(4), 690–709.

Stamou, E., Popov, A., & Soytemel, E. (2022). Normative multiculturalism and the limits of inclusion in school lives: Qualitative insights from three secondary schools in England. In L. H. Seukwa, E. Marmer, & C. Silla (eds.), *The challenge of cultural heritage and identity for inclusive and open societies: Young people's perspectives from European and Asian Countries.* Peter Lang.

The Stephen Lawrence Inquiry (1999). The Stephen Lawrence inquiry, report of an inquiry by Sir William Macpherson of Cluny, Advised by Tom Cook, the right reverend Dr John Sentamu, Dr Richard Stone. *Presented to parliament by the secretary of state for the home department by command of her majesty*. https://assets.publishing.service.gov.uk/government/uploads/system/uploads/attachment_data/file/277111/4262.pdf

Steven, V., & Wessendorf, S. (2010). Introduction: Assessing the backlash against multiculturalism in Europe. In *The multiculturalism backlash: European discourses, policies and practices* (pp. 1–32). Routledge.

Stiglitz, J. E. (2000). Democratic development as the fruits of labor. *Perspectives on Work*, 31–37.

Stiglitz, J. E. (2012). *The price of inequality: How today's divided society endangers our future*. WW Norton & Company.

Stiglitz, J. E. (2016). *Nobel Prize-winning economist Stiglitz tells us why 'neoliberalism is dead'*. www.businessinsider.com/joseph-stiglitz-says-neoliberalism-is-dead-2016-8?r=US&IR=T

Stockdale, M. S., & Crosby, F. J. (2004). *The psychology and management of workplace diversity*. Blackwell Publishing.

Sultana, F. (2018). The false equivalence of academic freedom and free speech. *ACME: An International Journal for Critical Geographies*, 17(2), 228–257.

Sung, S. Y., & Choi, J. N. (2021). Contingent effects of workforce diversity on firm innovation: High-tech industry and market turbulence as critical environmental contingencies. *The International Journal of Human Resource Management*, 32(9), 1986–2012. https://doi.org/10.1080/09585192.2019.1579243

Syed, J. (2010). *Introduction: Diversity management travels to under-explored territories*.

Syed, J., Klarsfeld, A., Ngunjiri, F. W., & Härtel, C. E. (2018). *Religious diversity in the workplace*. Cambridge: Cambridge University Press.

Syed, J., & Kramar, R. (2010). *What is the Australian model for managing cultural diversity?*. Personnel Review.

Syed, J., & Özbilgin, M. (2009). A relational framework for international transfer of diversity management practices. *The International Journal of Human Resource Management*, 20(12), 2435–2453.

Syed, J., & Ozbilgin, M. (eds.). (2015). *Managing diversity and inclusion: An international perspective*. Sage.

Syed, J., & Ozbilgin, M. (2019). *Managing diversity and inclusion: An international perspective*. Sage.

Szabados, K. (2019). Can we win the war on science? Understanding the link between political populism and anti-science politics. *Populism*, 2(2), 207–236.

Tajfel, H., & Turner, J. C. (1986). An integrative theory of intergroup conflict. In W. G. Austin & S. Worchel (eds.), *The social psychology of intergroup relations* (pp. 33–48). Greenwich, CT: JAI Press.

Tajfel, H., & Turner, J. C. (2004). The social identity theory of intergroup behavior. In *Political psychology* (pp. 276–293). Edited By John T. Jost, Jim Sidanius, New York: Psychology Press.

Taksa, L., & Groutsis, D. (2010). Managing diverse commodities: From factory fodder to business asset. *The Economic and Labour Relations Review*, 20(2), 77–98.

Taksa, L., & Groutsis, D. (2013a). Managing cultural diversity: Problems and prospects for ethnicity and gender at work. In A. J. Mills & G. Durepos (eds.), *Case study methods in business research – Volume 4 case study research from the traditions of the post and beyond*. London: Sage Publications.

Taksa, L., & Groutsis, D. (2013b). Managing diversity in the workplace: Considering the neglect of identity. In A. Jakubowicz & C. Ho (eds.), *'For those who've come across the seas . . .' Australian multicultural theory, policy and practice*. North Melbourne: Australian Scholarly Publishing.

Taksa, L., & Groutsis, D. (2017). Swings and roundabouts: Reconsidering equal employment opportunity, affirmative action and diversity management in Australia from an historical perspective. In M. Ozbilgin & J.-F. Chanlat (eds.), *Management and diversity*. Bingley, UK: Emerald Group Publishing Limited.

Taksa, L., & Thornthwaite, L. (2022). Organisations must stop shifting responsibility for harassment. *Sydney Morning Herald*. www.smh.com.au/business/workplace/organisations-must-stop-shifting-responsibility-for-harassment-20210525-p57v0f.html

Taksa, L., & Thornthwaite, L. (2023). Addressing and regulating bias: Law and management practice. *Comparative Labor Law and Policy Journal*, 42(3).

Tanriverdi, V. (2022). Cinsiyetler ve Cinsellikler. In V. Tanriverdi & S. Ercan (eds.), *Sosyal Psikolojide Çeşitlilik* (pp. 139–170). Ankara: Nobel Publishing.

Tanriverdi, V., & Gezici Yalçin, M. (2022). İnsanları hayvanlardan ve robotlardan ayıran özelliklerin atfedilmesinde kadınsı ve erkeksi cinsiyet ifadesinin etkisi. *Psikoloji Çalışmaları – Studies in Psychology*, 42(3), 667–698. https://doi.org/10.26650/SP2022-1067397

Taragin-Zeller, L., Rozenblum, Y., & Baram-Tsabari, A. (2020). Public engagement with science among religious minorities: Lessons from COVID-19. *Science Communication*, 42(5), 643–678. https://doi.org/10.1177/1075547020962107

Tatli, A. (2011). A multi-layered exploration of the diversity management field: Diversity discourses, practices and practitioners in the UK. *British Journal of Management*, 22(2), 238–253.

Tatli, A., & Özbilgin, M. F. (2009). Agency in management of change: bringing in relationality, situatedness and foresight. In *Handbook of research on strategy and foresight*. Edward Elgar Publishing.

Tatli, A., & Özbilgin, M. F. (2012a). An emic approach to intersectional study of diversity at work: A Bourdieuan framing. *International Journal of Management Reviews*, 14(2), 180–200.

Tatli, A., & Özbilgin, M. F. (2012b). Surprising intersectionalities of inequality and privilege: The case of the arts and cultural sector. *Equality, Diversity and Inclusion: An International Journal*.

Tatli, A., Vassilopoulou, J., Ariss, A. A., & Özbilgin, M. (2012). The role of regulatory and temporal context in the construction of diversity discourses: The case of the UK, France and Germany. *European Journal of Industrial Relations*, 18(4), 293–308.

Tatli, A., Vassilopoulou, J., Özbilgin, M., Forson, C., & Slutskaya, N. (2014). A Bourdieuan relational perspective for entrepreneurship research. *Journal of Small Business Management*, 52(4), 615–632.

Taylor, M. (2020). Extinction Rebellion launch campaign of financial disobedience. *The Guardian*, original 23 November 2020. www.theguardian.com/environment/2020/nov/23/extinction-rebellion-launch-campaign-of-financial-disobedience, accessed 25 March 2021.

Tchibozo, G. (ed.). (2012). *Cultural and social diversity and the transition from education to work* (Vol. 17). Springer Science & Business Media.

Thomas, D. A. (2016). Diversity as strategy. In *Readings and cases in international human resource management* (pp. 105–118). Routledge.

Thomason, B., Opie, T., Livingston, B., & Sitzmann, T. (2023). "Woke" diversity strategies: Science or sensationalism? *Academy of Management Perspectives*.

Tol, G. (2023). How corruption and misrule made Turkey's earthquake deadlier – Turkish President Recep Tayyip Erdogan hollowed out state institutions, placed loyalists in key positions, and enriched his cronies – paving the way for this tragedy. *Foreign Policy*. https://foreignpolicy.com/2023/02/10/turkey-earthquake-erdogan-government-response-corruption-construction/

Tollefson, J. (2019). One million species face extinction. *Nature*, 569(7755), 171.

Tomaskovic-Devey, D., & Lin, K. H. (2013). Financialization: Causes, inequality consequences, and policy implications. *NC Banking Inst*, 18, 167.

Topping, A. (2021). Women face significant jobs risk during Covid pandemic, UK analysis finds. *The Guardian Newspaper*, 4 May 2021. www.theguardian.com/world/2021/may/04/women-jobs-risk-covid-pandemic-uk-analysis

Traczyk, A. (2020). Can accent discrimination become a legal reality? *HR Magazine*, 24 January 2020. www.hrmagazine.co.uk/content/features/can-accent-discrimination-become-a-legal-reality

Trau, R., Brown, C., & O'Leary, J. (2018). Coming out at work is not a one-off event. *The Conversation*. https://theconversation.com/coming-out-at-work-is-not-a-one-off-event-101118

Tsouroufli, M. (2018a). 'Playing it right?' Gendered performances of professional respectability and 'authenticity' in Greek academia. *Journal of International Women's Studies*, August issue, 19(6), 53–69. https://vc.bridgew.edu/jiws/vol19/iss6/4/

Tsouroufli, M. (2018b). 'Migrant academic/sister outsider?' Feminist solidarity unsettled and intersectional politics interrogated. *Journal of International Women's Studies*, in press, January 2023.

Tsouroufli, M. (2023). Migrant academic/sister outsider: Feminist solidarity unsettled and intersectional politics interrogated. *Journal of International Women's Studies*, 25(1), 2. https://vc.bridgew.edu/jiws/vol25/iss1/2

Tsui, A. S., Egan, T. D., & O'Reilly III, C. A. (1992). Being different: Relational demography and organizational attachment. *Administrative Science Quarterly*, 37(4), 549–579.

Tunstall, R., Green, A., Lupton, R., Watmough, S., & Bates, K. (2014). Does poor neighbourhood reputation create a neighbourhood effect on employment? The results of a field experiment in the UK. *Urban Studies*, 51(4), 763–780. https://doi.org/10.1177/0042098013492230

Turkmenoglu, M. A. (2016). *Examining the responses and coping mechanisms of food leaders in the face of challenges: A case from Turkey* (PhD Thesis, Brunel University, UK).

Turkmenoglu, M. A. (2020). Exploring appearance-based discrimination in the workplace. In M. A. Turkmenoglu & B. Cicek (ed.), *Contemporary global issues in human resource management* (pp. 23–35). Bingley: Emerald Publishing Limited. https://doi.org/10.1108/978-1-80043-392-220201004

Tuzcu, P. (2021). Decoding the cybaltern: Cybercolonialism and postcolonial intellectuals in the digital age. *Postcolonial Studies*, 24(4), 514–527.

UN (2021). *OHCHR, UN experts Condemn UK commission on race and ethnic disparities report*. www.ohchr. org/EN/NewsEvents/Pages/DisplayNews.aspx?NewsID=27004&LangID=E

UN (United Nations) (2022). *World population to 2300*. www.un.org/development/desa/pd/sites/ www.un.org.development.desa.pd/files/files/documents/2020/Jan/un_2002_world_popula-tion_to_2300.pdf, accesses 28 March 2021.

The UN Convention on the Biological Diversity (2023). *The convention on biological diversity*. www.cbd. int/convention/

Underhill, E., Groutsis, D., van den Broek, D., & Rimmer, M. (2016). Migration intermediaries and codes of conduct: Temporary migrant workers in Australian horticulture. *Journal of Business Ethics*. https://doi.org/10.1007/s10551-016-3351-z

UNESCO (2005). *The convention on the protection and promotion of the diversity of cultural expressions*. https:// en.unesco.org/creativity/convention

Uslaner, E. M. (2006, April). Does diversity drive down trust? *FEEM Working Paper No. 69*. https:// ssrn.com/abstract=903051 or http://doi.org/10.2139/ssrn.903051

Usta, D. D., & Ozbilgin, M. (2022). Hidden side of migration: Understanding sexuality as an aspiration to migrate. *Frontiers in Sociology*.

Uygur, K. (2021). *Understanding a Hybrid Print Media and its influence on public opinion: The case of Armeno-Turkish Periodical Press in the Ottoman Empire, 1850–1875* (Unpublished PhD dissertation, University of Birmingham, Birmingham, UK).

Uygur, K. (2022). Intercultural encounters across millet boundaries in the late Ottoman Empire: The case of Armeno-Turkish print media. *Turkish Area Studies Review*, 39(2), 36–45.

Uygur, S., & Aydin, E. (2019). *Religious diversity in the workplace* (in Managing diversity and inclusion: An international perspective, eds. Jawad Syed and Mustafa Ozbilgin). Sage.

Uygur, S., Spence, L. J., Simpson, R., & Karakas, F. (2017). Work ethic, religion and moral energy: The case of Turkish SME owner-managers. *The International Journal of Human Resource Management*, 28(8), 1212–1235

Valsecchi, R., Anderson, N., Balta, M., & Harrison, J. (2021). Managing health and well-being in SMEs through an advice line: A typology of managerial behaviours. *Work, Employment and Society*, 1–18. Published online June 2021.

Van den Berghe, P. L. (1978). Race and ethnicity: A sociobiological perspective. *Ethnic and Racial Studies*, 1(4), 401–411.

van den Broek, D., Harvey, W., & Groutsis, D. (2016). Commercial Migration Intermediaries and the segmentation of skilled migrant employment. *Work, Employment and Society*, 30(3), 523–534.

Varshney, A. (2021). Populism and nationalism: An overview of similarities and differences. *Studies in Comparative International Development*, 56(2), 131–147.

Vassilopoulou, J. (2011). *Understanding the habitus of managing ethnic diversity in Germany. A multilevel relational study* (Doctoral dissertation, University of East Anglia).

Vassilopoulou, J. (2017). Diversity management as window dressing? A company case study of a Diversity Charta member in Germany. In *Management and diversity* (Vol. 3, pp. 281–306). Emerald Publishing Limited.

Vassilopoulou, J., Brabet, J., & Showunmi, V. (eds.). (2019). *Race discrimination and management of ethnic diversity and migration at work: European countries' perspectives*. Emerald Group Publishing.

Vassilopoulou, J., Da Rocha, J. P., Seierstad, C., April, K., & Ozbilgin, M. (2013). International diversity management: Examples from the USA, South Africa, and Norway. In *Cultural and technological influences on global business* (pp. 14–28). IGI Global.

Vassilopoulou, J., Kyriakidou, O., da Rocha, J. P., Georgiadou, A., & Mor Barak, M. (2018). International perspectives on securing human and social rights and diversity gains at work in the aftermath of the global economic crisis and in times of austerity. *European Management Review*.

Vassilopoulou, J., Kyriakidou, O., Özbilgin, M. F., & Groutsis, D. (2022). Scientism as illusio in HR algorithms: Towards a framework for algorithmic hygiene for bias proofing. *Human Resource Management Journal*.

Vassilopoulou, J., Merx, A., & Bruchhagen, V. (2019). An overview of diversity policies in the public and private sector that seek to increase the representation of migrants and ethnic minorities in the workplace: The case of Germany. *Race discrimination and management of ethnic diversity and migration at work.*

Verhulst, S., Engin, Z., & Crowcroft, J. (2019). Data & Policy: A new venue to study and explore policy – data interaction. *Data & Policy*, 1, E1. https://doi.org/10.1017/dap.2019.2

Vickers, L. (2017). Achbita and Bougnaoui: One step forward and two steps back for religious diversity in the workplace. *European Labour Law Journal*, 8(3), 232–257.

Villesèche, F., Meliou, E., & Jha, H. K. (2022). Feminism in women's business networks: A freedom-centred perspective. *Human Relations*, 75(10), 1903–1927. https://doi.org/10.1177/00187267221083665

Villesèche, F., Muhr, S. L., & Holck, L. (2018). *Diversity and identity in the workplace: Connections and perspectives.* Springer.

Villesèche, F., & Sinani, E. (2021). From presence to influence: Gender, nationality and network centrality of corporate directors. *Work, Employment and Society.* https://doi.org/10.1177/09500170211018579

von Doussa, H., Power, J., & Riggs, D. (2015). Imagining parenthood: The possibilities and experiences of parenthood among transgender people. *Culture, Health & Sexuality*, 17(9), 1119–1131.

von Doussa, H., Power, J., & Riggs, D. W. (2020). Family matters: Transgender and gender diverse peoples' experience with family when they transition. *Journal of Family Studies*, 26(2), 272–285.

Wacquant, L. J., & Bourdieu, P. (1992). *An invitation to reflexive sociology* (pp. 1–59). Cambridge: Polity.

Wagner, I. (2022). Equal pay for work of equal value? Iceland and the equal pay standard. *Social Politics: International Studies in Gender, State & Society*, 29(2), 477–496.

Waisbord, S. (2018). Why populism is troubling for democratic communication. *Communication Culture & Critique*, 11(1), 21–34.

Wajcman, J. (2006). Technocapitalism meets technofeminism: Women and technology in a wireless world. *Labour & Industry: A Journal of the Social and Economic Relations of Work*, 16(3), 7–20.

Wajcman, J. (2011). Gender and work: A technofeminist analysis. In *Handbook of gender, work and organization* (pp. 263–275).

Waldman, D. A., & Sparr, J. L. (2022). Rethinking diversity strategies: An application of paradox and positive organization behavior theories. *Academy of Management Perspectives.*

Wang, M., & Kelan, E. K. (2013). The gender quota and female leadership – Effects of the Norwegian gender quota on board chairs and CEOs. *Journal of Business Ethics*, 117, 449–466.

Wanjiru-Mwita, M., & Giraut, F. (2020). Toponymy, pioneership, and the politics of ethnic hierarchies in the spatial organization of British colonial Nairobi. *Urban Science*, 4(1), 6.

Watson, P. (2017). *Psychology and race.* Routledge.

Watson, W. E., Johnson, L., & Zgourides, G. D. (2002). The influence of ethnic diversity on leadership, group process, and performance: An examination of learning teams. *International Journal of Intercultural Relations*, 26(1), 1–16.

Webber, F. (2019). On the creation of the UK's 'hostile environment'. *Race & Class*, 60(4), 76–87.

Weichselbaumer, D. (2015). Testing for discrimination against lesbians of different marital status: A field experiment. *Industrial Relations: A Journal of Economy and Society*, 54(1), 131–161.

Wellalage, N. H., & Locke, S. (2013). Women on board, firm financial performance and agency costs. *Asian Journal of Business Ethics*, 2(2), 113–127.

Wieczorek-Szymańska, A. (2017). Organisational maturity in diversity management. *Journal of Corporate Responsibility and Leadership*, 4(1), 79–91. https://doi.org/10.12775/JCRL.2017.005

Wikhamn, W., & Wikhamn, B. R. (2020). Gender diversity and innovation performance: Evidence from R&D workforce in Sweden. *International Journal of Innovation Management*, 24(07), 2050061.

Wilchins, R., Nestle, J., Howell, C., Rivera, S., Wright, S., & Reiss, G. (2020). *GenderQueer-voices from beyond the sexual binary.* Riverdale Avenue Books LLC.

Willett, C. (2014). *Interspecies ethics.* Columbia University Press.

Williams, J. (1985). Redefining institutional racism. *Ethnic and Racial Studies*, 8(3), 323–348.

Williams, J., Meliou, E., & Arevalo, J. A (2017). Gender and sustainable management education: Exploring the missing link. In *Handbook of sustainability in management education: In search of a multidisciplinary, innovative and integrated approach* (pp. 307–330). Edward Elgar.

Wittenberg-Cox, A. (2013). Stop fixing women, start building management competencies. In *Handbook of research on promoting women's careers.* Edward Elgar Publishing.

Witz, A. (2013). *Professions and patriarchy.* Routledge.

Wolff, A. C., Ratner, P. A., Robinson, S. L., Oliffe, J. L., & Hall, L. M. (2010). Beyond generational differences: A literature review of the impact of relational diversity on nurses' attitudes and work. *Journal of Nursing Management, 18*(8), 948–969.

Woodhams, C., Lupton, B., & Cowling, M. (2015). The snowballing penalty effect: Multiple disadvantage and pay. *British Journal of Management, 26*(1), 63–77.

World Meteorological Organization (WMO). (2022). *Executive summary. Scientific assessment of Ozone depletion: 2022*. GAW Report No. 278, 56 pp., WMO, Geneva.

Wrench, J. (2005). Diversity management can be bad for you. *Race & Class, 46*(3), 73–84.

Wrench, J. (2016). *Diversity management and discrimination: Immigrants and ethnic minorities in the EU*. Routledge.

Wright, P. (2022). Woke corporations and worldview: Making moral proclamations from shaky moral foundations. *Academy of Management Perspectives*.

Yalkin, C., & Özbilgin, M. F. (2022). Neo-colonial hierarchies of knowledge in marketing: Toxic field and illusio. *Marketing Theory, 22*(2), 191–209.

Yamak, S., Ergur, A., Özbilgin, M. F., & Alakavuklar, O. N. (2016). Gender as symbolic capital and violence: The case of corporate elites in Turkey. *Gender, Work & Organization, 23*(2), 125–146.

Yang, J., Chuenterawong, P., & Pugdeethosapol, K. (2021). Speaking up on Black lives matter: A comparative study of consumer reactions toward brand and influencer-generated corporate social responsibility messages. *Journal of Advertising, 50*(5), 565–583.

Yavuz Sercekman, M. (2023). Managing differences in the workplace: Mindfulness-based interventions. In B. Kucukaltan (ed.), *Contemporary approaches in equality, diversity and inclusion: Strategic and technological perspectives*. Bingley: Emerald Publishing.

Yavuz Sercekman, M., & Ceviker, M. (2023). The new brave world of the neoliberal market: Mindfulness as a VIP product (or not)? In C. Yalkin & M. Ozbilgin (eds.), *Care and compassion in capitalism*. Bingley: Emerald Publishing.

Yip, A. K. (1999). The politics of counter-rejection: Gay Christians and the church. *Journal of Homosexuality, 37*(2), 47–63.

Yoo, H. S., Jung, Y. L., & Jun, S.-P. (2023). The effects of SMEs' R&D team diversity on project-level performances: Evidence from South Korea's R&D subsidy program. *R&D Management*. https://doi.org/10.1111/radm.12575

YouTube (2022). COMMONS, Suella Braverman blames 'Guardian-reading, tofu-eating wokerati' for disruptive protests. *The Guardian*. www.youtube.com/watch?v=rY79cDI-miA

Zanoni, P. (2011). Diversity in the lean automobile factory: Doing class through gender, disability and age. *Organization, 18*(1), 105–127.

Zanoni, P., Janssens, M., Benschop, Y., & Nkomo, S. (2010). Guest editorial: Unpacking diversity, grasping inequality: Rethinking difference through critical perspectives. *Organization, 17*(1), 9–29.

Zapata-Barrero, R. (2019). *Intercultural citizenship in the post-multicultural era*, Sage: London (pp. 1–152).

Zaraska, M. (2016). The genes of left and right. *Scientific American Mind, 27*(3), 9–10.

Zhang, L. (2020). An institutional approach to gender diversity and firm performance. *Organization Science, 31*(2), 439–457.

Zhou, Y., & April, K. (2020). BRICS workplace comparisons: Influence of Chinese and South African cultural orientations. *Effective Executive, 23*(1), 40–55.

Zoogah, D. B. (2016). Tribal diversity, human resources management practices, and firm performance. *Canadian Journal of Administrative Sciences/Revue Canadienne des Sciences de l'Administration, 33*(3), 182–196.

Zuckerman, A. J., & Simons, G. F. (1995). *Sexual orientation in the workplace: Gay men, lesbians, bisexuals, and heterosexuals working together*. Sage Publications.

INDEX

Printed in the United States
by Baker & Taylor Publisher Services